Advertising

Community Literacy Journal welcomes advertising. The journal is published twice annually, in the Fall and Spring (November and May). Deadlines for advertising are two months prior to publication (September and March).

Ad Sizes and Pricing
Half page (trim size 5.5X4.25): $200
Full page (trim size 5.5X8.5): $350
Inside back cover (trim size 5.5X8.5): $500
Inside front cover (trim size 5.5X8.5): $600

Format

We accept .PDF, .JPG, .TIF or .EPS. All advertising images should be camera-ready and have a resolution of 300 dpi. For more information, please contact Veronica House (housev@colorado.edu) and Paul Feigenbaum (pfeigenb@fiu.edu).

Copyright © 2021 *Community Literacy Journal*
ISSN 1555-9734

Community Literacy Journal is a member of the Council of Editors of Learned Journals.

Production and distribution managed by Parlor Press.

Publication of the *Community Literacy Journal* is made possible through the generous support of the English Department and the Writing and Rhetoric Program at Florida International University. The *CLJ* is a journal of the Coalition for Community Writing.

Editorial Board

Jonathan Alexander, *University of California Irvine*
Steven Alvarez, *St. John's University*
April Baker Bell, *Michigan State University*
Melody Bowdon, *University of Central Florida*
Kirk Branch, *Montana State University*
Stephanie Briggs, *Community College of Baltimore County*
Laurie Cella, *Shippensburg University*
David Coogan, *Virginia Commonwealth University*
Ellen Cushman, *Northeastern University*
Lisa Dush, *DePaul University*
Jenn Fishman, *Marquette University*
Linda Flower, *Carnegie Mellon University*
Diana George, *Virginia Technical University*
Beth Godbee, *Heart-Head-Hands.com*
Eli Goldblatt, *Temple University*
Laurie Grobman, *Pennsylvania State University Berks*
Shirley Brice Heath, *Stanford University*
Glenn Hutchinson, *Florida International University*
Tobi Jacobi, *Colorado State University*
Ben Kuebrich, *West Chester University*
Carmen Kynard, *Texas Christian University*
Paula Mathieu, *Boston College*
Seán Ronan McCarthy, *James Madison University*
Jill McCracken, *University of South Florida St. Petersburg*
Michael Moore, *DePaul University*
Beverly Moss, *The Ohio State University*
Steve Parks, *The University of Virginia*
Jessica Pauszek, *Texas A&M University Commerce*
Malea Powell, *Michigan State University*
Eric Darnell Pritchard, *University of Arkansas*
Jessica Restaino, *Montclair State University*
Georgia Rhoades, *Appalachian State University*
Elaine Richardson, *The Ohio State University*
Lauren Rosenberg, *University of Texas at El Paso*
Tiffany Rousculp, *Salt Lake Community College*
Iris Ruiz, *University of California Merced*
Donnie Johnson Sackey, *University of Texas at Austin*
Rachael W. Shah, *University of Nebraska-Lincoln*
Erec Smith, *York College of Pennsylvania*
Vanderlei de Souza, *Faculdade de Tecnologia de Carapicuiba, São Paulo, Brazil*
John Trimbur, *Emerson College*
Stephanie Wade, *Bates College*
John Warnock, *University of Arizona*
Christopher Wilkey, *Northern Kentucky University*

Mission

The *Community Literacy Journal* is an interdisciplinary journal that publishes both scholarly work that contributes to theories, methodologies, and research agendas and work by literacy workers, practitioners, and community literacy program staff. We are especially committed to presenting work done in collaboration between academics and community members, organizers, activists, teachers, and artists.

We understand "community literacy" as including multiple domains for literacy work extending beyond mainstream educational and work institutions. It can be found in programs devoted to adult education, early childhood education, reading initiatives, or work with marginalized populations. It can also be found in more informal, ad hoc projects, including creative writing, graffiti art, protest songwriting, and social media campaigns.

For us, literacy is defined as the realm where attention is paid not just to content or to knowledge but to the symbolic means by which it is represented and used. Thus, literacy makes reference not just to letters and to text but to other multimodal, technological, and embodied representations, as well. Community literacy is interdisciplinary and intersectional in nature, drawing from rhetoric and composition, communication, literacy studies, English studies, gender studies, race and ethnic studies, environmental studies, critical theory, linguistics, cultural studies, education, and more.

Subscriptions

Donations to the *CLJ* in any amount can be made with a check made out to "FIU English Department," with *Community Literacy Journal* in the memo line.

Send to:

Paul Feigenbaum
Department of English
Florida International University
DM462D
11200 SW 8th St.
Miami, FL 33199

Donors at the $40 level or above will receive a courtesy subscription of the academic year's issues. Donors will also be given electronic access to the *CLJ*'s present and past issues, upon request to Paul Feigenbaum at the mailing address above or at pfeigenb@fiu.edu.

Cover Art

The cover image is by artist and community activist Nyesha Clark-Young of Saginaw, Michigan. Part of a larger exhibit called "Blood, Sweat, and Gears," the image was taken at an abandoned auto parts factory and recognizes Saginaw's ties to the Rust-belt. Other works in Clark-Young's 2019 series merged historical and modern photographs; still others involved manipulating images of industrial sites into geometric designs. "Blood, Sweat, and Gears" was one of a series of community art events held in Saginaw in Fall 2019. These events celebrated a performance of Sweat, the Pulitzer Prize-winning play by Lynn Nottage. The performance was staged by the Mobile Unit of the Public Theater of New York as part of their efforts to bring theater to communities in the Midwest.

Submissions

Submissions for the articles section of the journal should clearly demonstrate engagement with community literacy scholarship, particularly scholarship previously published in the *Community Literacy Journal*. The editors seek work that pushes the field forward in exciting and perhaps unexpected ways. Case studies, qualitative and/or quantitative research, conceptual articles, etc., ranging from 20-25 manuscript pages, are welcome. If deemed appropriate, we will send the manuscript out to readers for blind review. You can expect a report in 8-10 weeks.

The *CLJ* also welcomes shorter manuscripts (8-12 pages) for two in-house sections:

Community Literacy Project and Program Profiles will discuss innovative and impactful community-based projects and programs that are grounded in best practices. We encourage community-based practitioners and non-profit staff to submit for this section. Profiles should draw on community literacy scholarship, but they are not expected to have the extended lit reviews that are customary in the articles section of the journal. If you are a community member wanting to submit, and it is your first time writing for an academic journal, we are happy to offer mentorship and answer questions. Pieces co-authored by multiple stakeholders in a project are also welcome.

Please submit using our online submission system. Contact the Project and Program Profiles Editor, Vincent Portillo, with questions at vportill@syr.edu.

Issues in Community Literacy will offer targeted analysis, reflection, and/or complication of ongoing challenges associated with the work of community literacy. Potential subjects for this section include (but are not limited to): building/sustaining infrastructure, navigating institutional constraints, pursuing community literacy in graduate school, working with vulnerable populations, building ethical relationships, realizing reciprocity, and negotiating conflicts among partners. We imagine this as a space for practitioners to raise critical issues or offer a response to an issue raised in a previous volume of the *CLJ*.

We encourage community-based practitioners and non-profit staff to submit for this section. If you are a community member wanting to submit, and it is your first time writing for an academic journal, we are happy to offer mentorship and answer questions. Pieces co-authored by multiple stakeholders in a project are also welcome. Please submit using our online submission system. Contact the Issues in Community Literacy Editor, Cayce Wicks, with questions at cwick003@fiu.edu.

COMMUNITY LITERACY Journal

Editors	Paul Feigenbaum, *Florida International University* Veronica House, *University of Colorado Boulder*
Senior Assistant Editor and Issues in Community Literacy Editor	Cayce Wicks, *Florida International University*
Journal Manager	Erin Daugherty, *University of Arkansas at Fayetteville*
Book and New Media Review Editor	Jessica Shumake, *University of Notre Dame*
Book and New Media Review Assistant Editor	Saul Hernandez, *Charlotte Mecklenburg Library*
Consulting Editor and Project Profiles Editor	Vincent Portillo, *Syracuse University*
Social Media Editor	Christian Ruvalcaba, *University of Arizona*
Senior Copyeditor	Sarah Hughes, *University of Michigan*
Copyeditors	Carlina Duan, University of Michigan Adam Hubrig, *Sam Houston State University* Charisse Iglesias, *University of Arizona* Kelly Whitney, *The Ohio State University*

community literacy journal

COMMUNITY LITERACY *journal*

Fall 2020
Volume 15, Issue 1

Guest Editors' Introduction

1   *Community Writing Centers: What Was, What Is, and What Potentially Can Be*
       Mark Latta, Helen Raica-Klotz, and Chris Giroux

Articles

7   *Detention/Writing Center Campaigns for Freedom*
       Glenn Hutchinson

28   *Resisting the "COVID-19 Scramble" by Writing Towards Black Transnational Futures*
       Wideline Seraphin

47   *You Can't Say Pupusa Without Saying Pupusa: Translanguaging in a Community-Based Writing Center*
       Stephanie Abraham and Kate Kedley

70   *Beyond 'Literacy Crusading': Neocolonialism, the Nonprofit Industrial Complex, and Possibilities of Divestment*
       Anna Zeemont

92   *A Network Approach to Writing Center Outreach*
       Thomas Deans

97   *Building a Community Literacy Network to Address Literacy Inequities: An Emergent Strategy Approach*
       Jeffrey Austin, Ann Blakeslee, Cathy Fleischer, and Christine Modey

112 *Write Here, Right Now: Shifting a Community Writing Center from a Place to a Practice*
Christopher LeCluyse, Nkenna Onwuzuruoha, and Brandon Wilde

121 *Whose House? A Dual Profile of Two Spaces for Writers in Camden, New Jersey*
Catherine Buck and Leah Falk

134 *Love and Poetic Anarchy: Establishing Mutual Care in Community Writing*
Emily Marie Passos Duffy and Ellie Swensson

147 *Neighborhood Writing: Developing Drop-In Writing Consultations in Philadelphia Public Libraries*
Dana M. Walker, Patrick Manning, and John Kehayias

157 *Reflection on "the Field"*
Tiffany Rousculp

Book Reviews

162 *From the Book and New Media Review Editor's Desk*
Jessica Shumake, Editor

163 *Writing Democracy: The Political Turn in and Beyond the Trump Era* edited by Shannon Carter, Deborah Mutnick, Stephen Parks, and Jessica Pauszek
Reviewed by Sarah Moon

175 *Transforming Ethos: Place and the Material in Rhetoric and Writing* by Rosanne Carlo
Reviewed by Jessica Nalani Lee

180 *Conceptions of Literacy: Graduate Instructors and the Teaching of First-Year Composition* by Meaghan Brewer
Reviewed by Jenna Morris Harte

184 *Beyond Progress in the Prison Classroom: Options and Opportunities* by Anna Plemons
Reviewed by Natalie Kopp

Guest Editors' Introduction

Community Writing Centers: What Was, What Is, and What Potentially Can Be

Mark Latta, Helen Raica-Klotz, and Chris Giroux

Welcome to the *Community Literacy Journal*'s special issue of "Community-Engaged Writing and Literacy Centers: A Critical Field Scan of Theory and History, Practice and Place." Our idea for this issue was a simple one. As the title suggests, we hoped to generate a "field scan," illustrating the ways in which community literacy programs draw upon theory, along with their respective regional geographies, past practices, and collective histories, to create community-engaged writing and literacy centers.

Specifically, we hoped to identify the current bodies of theories that guide community-based writing and literacy center work and make visible both the scholarship and humanizing practices that drive this emergent and growing field (Campano; Fine). Additionally, we hoped to showcase the different practices of community-based writing and literacy centers, exploring the ways that specific communities support and sustain this work. And finally, we wanted to trace the history of these various centers, so that we could begin to imagine what might come next.

Through our own experiences in creating and supporting community writing centers, we knew that the critical theories and posthuman practices of community work, social justice, and literacy education informed the planning, shaping, and overall direction of our own efforts. If we could offer our readers multiple models of similar community-engaged writing and literacy centers, then this issue would have value. Moreover, if we could begin to understand the history, context, and theory that informs these centers, we could not only envision possible futures for our own community writing centers but offer these same futures to the field itself. In short, we were excited. We were even more excited when the proposals arrived: a diverse mix of programs and centers from across the country, doing literacy work in a variety of different settings and drawing on a diverse set of practices and theory to do so.

However, the week we received our first draft of the articles in mid-March, COVID happened. Our universities closed, our classes abruptly shifted online, and our community writing centers shut down. Our personal lives shifted dramatically as well: Mark fell ill for a number of weeks and later tested positive for the virus; Helen's daughter, enrolled in a graduate program in the U.K., caught one of the last flights back to the States, where she found herself in long-term quarantine; and Chris, his daughter (a high school senior), and his spouse (a high school teacher) all found themselves on their home computers, trying to patchwork together the rest of their respective school years. At the end of March, we met on a Zoom call, looking at each other in despair. "I have to ask," Mark said, "at this point, does this issue even have any relevance?" It was a good question. After all, if this issue was based on the idea of "writing *for*, writing *with*, and writing *about* the community" (Deans), what happens when your community is shut away behind closed doors? A few months later, we watched George Floyd's violent death and the subsequent social uprisings sweep across the U.S. Marching with our neighbors to protest the systemic violence and racism that have pervaded our communities for decades, we paused to ask Mark's question again: during this time of COVID and social uprising, what relevance might a collection of articles on community-engaged writing and literacy centers have in the larger world?

We didn't necessarily know, so we decided to ask our writers this question. In our suggestions for revision of their original pieces, we asked our authors if they would consider how COVID-19 and the recent BLM protests might have informed or changed their work. In August, we got their answer: Yes, their work is relevant right now. In fact, it is more relevant than ever.

Many of these articles make the argument that community-engaged writing and literacy centers are uniquely positioned to respond to the needs of the community because of their grounding in the theories of social justice, their awareness of the inherent dangers of white power and privilege, their belief in the voices of people often silenced and oppressed, and their experience in creating communal vs. hierarchical structures. Moreover, many of our authors, particularly in the program profiles, demonstrate the ways that community-engaged writing and literacy centers exist in third spaces; therefore, they are more fluid and adaptable, much more able to hear and respond to the needs of their distinct communities. In this issue we see why the theory underpinning our work matters. It doesn't just inform our practice; it *is* our practice.

We also believe these articles help clarify some of the ways in which community-engaged writing and literacy centers remain so relevant during times of crises and unrest. Several of these articles point to and illustrate the crucial importance of a common element they all share: that of invitation. The community writing and literacy centers that have been invited into their respective communities were able to recognize immediately their continued relevancy because they were actively listening to the residents in the neighborhoods where they write.

During a roundtable discussion at the 2020 East Central Writing Association Conference (which concluded just two weeks before the Big Close), we, along with K.C. Chan Brose (administrative assistant at the Flanner Community Writing Center in Indianapolis), led a panel discussion related to the creation of community writing centers. Often, when we hold these conversations, we get questions related to funding, location, staffing, and marketing. These concerns are important, but they also focus predominantly on institutional and business logistics, and they neglect the importance of relationships. During the panel discussion, we hoped to encourage discussions related to community writing centers on the *who* and the *how*. With whom will we work? And, perhaps more importantly, how will we know when we have been invited into the communities with which we hope to write—to share their stories; to provide witness to their gifts; and to sit beside them as they lay bare their frustrations, concerns, and joys? How can we be *in* community together?

"Think about the person you hope will visit your community writing center," Mark told the small crowd during our panel talk. "When you have been invited by that person to have lunch or dinner with them, then you'll be ready to open up your community writing center." While COVID has changed the ways we think about gathering together, the larger point remains just as valid now. When we have been invited into a community, we are then part of the community. This "invitational validity" (Latta and Warren-Gordon) underscores the legitimacy and importance of the relational knowledge-making that community writing embodies. The articles within this issue demonstrate the power of relationships and the durability of invitation. Even in the midst of isolation and upheaval, our authors demonstrate that when we are fortunate enough to be invited into a community, the relevance of this work—while it should be continually negotiated and nurtured—is rarely questioned. As some of the authors point out, the relevance of relationships and invitations remains true even when these relationships may be fragile, when they are defined by moments of tension, or even when their authenticity should be called into question. Relationships are always relevant.

We're pleased to say the work continues. In the end, this collection of case studies and articles provides models grounded in critical and humanizing theories and practices that show us not only what was, but what is, and what potentially can be.

This potential is seen in Glenn Hutchinson's "Detention/Writing Center Campaigns for Freedom." Hutchinson challenges the idea that literacy programs serving the incarcerated are about traditional forms of education. Outlining an initiative linking Florida International University and Krome Detention Center in which students advocated for the release of ICE detainees, he argues such advocacy is also the work of community literacy centers.

Wideline Seraphin talks of her experiences teaching in a community education program for Haitian and Haitian American youth in "Resisting the 'COVID-19 Scramble' by Writing towards Black Transnational Futures." Providing examples of various workshop activities conducted with youth in Miami, Florida, she argues for the need for community literacy centers to meet participants where they are by privileging—and often destigmatizing—their own rich cultural histories and practices, their home languages, and the issues faced in their home communities.

Much like Serpahin's work, Stephanie Abraham and Kate Kedley's "'You Can't Say Pupusa Without Saying Pupusa:' Translanguaging in a Community-Based Writing Center" discusses the importance of place and home community in community writing center work. Beyond providing an overview of translanguaging, Abraham and Kedley offer examples of various literacy development activities undertaken in South Philly; these activities encouraged area youth to actively draw upon their home languages as well as the English used in school settings.

In "Beyond 'Literacy Crusading': Neocolonialism, the Nonprofit Industrial Complex, and Possibilities of Divestment," Anna Zeemont asks us to consider the power of language and place in yet another way. By using 826 Valencia as a case study, by analyzing the lore and cultural artifacts attached to it, and by thinking about the population and socio-cultural history of the community in which the flag-store center operates, Zeemont exhorts us to consider the messages we send based on our various partnerships and initiatives.

Thomas Deans and Jeffrey Austin, Ann Blakeslee, Cathy Fleischer, and Christine Modey talk of issues of networks. In "A Network Approach to Writing Center Outreach," Deans delineates the ways in which the larger network—rather than isolated binary partnerships—that the University of Connecticut's long-standing Secondary School Outreach Program has created operates, thrives, and adapts (and sometimes falters). Austin, Blakeslee, Fleischer, and Modey focus on another, newer network of literacy partners in southeast Michigan. In "Building a Community Literacy Network to Address Literacy Inequities: An Emergent Strategy Approach," Austin, Blakeslee, Fleischer, and Modey draw on the work of activist adrienne maree brown to discuss the importance of flexibility, adaptability, and interdependence in community literacy work particularly in this time of "twin pandemics."

Issues of flexibility and place are also apparent in many of our program profiles, starting with "Write Here, Right Now: Shifting a Community Writing Center from a Place to a Practice" by Christopher LeCluyse, Nkenna Onwuzuruoha, and Brandon Wilde. In this piece on Write Here, a community writing center in Salt Lake City, Utah, the authors provide an overview of their services and conceptualize their work (and all of our work), particularly during the pandemic, as one of practice rather than geographic location.

"Whose House?: A Dual Profile of Two Spaces for Writers in Camden, New Jersey" offers a glimpse into Writers House at Rutgers University-Camden and the Nick Virgilio Writers House, affiliated with Mighty Writers Camden. Authors Catherine Buck and Leah Falk relate the history, practices, and challenges of these sites; moreover, by examining them together, Buck and Falk remind us of the importance of collaboration and community in this time of social distancing.

Emily Marie Passos Duffy and Ellie Swensson give us a look into Writers Warehouse, a collective operating out of Boulder, Colorado, in their profile "Love and Poetic Anarchy: Establishing Mutual Care in Community Writing." Duffy and Swensson provide a history of the organization and overview of various projects with which Writers Warehouse has been affiliated, as well as their overriding philosophy, largely influenced by bell hooks, adrienne maree brown, and Gloria Anzaldúa.

In "Neighborhood Writing: Developing Drop-In Consultations in Philadelphia Public Libraries," Dana M. Walker, Patrick Manning, and John Kehayias round out the issue by relating their work in an embedded writing project in Philadelphia. They discuss the benefits and challenges of this "no-cost" project, started in 2003, in which faculty members at the University of Pennsylvania provide free writing consultations to community members at the Free Library of Pennsylvania.

Tiffany Rousculp concludes this issue by reflecting back on her initial work in this field over twenty years ago, the community she discovered doing work centered on community literacy, and the open invitation she received to come and "sit at the table." She outlines, in brief, the field's origins, key moments and players, and the tensions surrounding "who and what belongs."

Finally, we wanted to thank our reviewers—Lori Rogers, Grace Pregent, Nancy Grigg, Clayton Chiarelott, Elizabeth Geib, John Trimbur, Melissa Pavlik, and Thomas Deans—for their thoughtful feedback and suggestions to our authors. A thank you also to Nyesha Clark-Young for her photograph featured on the cover of this issue, featuring an image from an exhibit entitled "Blood, Sweat, and Gears." In Fall 2019, the Public Theater in New York City sponsored a touring production of *Sweat*, a play by Lynn Nottage, which was performed in 40 post-industrial towns in the Midwest. This project supported community dialogue and arts/writing-based projects centered around the inherent themes in the play, and the Saginaw Community Writing Center was fortunate to be one of the community partners for this project. Clark-Young's photograph of an abandoned auto parts factory in Saginaw, Michigan, demonstrates the themes of resilience, flexibility, and possibility found in forgotten spaces: another recurring theme in this issue of the *CLJ*. And lastly a special thank you to Paul Feigenbaum and Veronica House, senior editors of the *Community Literacy Journal*, for their support and encouragement.

Works Cited

Campano, Gerald. *Immigrant Students and Literacy: Reading, Writing, and Remembering*. Teachers College Press, 2007.

Deans, Thomas. *Writing Partnerships: Service Learning in Composition*. National Council of Teachers of English, 2000.

Fine, Michelle. *Just Research in Contentious Times: Widening the Methodological Imagination*. Teachers College Press, 2018.

Latta, Mark, and Kiesha Warren-Gordon. "Come On In: Invitational Validity As a Means To Relational Knowledge," (in progress).

Taylor, Carol. "Edu-crafting a Cacophonous Ecology: Posthumanist Research Practices for Education." *Posthuman Research Practices in Education*, edited by Carol Taylor and Christina Hughes, Palgrave Macmillan, 2016, pp. 5-24.

Editor Bios

Mark Latta is an assistant professor of English at Marian University in Indianapolis, IN. Latta also directs the Marian University Writing Center and Flanner Community Writing Center. His teaching, scholarship, and public narrative projects are framed around critical literacy perspectives and the use of writing as a humanizing social practice.

Helen Raica-Klotz directs the Writing Center at Saginaw Valley State University located in Saginaw, MI, and is the co-director of its Center for Community Writing, which supports two community-based writing centers, the first of their kind in Michigan. Raica-Klotz is also the director of the Saginaw Bay Writing Project, a National Writing Project site. Her scholarship focuses on embedded tutoring and on university and community writing centers.

Chris Giroux, Ph.D., is a member of the English Department of Saginaw Valley State University in Saginaw, MI. He serves as the co-director of the school's Center for Community Writing and as the assistant director of its Writing Center. Giroux is also the co-editor of the community arts journal *Still Life*, is the author of numerous published poems, and is interested in issues related to tutor training, community writing, and representations of trauma in contemporary American literature.

Articles

Detention/Writing Center Campaigns for Freedom

Glenn Hutchinson

Abstract

This essay will focus on student campaigns to stop deportations at Krome Detention Center between 2013-2017 in Miami, Florida. This advocacy work shaped a letter writing project between my university writing center and a detention center. Writing in this context, then, is a collective act, challenging a prison industrial complex that impacts both the classroom and community. The work of student organizers can challenge our field to work beyond our disciplinary boundaries and help us find new possibilities for community writing in the classroom and writing centers.

Keywords

community writing, organizing, immigration, undocumented students, prisons, detention centers

> *I deal with cases. I'm part of also the Education, Not Deportation Team . . . . you get a case and then we have to help the families try and get out from the detention center . . . He was a parent, a dad from Arizona. We heard about the case because . . . the daughter was an activist in Arizona, but for some reason they sent [him] to Miami. When we heard about the case, we did everything we could. We did vigils. We went to Krome detention center. I believe he was in Krome and then in Broward as well, in the BTC. And even though I did not know the guy, I had only seen him through fliers and pictures, and people had just talked to me about him, we were able to win his case. He came out of the detention center. When I finally saw him, I had never even met the guy, he just gave me a hug, a handshake and telling me how proud he was of us, he felt like we were his kids and we were his family, when he saw us and then I noticed that he was skinner I guess he wasn't eating as well they don't really each much or like rice and beans, I think, that's it. So the first thing we did was we went to go eat, and so he was telling us about it. Like that got to me. It could be my dad or my mom too that could be detained. Somebody hopefully helps them out like I did . . . So that's something that I learned from that . . .* — Francis Tume, Florida International University student and member of Students Working for Equal Rights

I really enjoyed the Broward campaign because that's the first time we put immigration on the defensive. They had to react to our allegations. They had to tell people that they're doing their job instead of us having to say you know it was a whole different spin and I think it's very rare that you're going to find any press release from ICE that mentions an organization and responds to their allegations and that's something we were able to do that was very—I mean it comes I think back to the thing of writing to an extent of, you know, we did our own internal investigation and put out the facts as to what they're doing. In their response, I think that gave a lot of credibility to our allegations and that would not have happened if it wasn't for us sort of manipulating the power of the press and our stories and using it for a greater goal beyond . . . —Mohammad Abdollahi, National Immigrant Youth Alliance and co-founder of Dream Activist

This was about families this whole time. This wasn't about what political party. This wasn't about any of that. It was always about the families—our community, the kids, the parents—that's what it's always about. —Viridiana Martinez, National Immigrant Youth Alliance and co-founder of NC Dream Team

Francis, Mohammad, and Viridiana, like youth organizers around the country, work on campaigns to get people out of detention centers. And as depicted in the documentary *The Infiltrators,* Mohammad worked with Viridiana and Marco to infiltrate the Broward Detention Center (BTC), located a few miles north of Miami. The documentary shows how they presented themselves to immigration authorities and purposely tried to get arrested. Since they were community organizers with the National Immigrant Youth Alliance, they wanted to get inside BTC and find out who was being held. Once inside BTC, both Viridiana and Marco collected stories and then did media interviews over the phone. They called for a full review of the cases at BTC. They discovered that there were hundreds of people being held without a criminal record, including people eligible for DACA. Most likely, no one would have known about these cases unless they were publicized. After their media interviews, Viridiana and Marco suddenly were released the next day (Sweeney). Because they were able to publicize their story and other people's stories who were being held in a detention center, they gained power through their actions. Once they were no longer invisible, the detention center released them. Mohammad helped with the organization of this project from outside the detention center and continues to work on campaigns for immigrant rights. As Mohammad notes, the rhetorical moves of "manipulating the power of the press and our stories" help people gain freedom.

These young organizers' work at detention centers shows that the struggle for immigrant rights isn't just about the right to an education. These leaders were addressing issues of mass incarceration and assisting other immigrants, some of whom were not receiving adequate medical care, including "a woman taken for ovarian surgery and returned the same day, still bleeding, to her cell, and a man who urinated blood for days but wasn't taken to see a doctor" (O'Matz). Therefore, this work with imprisoned immigrants contrasts with some of the traditional work of providing literacy classes inside prisons.

Immigrant rights organizers challenge the incarceration of immigrants and use complex rhetorical moves to work within a system to challenge it. Such advocacy speaks to a need for community writing projects that do more than provide a writing class/tutoring session or express solidarity with someone. Although there is a growing body of scholarship about teaching writing in prison (Jacobi, Berry, Cavallaro, et al.), these initiatives often struggle between focusing on individual rehabilitation and working toward changing the incarceration system (Plemons). The advocacy work of student organizers highlights the need for writing to make visible what the public sphere has left invisible. For those incarcerated in detention centers, their stories and cases often are silenced by an immigration system that does not provide them legal representation and limits their communication with the outside world. In essence, their imprisonment presumes their guilt and creates an almost impossible rhetorical situation, particularly for the majority who do not have access to legal resources. Such imprisonment has a direct impact on students, their families, and the community. In addition, their imprisonment reflects a fractured democracy where millions are disenfranchised from the political process and lack the same legal rights as documented people because of their immigration status.

This essay will discuss how neoliberal policies limit the public sphere and help to create a system of mass incarceration. In response, the dominant models of prison literacy initiatives often are marketed to the prison as rehabilitation for participants, which sometimes can conflict with goals of challenging a system of mass incarceration. In contrast to traditional prison literacy classes/tutoring, student advocacy campaigns focus on stopping deportations and releasing people from detention centers. The essay will focus on Education Not Deportation (END) campaigns at Krome Detention Center between 2013-2017 and how this advocacy work shaped a letter writing project started between my university writing center and a detention center. Writing in this context, then, is not just a personal letter expressing sympathy or support; this writing is a collective act, challenging a prison industrial complex that impacts both the classroom and community. The work of student organizers can challenge our field to work beyond our disciplinary boundaries and help us find new possibilities for community writing in the classroom and writing centers. This essay is part of a longer work that focuses on how volunteering with student organizers in the immigrant rights movement shaped my pedagogy. I am not advocating for one pedagogical approach for all writing centers, because my own positionality as a white male citizen shapes and limits my perspective. However, I argue that the rhetorical skills of student organizers need to be more central in the writing classroom and writing center, including the work of immigrant rights organizers in challenging a racist, exploitive immigration system.

Public Imprisoned

Neoliberal policies have changed our relationship with the public sphere and placed limits on participation in it. As Tony Scott and Nancy Welch argue in *Composition in the Age of Austerity*, "From schools to garbage pickup to prisons, we have seen over the past forty years a sea change toward privatization and the economization of public services, and this change is often called neoliberalism" (7). This emphasis upon private enterprise is guided by a belief that "[g]overnment best achieves the greater public good by serving private interests and privatizing government functions" (Scott and Welch 7). Examples of such policies include legislatures diverting funding from public schools to private charter schools and Congress hiring private corporations to run detention centers. And this movement affects academia with a growing market-like emphasis upon rankings and performance even as government funding decreases. As support for social programs decreases, government policies favor corporations, contributing to a shrinking of the public sphere. Democracy, then, becomes more of a place for private sector economic policies and less of a place for representative democracy. With unrestricted campaign contributions to candidates from corporations, it seems, super pacs control the discourse on media channels in support of certain policies.

It is difficult, then, to enter the public sphere when the physical space and media are controlled by a few corporations. As Nancy Welch argues, many public spaces have become private spaces, and free speech zones limit when and where people can share their ideas: "[f]rom the malling of suburbia to the vertical integration of radio, television, cable, film, music, and print outlets into a few media monopolies—we face dramatically shrinking material and virtual space . . ." ("Living Room" 474). Susan Wells discusses this broken public sphere as a "prison visiting room," a metaphor used by German scholars Oskar Negt and Alexander Kluge: "The visiting room allows communication between inside and out. It represents the prisoner's participation in both worlds" ("Rogue Cops" 335). Therefore, when we write, it is an "exchange between the private, the domain of production, and some approximations of the public sphere" (335). And in this prison visiting room for communication, "[b]oundaries are put in play for both prisoner and guest" (335).

And in the context of immigrant rights and the writing classroom/center, this prison visiting room is more than just a metaphor. As more people are placed in prisons/detention centers, immigrants are physically restricted in their communications with the outside world. Visitation is closely monitored and regulated, and private corporations charge fees for the use of a phone. In addition, raids on immigrant communities and imprisoning people in detention centers reflect neoliberalism's "reliance on crisis" (Scott and Welch 8). As the state and private corporations place immigrants behind bars, immigrants' rights are taken away as they are criminalized. As Jennifer Wingard notes, "[I]CE has developed an evolving threat matrix where anyone can move from a misdemeanor to a felon in one step" (Wingard 54). In addition, as Tobi Jacobi points out, "Many universities are inextricably tied to the prison industrial complex through everything from investment in Corrections Corporation of America (CCA) market shares to UNICOR (Bureau of Prisons) dorm furniture contracts" ("Austerity Behind Bars" 108).

The prison industrial complex's restrictions on communication are significant, particularly since the United States has the highest rate of imprisoning its people, more than any country in the world. Starting in 1972, the U.S. prison population has increased from 350,000 people to more than two million (Alexander 8). In *The New Jim Crow: Mass Incarceration in the Age of Colorblindness*, Michelle Alexander emphasizes the problems with the system:

> One way of understanding our current system of mass incarceration is to think of it as a birdcage with a locked door. It is a set of structural arrangements that locks a racially distinct group into a subordinate political, social, and economic position, effectively creating a second-class citizenship. Those trapped within the system are not merely disadvantaged, in the sense that they are competing on an unequal playing field or face additional hurdles to political or economic success; rather, the system itself is structured to lock them into a subordinate position. (Alexander 185).

Similarly, the immigration system reflects this "birdcage with a locked door" that puts people—because of their ethnic and racial identity—in "a subordinate position" (185). As Partrisia Marcías-Rojas argues in *From Deportation to Prison: The Politics of Immigration Enforcement in Post-Civil Rights America*, the system profits off criminalizing immigrants: "Immigration has surpassed drug violations as the leading charge that sends people to prison . . ." (18). Detention Centers have a long but changing history in the United States. Ellis Island in 1892 was the first detention center that kept immigrants "between a few days and several weeks" (AIJ 5); however, the U.S. "largely did not detain immigrants in the past" (AIJ 5) compared to the practices now. Detention started to grow with legislation like the 1996 Illegal Immigration Reform and Immigration Responsibility Act (IIRIRA) and the Department of Homeland Security Appropriations Act, 2010. This bi-partisan 2010 bill, often using private prison companies like GEO Group, requires at least 33,400 beds be filled with immigrants.

This system has been supported by administrations from both sides of the aisle, and when Donald Trump became president, prison companies CoreCivic and GEO's stock prices soared. In 2017, GEO gave $1.7 million to politicians in their lobbying efforts (AIJ 6), and the number of immigrants imprisoned increased:

> On a given day in August 2019, U.S. Immigration and Customs Enforcement (ICE) held over 55,000 people in detention – a massive increase from five years ago when ICE held fewer than 30,000 people. Unsurprisingly, the United States has the largest immigration incarceration system in the world. (AIJ 2)

The mass incarceration of immigrants was a $3 billion industry in 2018, and Florida, where my university resides, has a large number of immigrants imprisoned. According to Americans for Immigrant Justice, "As of April 2019, Florida had the sixth-largest population of people detained by ICE in the United States" (2). The conditions of detention centers are dangerous, including "inadequate medical and mental health care, lack of accommodations for and discrimination against individuals with disabilities, and overuse of solitary confinement" (AIJ 2). In addition, imprisoning children is part of this system. For example, there is an immigrant prison for children in Homestead, which is about thirty miles from FIU, which can imprison over two thousand immigrant children requesting asylum (Kennedy). And as children are separated from their families, "The trauma that unaccompanied children experience pre-migration, during migration, upon arrival to the US, and within communities can threaten their short- and long-term health and well-being" (Linton et al. 129). Incarceration can affect an entire family. Immigrants imprisoned in detention centers do not have the right to an attorney and have limited communication with the outside world.

As a result of neoliberal economic policies, the detention center is a space regulated often by private prison companies. Visitors must be approved for their visit, arrive at least an hour or more before the scheduled time, go through security, and place all personal belongings in a locker. A visitor may not even have a pencil or piece of paper for fear it could be used as a dangerous tool. The conversation between the visitor and the imprisoned immigrant is through a telephone as they see each other only through a protective glass barrier. And of course, anything they say can be monitored and perhaps recorded by guards. Immigrants must pay fees to use the phone to call someone outside the center and can only earn money—$1/day at Krome and other centers—to work various jobs at the center. In this space, the public sphere has no freedom, and immigrants' ability to see other people, communicate, and work is controlled by a private company or ICE.

In response to this mass incarceration and neoliberal environment, writing teachers have often focused on prison education, including writing courses/writing centers (Jacobi; Berry; Cavallaro; Hinshaw; Plemmons). Over the past decade, the Prison Studies Project has created a directory of prison education programs (http://prisonstudiesproject.org) even though Pell grants for prison education programs ended under the Clinton administration in 1994 (Pettit, "Ending Ban"), making the sustaining of such programs difficult. In *Beyond Progress in the Prison Classroom: Options and Opportunities*, Anna Plemons discusses how the "liberatory" goals of education can contrast with the realities of a prison system, showing "[t]he tension between complicity and confrontation . . ." in prison education programs (10). A prison writing course, for example, often includes the transformational narrative where writers talk about how they have worked to become a better person. However, as Plemons notes, there are problems with such an assignment: "A program that presumes a writer's highest goal to be individual transformation requires incarcerated scholars to produce texts that exemplify individual meaning-making, thereby foreclosing a critical examination of the wider enterprise" (Plemons 49-50). Although there are different approaches to teaching writing classes in prisons, this dominant model of a writing assignment places blame and emphasis upon the individual writer to transform and ignores the larger social factors of the prison industrial complex. Our writing assignments, then, can be shaped by neoliberal policies and replicate an ideology of individual responsibility rather than an examination of the private sector's profit motive in criminalizing more and more people.

Prison writing scholarship explores that tension between how to teach a course justified as rehabilitative by the prison system and the goal of challenging neoliberal incarceration. For instance, Tobi Jacobi sees such writing as "[p]art of a collective voice and social movement that demands viable alternatives to incarceration" (Jacobi 52). Cavallaro et al. "[r]eject the idea that our work in the prison classroom is aimed at reforming or saving our students . . ." And Patrick W. Berry questions when people turn to "[e]ducation and literacy as the answer to a myriad of social problems" like mass incarceration (11). However, Plemons argues we need a shift in our thinking about prison education, favoring a decolonizing approach and pointing out, "Much of the scholarship on prison education highlights the struggle among academics to transcend colonial logics when describing the value of literacy in prison" (Plemons 52).

Similarly, university/community writing centers also have engaged with prisons, focusing often on educational initiatives of individual writers. In *Rhetoric of Respect: Recognizing Change at a Community Writing Center*, Tiffany Rousculp discusses how community writing centers can consider a mission of "change" (91). Rousculp's Salt Lake Community College Community Writing Center, for example, includes writing projects inside jails. In addition, University of Miami and Goucher College's prison initiatives have featured a writing center where university tutors give individual writing consultations inside the prison. Some of these projects are started by non-profits like Exchange for Change in Miami, where faculty from Florida International University and other schools volunteer to teach creative writing courses (Hinshaw). Like the writing classes critiqued by Plemons, such projects are constrained by a neoliberal system that continues to place more and more people behind bars for profit and restricts their ability to communicate beyond the prison yard other than these educational initiatives.

What's even more striking is that such educational initiatives are not even allowed in a detention center like Krome, located near my university in Miami. First, a writing class or writing center partnership with a detention center is not allowed by ICE. Theoretically, a detention center is supposed to be a temporary imprisonment for immigrants as they resolve their immigration cases, so authorities deny education even though many immigrants are imprisoned for years as they challenge their deportations. Krome Detention Center only offers detainees the ability to watch anger management videos or attend a religious meeting.

Writing classes, as described by Jacobi, Berry, and others, might find some interested participants in a detention center, but the political/economic reality of a detention center complicates such a pedagogy. Unlike a prison where people have received their sentences, immigrants in a detention center are stuck in a legal limbo as they await a decision on their ability to stay in the country. They often lack legal representation and have few rights. There is no pretense that the detention center is striving to be rehabilitative like a prison. There are no positive public relations and news stories like there can be about prison education; instead, detention centers want to make immigrants less visible to the public. Jennifer Wingard comments on this strategy of creating fear from perceived threats: "Therefore all citizens of the United States must be aware that there are invisible enemies who are waging invisible wars against us who must be stopped, even though we cannot see them" (59). Making immigrants invisible reflects neoliberalism's emphasis upon crisis grounded in fear. Therefore, a traditional prison literacy initiative conflicts with such neoliberal policies and doesn't address the immediate needs of immigrants contesting their deportations.

Project Background: FIU and Krome, Nine Miles Apart and a World Away

Calle Ocho is the street of Little Havana, where Cuban immigrants made their home after escaping Castro's communist regime in the 1960's. From Little Havana, go further west and there's Florida International University. Started in 1972, FIU was built on what was once an airport, and now has become the university that awards the most bachelors and master's degrees to Hispanic students in the country. There are over fifty thousand students representing at least one hundred countries. Fifteen minutes further down 8th Street, before the alligators of the Everglades, there's Krome Detention Center, where immigrants are detained—imprisoned—for weeks, months, and years. Only nine miles separate Krome Detention Center from FIU, and there's no sign pointing to the long gravel road leading to a giant prison security gate there in the Everglades. Inside there are often five hundred to six hundred immigrants imprisoned because of their citizenship status. The name of this place has so much negative power. In a conference with one of my students, the word "Krome" is mentioned, and my student starts to cry because she remembers a family member's prolonged stay there.

The placement of Krome—both its physical location and historical context—reflects policies that attempt to make foreign policy and immigrants invisible to the public. First, Krome Detention Center was a nuclear missile base during the Cold War. According to Jana K. Lipman's historical account, residents of Miami were largely unaware at the time that there were nuclear missiles within a few miles of downtown (Lipman 119-20). After the 1962 Cuban Missile Crisis, the United States installed a missile launch center in South Florida (National Park Service, "HM69 Nike Missile Base"). At first, the missiles were conventional weapons but were replaced with nuclear missiles in 1965 (Lipman 118). Because the missile site was in the Everglades, they built it above ground because it was a swamp. The soldiers guarding the base experienced tough living conditions, particularly because of the plentiful mosquitoes that still persist today. After the last missiles were removed in 1979, the military base became a place for refugees (Lipman 118-19). According to Lipman, there was not much public discussion about transforming a nuclear base into a camp or prison for refugees, but when thousands of Cubans and Haitians fled persecution in their home countries, the United States government decided to use Krome as one of the places to house them.

The 1980 Mariel Boat Lift had brought Cuban immigrants wanting to leave Castro's regime, and at the same time, thousands of Haitian immigrants were escaping Duvalier's regime in Haiti. Cubans were treated mostly as political "refugees" because of the United States' Cold War relationship with Cuba. However, Haitians making the journey to the United States often were treated as if they were only leaving the island because of economic reasons, even though the brutal Duvalier killed and tortured many Haitians. Edwidge Danticat's powerful memoir, *Brother, I'm Dying*, tells the story of her elderly uncle traveling to Miami because of the violence in Haiti. Her uncle had a travel visa, but because he mentioned the desire for temporary asylum at the airport, he was arrested and sent to Krome. Without his proper medication, he died a few days later. This violent treatment has continued. In 1982, thirty-three Haitian women held a hunger strike to protest their conditions, and Krome force-fed some of them (Jaynes). In the 1980s and 90s, there were widespread reports of guards physically abusing and raping detainees at Krome (Bach). Now an all-male facility, Krome continues to abuse.

Besides refugees seeking asylum, Krome is a place where a resident without the right papers can end up. A man moves here when he is four years old, grows up and graduates high school or college, gets a job, but he never is able to become a citizen because of a racist immigration system that prevents many people from becoming citizens. He's now forty-something years old, and at a traffic stop, or some other run-in with the law, he is arrested. Or it could be someone who is a college student but isn't able to become a citizen. When it's discovered that these community members are undocumented, they can be given an order of deportation and sent to a detention center like Krome.

A visitation project affiliated with a national group called CIVIC—now named Freedom For Immigrants—started in 2013. To end the isolation at this all-male detention center by talking to someone for an hour, the local group—Friends of Miami-Dade Detainees—organizes visitations. Such a project requires approval by the detention center, and it always has the threat of being ended or suspended. The initial tour of the facility took place in October 2013. As volunteers walked from the parking lot to the entrance, we could hear the sound of gunshots in the air from the nearby firing range. Then inside, we got to see where the men—usually five hundred to six hundred—slept and ate. There was a room with padded walls where guards can lock people up when they have mental breakdowns. Men were dressed in different color prison uniforms: blue, orange, or red. The color indicates how serious the offense is. Of course, the offense that everyone has made is not having the right papers. Although a blue uniform is supposed to represent someone whose only offense is not having the right papers, and someone dressed in red means they were accused of committing a felony, the colors aren't always accurate. Some men at Krome had lived in the U.S. for many years but their countries of birth included Cuba, Ethiopia, Eritrea, Bangladesh, Brazil, Colombia, Honduras, El Salvador, England, Mexico, Jamaica, the Bahamas, and Haiti. During weekly visitations from 2013-2017, detainees discuss participating in hunger strikes and other forms of civil disobedience at Krome. Similar to what happened in the 1980s, a judge ruled in 2015 that Krome officials could use "nasal-gastric tubes" to force feed refugees from Bangladesh who went on a hunger strike to protest being held for years in detention (Alexandra Martinez).

Usually all communication is through a glass barrier and phone, but on that first tour, as we walked through the facility, a man wearing red handed us a letter and asked for help. Wally was born in Mexico but had lived in the U.S. since he was fourteen years old. He had an eleven-year-old son who was a citizen. In February 2012, Wally was arrested at his house in Bradenton, near Tampa, because he was undocumented. He had no criminal record. The only reason he was being detained is because he overstayed his visa and then re-entered the country four times to be with his son. He crossed the desert in Texas, near Brownsville, and spent four days and four nights trying to get back to his eleven-year-old boy. Wally nearly died from lack of water and exhaustion.

Even though he didn't have a lawyer, he was fighting his case and representing himself. He read up on immigration law with whatever resources they had at the detention center, and he was doing everything he could to stop his deportation so he could return to his son. He said the men called him the "jailhouse lawyer" as he helped them with their cases too. He wanted the help of student organizing groups like Students Working for Equal Rights (SWER), Dreamactivist, or United We Dream who conduct END campaigns to stop deportations.

Francis, a member of SWER and whose words begin this chapter, along with other students, agreed to help, because Wally wanted to go public and use the press to share his story and connect with the community. Students spoke with Wally's family to implement an END campaign that included various actions, including a call-in campaign, social media, press releases, rallies outside the detention center, and an op-ed. SWER leaders planned and held a rally outside a detention center where Wally's brother made a speech in front of the media. Wally wanted a petition, and he asked his brother to send a photograph that could be used. In this collective effort, student organizers from SWER and I worked on drafting an online petition and posting it on change.org (please see appendix A). This petition has a rhetorical strategy of emphasizing the person's connection to family and the community, invoking Americanisms as part of its argument. Wally is a father, and he wants to pursue his education and career. Also, he is a member of a church. Part of the argument is discussing American ideals and stressing that the person is a valuable member of the community. And besides asking people to sign, the petition encourages them to call ICE and support the person and use their Alien Registration Number (A#). Importantly, the purpose of telling Wally's story is not a story of transformation that might take place in a literacy class. The purpose is not to share his story with a university class to create an exchange between people on the inside of the prison and on the outside in the classroom. The purpose of the petition is to take action—to raise the profile of a case.

As the campaign progressed, there were conversations between Wally, the pro-bono lawyers, the family, and the organizers. In these conversations, the END campaign sets a strategy about how to go public and to what extent the campaign is private or public. As he appealed his deportation, court dates were set and the call-in campaign intensified. Then in November, he was transferred to another detention center in Wakulla County, outside of Tallahassee, as his case/appeal was pending. This move shows how the detention center system continues to disrupt detainees' lives. When people are transferred to a new detention center, they often lose contact with family and friends who are able to visit them. And if they do have a lawyer, then that lawyer would not be able to visit them in-person. Their court case would likely be conducted through video conferencing. In consultation with Wally's family, the SWER group made a plan to call ICE, plan protests, contact representatives, and involve members of Wally's church (please see appendix B for SWER email). This call to action includes specific ICE targets for the campaign and the use of social media hashtags to raise the visibility of Wally's case. In addition, congressional representatives were contacted to see if they could help. In December of 2013, The Progressive Media Project (PMP) welcomed an op-ed to tell Wally's story and how it connected with many other immigrant parents. With help from SWER and other groups, the petition gained nearly five thousand signatures, and the op-ed was published in several newspapers around the country. People wrote online comments from different states and countries in support of Wally. After the op-ed was published, the call-in campaign continued in January and February. The campaign reflected a collective effort combining writing and action to advocate for Wally and his family. Because Wally was imprisoned inside the detention center, he lacked access to participate in these advocacy events. Neoliberal policies of incarceration make it extremely difficult for immigrants facing deportation to participate in the public sphere at all.

Then in March, Wally was transferred back to Krome and tried for a final stay of removal. The next week, the online detainee locator (locator.ice.gov/odls/) indicated that Wally was "not in custody." Wally's family members called to confirm what it meant: Wally was deported in March 2014 after being held in detention for two years and one month. Since Wally had re-entered the country after being deported, his offense was treated as a felony. He wore the red uniform, not the blue. Wally had not committed a crime other than wanting to be with his son. At the next SWER meeting on campus, students discussed the campaign for Wally and shared how deportations affected their own families. One student shared how he and his brother had to live without their mother. He continues to attend college, and he wants to change the laws to make it possible for his mother to return to the United States. Even though the campaign wasn't successful, organizers continue to work on ending deportations.

The project was led by community organizers and did not have any direct link with a particular class or university department. However, student organizers' rhetorical skills combined with action give a different framework than traditional prison literacy initiatives. Although Berry, Jacobi, and other scholars discuss the tension between teaching a rehabilitative prison literacy course and social activism, this project focused more on organizing and connecting people for campaigns to escape incarceration. Instead of teaching writing, this student-led project challenged neoliberal incarceration policies. The goal for such a project is to make visible what the public sphere makes invisible: the incarceration and deportation of immigrants. Although the campaign to stop Wally's deportation wasn't successful, student organizers have achieved many victories with other END campaigns throughout the country. These organizing efforts inspired a letter writing project between our writing center and Krome Detention Center.

Writing Centers, Social Justice, and Letters

The letter writing project between our university writing center and Krome focused on connecting imprisoned immigrants to resources and groups that would advocate for their release. In addition, when given permission by incarcerated immigrants, the media could be contacted to profile cases. Instead of organizing a literacy class, which was forbidden by Krome, this project aimed to follow some of the activist rhetorical approaches of student organizers.

In many projects, letter writing with those who are incarcerated often begins with a goal for greater understanding and sympathy from those on the outside. Amnesty International has a letter writing campaign every December to show solidarity with people who are imprisoned and whose human rights have been violated. Wendy Hinshaw discusses letter exchanges between writing classrooms and those incarcerated in prison as part of the Exchange for Change program: students on the inside (the prison) and students on the outside (the university classroom) write about similar topics and have a conversation through writing letters to one another, using pseudonyms. She points out that such exchanges can help "build community through listening" to one another (69). Another example of letter writing with imprisoned people, Detainee Allies, is an organization started by several San Diego State professors. They have created an online collection of letters from immigrant detainees (Pettit, "Begging"). The purpose of the project is not to "solve" the issue, but to "document" what is happening (Pettit, "'Begging'"). A project called "Vision From The Inside" turns letters written by detained people into art. The goal of their project is to publicize what many immigrants are experiencing inside detention centers and how people are coping. Such projects have value in creating conversation between those incarcerated and those on the outside, a way to end isolation and show solidarity. Some detainees have not had direct contact with family members or friends for years, and several commented how they valued and were thankful for receiving a letter in the mail, including those from the volunteers in the visitation program. In addition, sometimes detainees write back about their desire to go to college and what they would like to study, asking for books that they can read while they are confined. The tutors at the writing center, for example, donated novels, dictionaries, GED preparation books, and atlases. However, besides showing solidarity and responding to these requests, we wanted to add an activist component to this letter writing project and help challenge incarceration policies. Most letters from the detention center focused on people's frustration with why they are being imprisoned and also their need for legal help.

The project started with volunteers who visited Krome Detention Center composing letters to those they had visited. With support from the writing center director, Dr. Paula Gillespie, FIU-affiliated visitors could use the writing center mailbox to send and receive mail to the detention center. More letter writers, who did not visit Krome, volunteered to help when the project was discussed during a writing center staff meeting and during my class. The organizers of Friends from Miami Dade had a list of people who wanted visitations at the detention center, and once we had their A#'s, then we could write a letter. Student volunteers and I composed letters in English, Spanish, and French to detainees, telling them about the hotline started by the advocacy group, a four-digit number they could use to call their families that was free and therefore wouldn't charge money that many don't have. Students would write the letters by hand in the writing center, or I would type them in my office. Also, letter writing events encouraged others to correspond, including an action with the Mass Story Lab hosted by the University of Miami in February of 2017. This traveling project aims to raise awareness through featuring five-minute stories from people who are directly affected by mass incarceration. FIU's chapter of Student Alliance for Prison Reform, which has coordinated a variety of activities on campus to raise awareness about the prison system, also joined the project and set up a letter-writing table in the FIU student center (please see appendix C for sample introductory letters). Students and I then followed up these introductory letters with more personal letters based on the responses. Also, some men would share their stories when people would visit them at the detention center. But in the process of writing letters, there's a possibility of not getting a response and the letter could be returned for various reasons—the person could be transferred to another center or deported.

After these initial letters, we tried to connect detainees with people who could help. The letter writing project became more than just writing to show solidarity; it became part of different kinds of action modeled by student organizers. The FIU law school was one resource with its immigration clinic and represents some detainees pro-bono, as many cannot afford legal representation. In their letters, detainees would sometimes ask someone to attend their court hearing that takes place at the detention center. In some hearings, for example, there was no one in the courtroom other than the judge, prosecution, defense attorney if the detainee has one, and the detainee. Having a family member or friend present is a show of support from the community and lets the court know the person is not alone. Also, if family members couldn't be present, the letter writing project sometimes meant speaking with their family members and passing along or relaying information to them. One man worried about his access to HIV medication if he was deported. Other men feared that if they were deported back to their birthplace that they would be killed because of their political beliefs or other aspects of their identity, including their sexual orientation.

In responding to some of these cases, student organizers from SWER assisted in crafting and sharing petitions about detainees and contacting the media. For example, in July 2015, Nina Agrawal, a reporter for the local NPR station (WRLN) received permission to bring in a camera and recording equipment, and ICE officials gave consent forms to detainees for an interview, three of whom were people we had been visiting for several months. There was much concern about the consent forms, because at Krome, signing something can have great significance, including agreeing to one's own deportation. The men signed the forms after analyzing them closely, but right before the interview, two of the men were suddenly released who had been held for several months. Therefore, the men were not interviewed, because they were freed from Krome. The power of the press or going public gave them freedom; their stories were no longer invisible. At the interview, several ICE officials, including the director of Krome, greeted us in the lobby. NPR was able to interview two detainees, including a man profiled in the story who was being deported to Brazil after living in the States for twenty years.

Arranging such media visits is a bureaucratic challenge, and so student organizers and I drafted petitions for other men, including those requesting asylum from Bangladesh and Ethiopia who waited sometimes years in the detention center for a decision on their case. For example, in January 2017, Abdul was released after being incarcerated for fifteen months. We had created a petition for him, telephoned ICE, and connected him to a pro-bono attorney. However, the work of student organizers shaped this letter writing project into something different than many traditional prison literacy efforts. The rhetorical and advocacy work of student organizers in assisting people who are imprisoned in detention centers shows a sophisticated use of media. Such campaigns often require publicizing a case so that people can speak out and pressure ICE and/or their elected representatives to act. This letter writing project was shaped, then, by the work of student organizers and found a connection with our writing center and other interested student groups on campus.

Conclusion

Making visible what the public sphere has made invisible may be a guiding principle for such advocacy work. Instead of being in the shadows, people gain a power through using a public voice. Doing so is difficult, particularly when confronting a neoliberal system of incarceration that profits off of immigrants being behind bars. In addition, neoliberal policies are often fueled by the fear of the unknown, creating a perpetual sense of crisis and threats with the rhetoric of elected leaders demonizing immigrants as invaders.

Such work raises questions about community writing projects. Writing partnerships can be effective in showing support of a group and engaging in an educational initiative like teaching a class or conducting a writing center inside a prison. At the same time, though, such partnerships can be limited and sometimes not permitted by a system that incarcerates and exploits immigrants. As Shannon Carter, Deborah Mutnick, Stephen Parks, and Jessica Pauszek comment in *Writing Democracy: The Political Turn in and Beyond the Trump Era*, "[c]ommunity engagement work—despite the best of intentions—too often underscores the problem of supporting social justice movements absent a critique of systemic inequality, escalating state repression and surveillance, and a rapacious market indifferent to human suffering" (13). A writing project connected to a detention center, then, is encountering a system of mass incarceration that exploits immigrants. Community writing becomes less of an opportunity for participants to become "better" writers. Instead, this kind of community writing combined with advocacy has goals that extend beyond our disciplinary boundaries. Letter writing is being guided by community organizers who enact campaigns to challenge deportations. In addition, letter writing can be a way to share contact information of the law school and other pro-bono attorneys that can help navigate this system. Such work pushes us to think beyond our discipline and recognize writing as one tool for community organizing. By foregrounding student voices, the writing classroom and center become spaces where students can have a conversation and engage with projects that focus also on organizing rather than just volunteering.

Not all campaigns and petitions succeed, as seen with Wally's case. In addition, some letters didn't lead to an activist campaign, because there wasn't enough time before the person was deported. At one point, the hotline was suspended. These institutional barriers are increased even more by anti-immigrant policies passed by the Trump administration and the suspension of in-person visitation during the coronavirus pandemic. Although petitions and media campaigns continue to be tools for challenging incarceration, organizers continue to adapt their tactics and strategies. For example, in 2019 *The Infiltrators* received premiers in various film festivals across the country, including Sundance. As the film about how undocumented people organized within a detention center gained notoriety, one of the detainees who helped the youth organizers inside Broward Detention Center, Claudio, was deported to Argentina shortly after the premier. Such an act by ICE shows the complex and dangerous landscape of immigration in the United States seven years after the action at Broward. Publicity and rhetorical advocacy work can make such a big difference in helping to stop deportations; however, the anti-immigrant system continues to marginalize and exploit people and strategies must adapt as more change is needed. As García Hernández comments, "The United States should shut down its immigration prison system. The federal government should redirect the billions of dollars it spends jailing migrants—$2.7 billion alone in 2017 for ICE's detention system—to helping them navigate the labyrinthine legal process."

If universities and writing programs/centers can engage in community organizing initiatives, we can challenge a system of incarceration that exploits people. This work moves us beyond the prison visiting room metaphor of public discourse and engages with different ways of participating in the public sphere. Advocacy groups like Dreamactivist.org and United We Dream can be good places to learn about immigrant rights campaigns, including END campaigns. However, on our own campuses, there may be student groups that can connect directly with the writing center and classroom. In addition, this work connects with our mission as educators too. This kind of work can represent university community engagement that challenges incarceration. For instance, the night that Abdul was released, he walked down the isolated road from the detention center, and when picked up, he asked if he could see FIU. He had heard talk about FIU for several months through visits and letters. That night he was released was rainy, but we drove around the campus and looked at some key buildings, and he commented on the beauty of the campus. We saw the giant palm trees lining the front entrance, the towering library at the center of campus, and all the new buildings built on this place that was once an airport. After gaining freedom and joining his family in the northeast, Abdul plans to attend college.

Appendix A

Petition:
Please stop the deportation of Wally, a father who wants to take care of his 11 year-old son.

Wally is currently being held in the Krome Detention Center in Miami.

Wally came to this country for a better life. In 1990, Wally left Guanajuato, Mexico when he was 14 years old. He earned his GED and studied air conditioning repair at Manatee Technical Institute in Bradenton, Florida. He has worked in construction. He is a Christian and a member of Vida Nueva Church in Bradenton.

Wally has spent 14 months in two different detention centers and fears he will be deported soon. Wally has no criminal record. The only reason he is being detained is because he overstayed his visa and then re-entered the country four times to be with his son.

Because of the psychological stress of his father being away, Wally's son has gotten sick. Missing his father has affected his son's schoolwork and mental health. He even wrote a letter to the deportation officer asking for help to bring his father home. He goes to sleep at night wanting to see his father again.

In February 2012, Wally was arrested at his house in Bradenton, Florida because he was undocumented. And the last time he saw his son was July 24, 2012.

Wally says that the reason he keeps coming back to the United States is to be with his son. He crossed the desert in Texas, near Brownsville, and spent 4 days and 4 nights trying to get back to his 11 year-old. Wally nearly died from lack of water and exhaustion.

Wally wants to become a civil engineer like his brother and father. His son is a U.S. citizen. His brother is a U.S. citizen. Give Wally a chance to be with his son.

Take action: SIGN the petition and call ICE @ 202-732-3000 or 202-732-3100!
Sample Script: "Hi, I was calling to ask that ICE stop the deportation of Wally: A#XXXXXXXXX. Wally has been living in the U.S. since 1990 and has an 11 year-old son. Please don't deport Wally!

Appendix B

Good Morning everyone,

A family needs your help!

Wally came to this Country when he was 14 years old. Harvey, Wally's 11 year old U.S. Citizen has become sick waiting for his father who has spent the past 14 months at a detention center. Please help us bring back Wally back to his son!

You can take action by:

1) Calling ICE and asking for Wally to be released and be reunited with his son for the holidays.

Numbers to call:

Acting Director, John Sandweg **(202) 732-3000**

AND

Assistant Field Office Director (Detention): Conrad C. Agagan

Assistant Field Office Director Line: **(407) 440-5100**

Script:
"Hi, My name is_____ I am calling to ask that ICE stop the deportation of Wally: (A#XXXXXXXXX). Wally has been living in the U.S. since 1990 and has an 11 year-old son who needs his father Please don't deport Wally and let him spend the Holidays with his 11 year old son.

2) Posting his picture and script through social media to get the word out.

Hastags: #Not1More #ENDOurPain #StopICE

*Picture attached below

We Thank you for your support!

Appendix C

Spanish Sample First Letter

El 14 de agosto, 2014

XXXXXXXX (A#XXX-XXX-XXX)

Estimado Señor XXXXXXX ,

Le escribo para mandarle un saludo. Siento mucho que se encuentre en esta situación tan difícil. No soy un abogado. Soy un voluntario para el grupo, "Friends of Miami-Dade Detainees."

Cada semana, nosotros (con "Friends of Miami-Dade Detainees) visitamos a los hombres en Krome. Para hacer esto, se necesitaría que usted diera permiso y firmara la lista para aprobar visitantes que Krome le provee ("Friends of Miami-Dade Detainees"). La lista está en tu pod (donde tú vivas).

Si quisiera, "Friends of Miami-Dade Detainees" provee una línea telefónica en la cual usted se puede comunicar con una amistad o familiar. Es gratis y el número es *9233. También, usted puede escribir una carta a mi dirección..

Le deseamos lo mejor.

Atentamente,

English Sample First Letter

August 8, 2014

Dear XXXX (A#: XXX-XXX-XXX),

Hello. My name is _____. I am not a lawyer, but I am a volunteer for the group, "Friends of Miami-Dade Detainees."

Each week, we visit men in Krome. If you would like for us to visit you, please sign our visitation list. The list is in your pod.

Also, we have a free hotline (*9233) that you can call to leave messages or to connect with family members and friends. The phone call does not cost you anything.

I hope things improve for you, and I hope to talk to you soon.

Sincerely,

Works Cited

Abdollahi, Mohammad. *Personal Interview.* 28 July 2016.

Agrawal, Nina. "Krome Corps: Volunteers Reach Out To Immigrants In Detention." *WLRN,* 27 July 2015, wlrn.org/post/krome-corps-volunteers-reach-out-immigrants-detention.

Alexander, Michelle. *The New Jim Crow: Mass Incarceration in the Age of Colorblindness.* New P, 2010.

Americans for Immigrant Justice. "Prison by Any Other Name: A Report on South Florida Detention Facilities." 9 Dec. 2019, www.aijustice.org/prison_by_any_other_name_a_report_on_south_florida_detention_facilities.

Bach, Trevor. "Guards and Immigration Detainees Describe Widespread Abuse at Krome Processing Center." *Miami New Times,* www.miaminewtimes.com/news/guards-and-immigration-detainees-describe-widespread-abuse-at-krome-processing-center-7829882.

Berry, Patrick W. *Doing Time, Writing Lives: Refiguring Literacy and Higher Education in Prison.* Southern Illinois UP, 2018.

Carter, Shannon, et al, editors. *Writing Democracy The Political Turn in and Beyond the Trump Era.* Routledge Research in Writing Studies, Kindle Edition. 2020.

Cavallaro, Alexandra J, et al. "Inside Voices: Collaborative Writing in a Prison Environment." *Harlot: A Revealing Look at the Arts of Persuasion,* no. 15, 2016, http://harlotofthearts.org/index.php/harlot/article/view/323/188.

Danticat, Edwidge. *Brother, I'm Dying.* Vintage P, 2008.

Department of Homeland Security Appropriations Act, 2010. United States Government Publishing Office, www.gpo.gov. PUBLIC LAW 111–83—28 OCT. 28 2009 123 STAT. 2149.

García Hernández, César Cuauhtémoc. "Abolish Immigrant Prisons." *The New York Times.* 2 Dec. 2019, www.nytimes.com/2019/12/02/opinion/immigration-detention-prison.html.

Hinshaw, Wendy Walters. "Writing to Listen: Why I Write Across Prison Walls." *Community Literacy Journal,* vol. 13, no. 1, 2018: pp. 55-70.

Jacobi, Tobi. "Austerity Behind Bars: The 'Cost' of Prison College Programs." *Composition in the Age of Austerity,* edited by Nancy Welch and Tony Scott, UP of Colorado, Boulder, CO, 2016, pp. 106–119. JSTOR, www.jstor.org/stable/j.ctt1b3h9ts.10.

—. "Speaking out for Social Justice: The Problems and Possibilities of US Women's Prison and Jail Writing Workshops." *Critical Survey,* vol. 23, no. 3, Sept. 2011, p. 40. *EBSCOhost,* search.ebscohost.com/login.aspx?direct=true&db=edsglr&AN=edsgcl.286253802&site=eds-live.

Jaynes, Gregory. "U.S. is Remaining Adamant as Detained Haitians Press Appeals for Asylum." *New York Times,* 24 Apr. 1982, www.nytimes.com/1982/04/24/us/us-is-remaining-adamant-as-detained-haitians-press-appeals-for-asylum.html.

Kennedy, Thomas. "Homestead detention center is no kids' summer camp." *Miami Herald,* 14 June 2019, www.miamiherald.com/opinion/op-ed/article231550468.html.

Linton, Julie M., et al. "Unaccompanied Children Seeking Safe Haven: Providing Care and Supporting Well-Being of a Vulnerable Population." *Children and Youth Services Review*, vol. 92, Sept. 2018, pp. 122–132. EBSCOhost, doi:10.1016/j.childyouth.2018.03.043.

Lipman, Jana K. "'The Fish Trusts the Water, and It Is in the Water That It Is Cooked': The Caribbean Origins of the Krome Detention Center," *Radical History Review*, vol. 115, 2013, pp. 115–141. doi: https://doi.org/10.1215/01636545-1724742

Marcías-Rojas, Partrisia. *From Deportation to Prison: The Politics of Immigration Enforcement in Post-Civil Rights America*. NYU P, 2016.

Martinez, Alexandra. "Judge's Order to Force-Feed Ten Hunger-Strikers at Krome Sparks Immigration Protest." *Miami New Times*, 28 Dec. 2015, www.miaminewtimes.com/news/judges-order-to-force-feed-ten-hunger-strikers-at-krome-sparks-immigration-protest-8138104.

Martinez, Viridiana. *Personal Interview*. 17 Nov. 2014.

National Park Service. "HM69 Nike Missile Base." www.nps.gov/ever/learn/historyculture/hm69.htm.

Negt, Oskar, and Alexander Kluge. *History and Obstinacy*. Translated by Richard Langston, Zone Books, 2014.

O'Matz, Megan. "Broward Transitional Center: Immigrants With No Criminal History Get Lengthy Stays At Little-Known Jail." *Sun Sentinel*. 7 March 2013, articles.sun-sentinel.com/2013-01-05/news/fl-private-immigration-jail-20130105_1_illegal-immigrants-deutch-human-rights-abuses.

Ortiz, Gabe. "Guards block children from delivering letters of support to migrant kids jailed at prison camp." *Daily Kos*, 28 May 2019, www.dailykos.com/story/2019/5/28/1860903/-Guards-block-children-from-delivering-letters-of-support-to-migrant-kids-jailed-at-prison-camp.

Pettit, Emma. "'Begging to Have Their Stories Told': San Diego State Professors Create Living Archive of Migrants' Letters From Detention." *The Chronicle of Higher Education*, 13 Feb. 2019.

—. "Ending Ban on Pell Grants for Prisoners Is Said to Yield 'Cascade' of Benefits." *The Chronicle of Higher Education*, 16 Jan. 2019.

Plemmons, Anna. *Beyond Progress in the Prison Classroom: Options and Opportunities*. NCTE, 2019.

Rousculp, Tiffany. *Rhetoric of Respect: Recognizing Change at a Community Writing Center*. NCTE, 2014.

Scott, Tony, and Nancy Welch. "Introduction." *Composition in the Age of Austerity*, edited by Nancy Welch and Tony Scott, UP of Colorado, 2016, pp. 3–18. JSTOR, www.jstor.org/stable/j.ctt1b3h9ts.3.

Sweeney, Chris. "Two Activists Infiltrate a Center Where Illegal Immigrants Are Held." *Miami New Times*, 25 Oct. 2012, www.miaminewtimes.com/news/two-activists-infiltrate-a-center-where-illegal-immigrants-are-held-6389574..

The Infiltrators. Directed by Cristina Ibarra and Alexa Rivera, 2019.

Tume, Francis. *Personal Interview*. 20 Nov. 2014.

Welch, Nancy. "Living Room: Teaching Public Writing in a Post-Publicity Era." *College Composition and Communication*, vol. 56, no. 3, Feb., 2005, pp. 470-492.

—. *Living Room: Teaching Public Writing in a Privatized World*. Boynton/Cook P, 2008.

Wells, Susan. "Rogue Cops and Health Care: What Do We Want from Public Writing?" *College Composition and Communication*, vol. 47, no. 3, Oct. 1996, pp. 325-341

Wildes-Muñoz, Laura. *The Making of a Dream: How a Group of Young Undocumented Immigrants Helped Change What it Means to Be American*. Harper, 2018.

Wingard, Jennifer. *Branded Bodies, Rhetoric, and the Neoliberal Nation-State*. Lexington Books, 2013. *EBSCOhost*, search.ebscohost.com/login.aspx?direct=true&db=cat06026a&AN=fiu.031010237&site=eds-live.

Author Bio

Glenn Hutchinson teaches rhetoric/composition and directs the writing center at Florida International University in Miami. Since 2007, he has volunteered with different immigrant rights organizations in North Carolina and Florida. His book, *Writing Accomplices with Student Immigrant Rights Organizers*, will be published in 2021 by NCTE/Studies in Writing & Rhetoric. Glenn also writes plays and op-eds.

Resisting the "COVID-19 Scramble" by Writing Towards Black Transnational Futures

Wideline Seraphin

Abstract

This case study demonstrates how a community-based literacy program, HELP, took up Black literate traditions, endarkened transnational feminism, and anticolonial practices to construct emancipatory literacy experiences for Haitian and Haitian American middle schoolers in Miami, Florida. Overall, the institutional practices of HELP worked to destigmatize the discourses of Haiti, center Black Haitian women's stories, and develop spiritual consciousness. Furthermore, this article discusses the "COVID-19 scramble" and its ability to detract from building socially just futures for Black transnational students. Lastly, the article ends with questions for consideration when confronting the cyclical violence of white supremacy in literacy programs.

Keywords

literacies, Black transnational youth, emancipatory curriculum, COVID-19, Haiti, middle school

Introduction

The murder of Trayvon Martin on February 26, 2012, and the subsequent birth of Black Lives Matter defined my first year as a literacy educator in Miami, Florida. As a Black female teacher in my early 20s, I felt a particular form of anguish—he was from the neighborhood in which I taught. Upon learning of his death, I remember surveying my classroom of predominantly Black and Brown fourth and fifth grade children. To me, they were just as extraordinary, and somehow, as easily disposable as Trayvon. I made the decision to wear a black hoodie to school. It was my first political undertaking as a brand-new teacher. I wanted to show solidarity and bring attention to Trayvon's death to our school of predominantly Black and Brown students, teachers, and administrators…and nothing really happened. My hoodie, Trayvon's death, and the perilous conditions of Black life did little to interrupt our daily schooling routines steeped in deficit orientations of testing, interventions, and the remediation of Black and Brown children. My good intentions as an aggrieved Black teacher were ineffectual and nowhere near enough. My school's silence around Trayvon's death, despite our geographical connection to his killing, perpetuated the legacy of anti-Black violence and harm.

In June of 2013, I began my first year as a literacy instructor at the culturally based, spiritually grounded, out-of-school literacy program called the Haitian Empowerment Literacy Project (HELP). By this point, heated protests denouncing racist policing in the United States engrossed Florida and much of the nation. Intergenerational racial traumas all came to a head during the criminal and public trial of ~~George Zimmerman~~ Trayvon Martin. I, like many, closely followed the media frenzy of the trial. As a Haitian American woman, I also felt the sting of the wildly racist linguistic dismissal of Haitian American teenager, Rachel Jeantel's Miami-bred Black Vernacular English. I remained glued to the news channels, desperately awaiting the jury's verdict. And late Saturday evening, on July 13, 2013, a jury acquitted the man charged with Trayvon's murder, and I was absolutely stunned. Suspended in a state of disbelief, I did not sleep that night or the following night. On Monday, July 15, 2013, week six of HELP's summer institute, I returned to my classroom of twenty-five Haitian and Haitian American rising sixth graders. That morning, I was not preoccupied with staying on target with the district's curriculum pacing guide. I was not scrambling to print off performance reports from benchmark exams. I did not teach a single test taking skill. On that morning, I asked my students to respond to the following questions in their daily journals: "What is your understanding of the events that happened between Trayvon Martin and George Zimmerman? What is your reaction to the not guilty verdict of the Zimmerman trial? How does the verdict affect your thinking as a Black student?" One young boy wrote, "I felt like George Zimmerman supposed to be locked up in jail. He killed some 17-year-old boy. So, if I had a gun, do I have the power to kill a white man? I'm Black so of course I'm going to jail automatically." To the last question, "how does the verdict affect your thinking as a Black student?," Manoucheca, a sixth grade girl, shared, "It effects me because, I feel like they think we are nothing." From there, I had one of the most powerful classroom discussions as a novice teacher. To be clear, Trayvon Martin was not our first curricular encounter with global anti-Black racism. In the five weeks leading up to this moment, students in the entire program wrote and read tirelessly about the Middle Passage, Haiti's colonial past, and its historical significance in the movement for Black liberation across the African Diaspora. By then, the rising sixth graders were skilled in naming the racist entanglements projected onto Blackness and Haitianness because of diverse literacy experiences defining their intersectionality as Black transnational young people. Each week brought opportunities to develop rich counternarratives of their ancestors and of themselves. Hence, our process of writing, speaking, listening, and embodying the life and death of Trayvon Martin ran congruent with the curricular philosophies of HELP to dignify and celebrate Black life. The learning space was especially designed to support both my students and myself during a wrought experience of racialed violence.

I open this article with my first-year teaching narrative to emphasize a few points. First, the murder of Trayvon Martin, a young Black boy from Miami, Florida, taking a walk to the corner store, was a transformative moment. It spurred the clarion call of Black Lives Matter, and activated a whole new generation of advocates, organizers, and civil servants. Those calls are even louder today at the intersection of COVID-19 and murders of Breonna Taylor, Ahmaud Arbery, and George Floyd. Second, juxtaposing these two schooling experiences within the context of Trayvon's death and his murderer's acquittal presents an opportunity to reemphasize how schooling spaces actively neutralize humanizing literacy instruction that advocates for Black children. My school, with its explicitly fixed notions of literacy for Black and Brown children, was never designed to nurture their dynamic diasporic literacies. Third, by illustrating the stark differences in my early work as a Reading/Language Arts educator, I want to assert the power of establishing literacy experiences for Black transnational youth that are deeply committed to emancipatory projects.

Black transnational youth, such as Haitians and Haitian Americans in the US, are coming of age in an era wrought with open hostility and state-sanctioned violence against Black people, women, members of the LGBTQ+ community, and immigrants. The discourses of anti-Blackness and white supremacy have been especially potent in the rhetoric and policies of the forty-fifth President of the United States describing Haiti as a "shithole" country while simultaneously seeking to gut the Temporary Protected Status of Haitian immigrants. For transnational Haitian youth, these messages are caustic and embedded in their everyday lives as children.

In its destruction of human life, the global pandemic of COVID-19 has hyper-magnified thinly veiled colonial logics and structures of white supremacy. It comes as no surprise to critical scholars that the most vulnerable communities prior to the outbreak of the coronavirus are paying the highest price in terms of loss of life, barriers to care, debilitating unemployment, housing and food insecurity, and widening gaps in equitable schooling experiences for children. It should also be no surprise that the global pandemic of 2020 has exacerbated centuries-long tensions regarding state-sanctioned violence and extrajudicial killings of Black people. The onslaught murders of Taylor, Arbery, and Floyd drew thousands of Americans onto the streets to demand justice and the abolishment of police as we know it.

Since Trayvon's death, my adulthood and teaching career have been punctuated, in rapid succession, by the footages, hashtags, protests, and headlines documenting the brutal violence lobbied against Black people. COVID-19 and the current demands for Black liberation represents our greatest challenge yet. Let us not forget, however, white supremacy is able to sustain generational cycles of anti-Black violence because of its remarkable adaptability to social progress. In his posthumous farewell, John Lewis aptly remarks, "Emmett Till was my George Floyd. He was my Rayshard Brooks, Sandra Bland and Breonna Taylor." To be frank, none of this is new. What I hope to accomplish in sharing this case study of HELP is to imbue readers with the urgency of establishing emancipatory curriculum in out-of-school literacy institutions that intentionally name the cyclical nature of global anti-Blackness and reconnect Black children to their literate traditions of liberation.

This paper intends to demonstrate how a community-based literacy program took up emancipatory approaches rooted in Black literacy traditions, Black transnational feminism, and anticolonial practices to generate liberatory experiences for Black Haitian and Haitian American middle schoolers. In doing so, this case study will provide opportunities for you to observe Black transnational youth wrestling with modern categories of Blackness and gender. It will also be an opportunity to glimpse how students take up spiritual tools to redefine their intersectional identities outside the confines of colonialist conceptualizations of Truth, science, and race (Ferreira da Silva 82).

In sharing the work of HELP and its emancipatory curriculum, I also want to urge against what I call *"the COVID-19 scramble"* where, in our rush to address the weight of this moment, we generate a patchwork of solutions aimed at "consciousness raising" (Grundy) that circumvent the work of redressing or outright dismantling institutions that disappear Indigenous people and extinguish Black and Brown life (Grande and Anderson 140). Breaking the generational cycles of white supremacy requires deliberate and intentional literacy practices dedicated to its eradication.

As a case study, this paper specifically focuses on the curricular practices of HELP, a middle school-level, out-of-school literacy program in Miami, Florida, where I served as a literacy instructor and researcher for three years. My primary question is "How can Black literate traditions, transnational feminist praxis, and anticolonial frameworks inform curriculum?" To engage this question, I methodologically triangulate Winn's (née Fisher) ethno-historiographical conceptualization of independent Black institutions (IBI), transnational feminist scholars, and anticoloniality to interpret HELP's curricular design and implementation.

The data for this case study was collected during my dissertation research during the summers of 2013, 2014, and 2015. For this piece, I pored over curriculum guides, lesson plans, weekly schedules, journal responses, and recorded classroom discussions. The goal was to examine how the curricular philosophies of the program supported my pedagogies as a literacy educator. I am specifically interested in how broad concepts such as race, gender, culture, place, and spirituality manifested in HELP's curriculum and facilitated Black transnational youth literacies. Overall, I determined HELP functioned as a transnational IBI by 1) disrupting neocolonial discourses of Haiti, Blackness, and Black womanhood, 2) strengthening students' cultural bridge to Haiti, and 3) encouraging spiritual consciousness that encompassed Haitian Vodou principles. By doing so, this community-based literacy center exercised transnational anticolonial pedagogy congruent with the African Diaspora's long traditions of literacy as resistance and liberation (Richardson, *African American Literacies* 16). In the sections that follow, I briefly overview HELP's inception, followed by theoretical perspectives of Black literacies and cultural institutions, Black transnational feminism, and anticolonialism. Next, I recount my teaching and learning experiences within the program while applying the triangulated methodological framework for analysis. Lastly, this piece maps twenty-first century implications for literacy programs committed to serving diverse Black transnational youth especially during moments of heightened racial violence.

Tools to Center Black Ways of Knowing and Liberation

Black literate traditions, Black transnational feminism, and anticolonial perspectives provide the necessary tools to decipher how HELP generated emancipatory curriculum for its Black transnational students. Collectively, these histories and perspectives center Black ways of knowing for the express purpose of global Black liberation. Black literate traditions credit the literacy practices of Black people across space and time. Black transnational feminism recognizes the work Black women do across the world to disrupt and resist racist and sexist colonial logics. Lastly, anticolonial projects interrogate coloniality's dehumanizing categories for Black people and its anti-Black knowledge productions. Thus, I turn to these histories and perspectives to inform my analysis of HELP's curricular practices and how they support the literacies and identities of Haitian and Haitian American middle schoolers.

The work of IBIs is best understood through an expansive conceptualization of literacy. In her exploration of the historical foundations of literacy in nineteenth-century Black communities, Gholdy Muhammad emphasizes, "literacy among Black people was not just tied to skills and proficiencies…but it was also defined as liberation and power. In this way, literacy was connected to acts of self-empowerment, self-determination, and self-liberation" (22). Similarly, Winn's ethno-historiographical research of the literacy practices of Black institutions in the mid to late twentieth century highlights the ways "people of African descent have employed literate practices to create and sustain independent institutions in the United States and abroad that focus on the production and preservation of written and spoken words while generating a discourse of self-reliance among Black people" (Fisher 3). I synthesized Winn's evaluation of the print news publication *Black News* and the after-school spoken word club at Benjamin Banneker Academy for Community Development in Brooklyn, New York, facilitated by veteran public-school teacher and literacy coach, Cathie Wright-Lewis, "Mama C," to deduce the most salient characteristics of IBIs. The core principles of IBIs illustrated in Winn's inquiry included building safe spaces for Black people to engage their concerns throughout the African Diaspora, connecting the local to the global by including issues that impact Black people all over the world; challenging community members, both elders and youth, to name and define their purposes for learning; and sustaining the literate lives of community members.

To better contextualize Black language use, I turn to Geneva Smitherman's observation of both Black religious and secular cultural institutions. Her work demonstrates how these Black cultural institutions employ literacy as liberation. As Smitherman explains, African American language "functioned as both a resistance language and a linguistic bond of cultural and racial solidarity for those born under the lash" ("'The Chain'" 8), and can be traced to seventeenth-century pidgin English which was the *lingua franca* of linguistically diverse enslaved African communities in Britain's North American colonies. Smitherman highlights communicative features that are prominent in African American language, especially in Hip Hop, such as narrativizing, the aspectual be, sampling, and semantic inversion as Black communication patterns of syntactic resistance, which "covertly reinforces Black America's 400-year rejection of Euro-American cultural, racial—and linguistic—domination" (11). Within the Black traditional church, Daniel and Smitherman's work note how Black communication dynamics are diasporic in nature and can be better defined through the cosmological lens of Traditional African World Views (27). Traditional African World

View is the "African formulation about the workings of the universe . . . that is of a dynamic, hierarchical unity…between God, man, and nature, with God serving as the head of the hierarchy" (29). They argue that this world view sustains a strong current in the African Diaspora and shapes the communication dynamics of Black people in the United States. By connecting Black literacies to Traditional African World View, it can also be argued that Black literacies are deeply spiritual and maintain connections to God, spirit, people, ancestors, and the material world. For Haitian communities especially, spirituality configures all aspects of life, which is aligned with Vodou's African-rooted principles (Bellegarde-Smith 103). Overall, historical and contemporary Black institutions center Black communicative dynamics of solidarity, spirituality, resistance, and invention. Thus, it is paramount to consider ways to incorporate the traditions of Black institutions when creating generative literacy experiences designed for Black transnational students.

It is vital for emancipatory literacy curriculum to name and dismantle the numerous ways race and gender are naturalized according to modern colonial categories (Ferreira da Silva 81). Coloniality can be understood as "centuries-long projects of delineating statuses of humanity, and from those categories of human and not, the ability to own land and others" (Wynter qtd. in Patel 359). These categories are normed by whiteness, masculinity, and heteronormativity and justified what C.L.R. James calls the "calculated total violence" of enslavement produced by colonial juridic, economic, and symbolic architectures (qtd. in Ferreira da Silva, 83). Ferreira da Silva further argues, "the total value produced by slave labor continues to sustain global capital" (83). Thus, transnationality can, in part, be understood as "a set of unequal relationships among and between peoples, rather than as a set of traits embodied in all non-U.S. citizens (particularly because U.S. citizenship continues to be premised within a white, Eurocentric, masculinist, heterosexist regime)" (Alexander and Mohanty 24). Nagar and Swarr propose several undertakings of transnational feminist praxis; however, for the scope of this case study, I focus on transnational feminism's ability to "attend to racialized, classed, masculinized, and heteronormative logics and practices of globalization and capitalist patriarchies, and the multiple ways in which they (re)structure colonial and neocolonial relations of domination and subordination" (5). Ferreira da Silva describes this process as "hacking," or the means to "disrupt the elements of sexual-gender signification that support the patriarch-form, even if she always comes into signification with/in the patriarch-form" ("Hacking" 26). In doing so, we emancipate Blackness from scientific and historical ways of knowing and allow an emancipated Blackness to open to other ways of knowing imagination (Ferreira da Silva, "Toward" 82).

Another key component in centering the racialized and gendered realities of Black women in global contexts is the spiritual discourses necessary to sustain diasporic ties to African-centered knowledge productions (Dillard and Okpalaoka 149). As Dillard highlights, academic spaces are often sites of universal generalizations which foreground White male knowledges to describe everyone's realities, including those Black and female (17). This leaves little room to ground research in the experiences and outside knowledges of Black women and dismisses spiritual consciousness. Endarkened feminist epistemologies advocate for self-defined Black female consciousness, which embraces both "a culturally centered worldview and a feminist sensibility" (Dillard 19), but also grounds spiritual consciousness as a "legitimate frame from and through which to participate in the social and political struggles of the world" (41). In sum, Black transnational feminist praxis and endarkened feminist epistemologies encourage the processes of naming colonial structures that create racialized and gendered social categories across the world, while honoring the Black women's ways of knowing and imagination that are grounded in diasporic experiential and spiritual knowledges. For that reason, I incorporate these perspectives in my work of contextualizing emancipatory curriculum for Black transnational students.

Postcolonial theory in education is largely committed to "decolonizing knowledge and the production of transformative knowledge" (Subedi and Daza 2). However, Tuck and Yang (2012) admonish the notion of decolonization as a metaphor for other civil rights and human rights social justice projects. Their argument is that decolonization projects cannot be detached from remitting Indigenous land and sovereignty. In thinking about the literacy practices engaged at HELP, I find it difficult to position our learning community as decolonial in nature because it does not intentionally center the return of land to Indigenous communities. However, the African Diaspora's complicated relationship to land, space, and time, alongside Haiti's own entrenched history with French coloniality, necessitates tools to deconstruct colonial power structures, center the lived experiences of historically silenced communities, and create motives for reimagination and transformation. Thus, I lean into Patel's conceptualization of anticolonial projects as it more accurately describes the intent and practices of HELP's curriculum.

As a concept, anticoloniality locates "the genealogies in contemporary colonial relationships to learning, knowledge, and knowledge production" while avoiding "the unmet promises of stripping away colonization, as the term *decolonization* gestures to do" (Patel 360). Characteristics for anticolonial projects include, being "vigilant about the deeply colonial structures of institution, thought," and interrupting relationality deeply tied to land ownership" (Patel 360). As Patel explains, settler colonialism actively "seeks to place land ownership in the hands of a few" and, therefore, "our relationships to the land, to each other, and to knowledge and learning, are shaped by this settler colonial structure (361). Equally important in anticolonial efforts is the denaturalization of English as the primary language and performance of knowledge production and meaning making (Cushman 236). The language use of Haitian and Haitian American students creates an intersection of linguistic resources and marginalization. As Richardson highlights, historically, language education in the US consisted of a continuous push towards monolingualism and monodialecticalism, a process which teaches Black children to "devalue the Black cultural aspects of [their] identity, including [their] language use" ("Race" 63). When navigating traditional institutions of education, which are constituted by institutional racism, some Black students learn to cope by "adopting or adapting dominant cultural values" (Richardson, "Race" 41). As Black transnational youth situated within the United States, the students at HELP spoke both African American Vernacular English and Haitian Creole.

To unseat white monolingual culture, an anticolonial project must also recognize students' right to their own language and culture (Smitherman, "'Students'" 25).

In summary, anticolonial teaching and learning in a literacy context resembles centering lived experiences of the marginalized, disrupting text enmeshed in white settler colonialism imaginations of the Caribbean, and modeling epistemic disobedience—questioning categories, acknowledging the existence of racist institutions, and connecting the local and global to colonial projects (Krueger-Henney 90-92). With this stance, I can more accurately locate teaching and learning practices rooted in tearing down colonial categories and knowledge production within the context of a middle school literacy program. In the grand scheme of community-based writing and literacy programs, why do Black literacy traditions, Black transnational feminist praxis, and anticolonial projects matter? As Grande and Anderson point out, when the world continues to unravel due to climate change, immense debt, and unprecedented inequality and violence, these perspectives provide students a context and framework to make sense of their lives and imagine different possibilities (141-42). As COVID-19 continues to ravage our most vulnerable communities and expose deep fissures of injustice in all of our social institutions, we should further challenge the fundamental philosophies of literacy education by looking to the scholarship and lived experiences of people of color to drive literacy experiences with young people.

The Haitian Empowerment Literacy Project (HELP)

The literacy program, HELP, was founded by Drs. Charlene Désir and Pamela Hall. Dr. Charlene Désir is a Haitian American scholar, co-founder of The Empowerment Network Global (T.E.N. Global), and an associate professor at Nova Southeastern University's Fischler College of Education. Dr. Pamela Hall is the associate dean of Graduate Studies in the College of Arts and Sciences and associate professor of psychology at Barry University. As community-oriented psychologists and researchers, the two created HELP's high school-serving predecessor, the Literacy Initiative for Empowerment (LIFE) Program, with a grant from The Children's Trust in 2009. HELP was formed to provide socioemotional support to the influx of Haitian children to South Florida after Haiti's devastating earthquake in 2010. The program began serving the middle grades to maintain grant requirements. HELP completed its seventh and final institute in the summer of 2015.

The purpose of the program was to mentor Haitian adolescents by empowering them to make positive life choices, develop sociocultural awareness, and build literacy skills in order for them to maximize their potential ("Pamela"). As a culturally based literacy program, HELP employed a holistic approach that provided students with "practical" literacy skills, explicit spiritual education, and cultural education. The program focused on cultivating the minds, bodies, and spirits of students. Each summer institute was shaped by a large overarching slogan which grounded the foundations for the cognitive, physical, and spiritual work to be accomplished during the summer institute. The slogans during my three years at the program were as follows: The School is the Church, the Church is the School: "Spiritual Consciousness Connects us with the Divine Mind" (2013); Mystical Imagination: "Zero Curriculum: From Nothing Comes Everything" (2014); and "Beyond Liberation" (2015). Each week was led by a smaller guiding principle related to different aspects of the broader summer slogan. The program convened Monday-Friday from 8:00am-4:00pm. Each summer, HELP enrolled approximately one hundred students between the grades six through eight. I began as one of two sixth grade literacy instructors and rose with the same cohort of students until my final year as an eighth grade literacy instructor. By then, my classroom consisted of twenty-seven seventh and eighth grade students: twenty-two girls and five boys. Based on the theoretical perspectives framing this case study inquiry, I asked three analytical questions of HELP's curricular data. First, how does Black liberation inform the literacy practices of the program? Second, in what ways are the experiences of Black women and African-centered spiritual ways of knowing centered in the curriculum? And third, how does the program name and disrupt colonial discourses of Haiti?

Teaching and Learning at HELP

Creating New Narratives for Haiti and Blackness

As a curricular practice, HELP disrupted neocolonial discourses of Haiti and Blackness by offering students multiple literacy experiences to explore Haiti and Blackness within Black epistemologies. Students generated multiple reflective journal entries to articulate who they were; the relationships between Blackness, Haitianness, and Americanness; and how they situate themselves within these frames. Each summer, every student crafted "Who am I?" poems. Some students revised these poems into performance pieces for the end-of-summer celebration. The activities prepare students to take on new narratives of Haiti and are particularly important at the sixth grade level because, often times, it is their first introduction to Haiti in a schooling space that does not engage the tired trope "Haiti is the poorest country in the Western Hemisphere." In the first week of the program, our sixth graders reflect on their imaginations of Haiti. In one journal prompt, "Haiti on my Mind," I asked my students to complete the following phrase: "When I think of the island Haiti, in my mind I see/think/feel…." I like to use the example of Manoucheca, the sixth grade girl referenced in my teaching narrative at the beginning of this article. I presented students with this prompt in the first week of the program, and on June 13, Manoucheca wrote, "When I see Haiti on TV, I feel sad for them. Sometimes, I think of doing a fundraiser to help Haiti." Her entry reveals even as a young Haitian girl who grew up in Miami, surrounded by a thriving Haitian community, she too, was unable to conceptualize the location of her ethnic heritage outside racist globalized pathologies that blame Haitian people for their current devastating realities (Krueger-Henney 91).

However, through close readings of the sixth grade text, and enrichment activities with local spoken word artist and musician, Mecca "Grimo" Marcelin, students gained entry into Haiti's remarkable histories and migration narratives through performative historical retellings of Haitian Revolution, poetry writing, and defining terms such as the Middle Passage and the African Diaspora. Four weeks later, I asked my sixth graders to describe what they had learned so far in the program. By then, Manoucheca demonstrated the breadth and depth of learning in her short time in HELP. She shared the following:

> I'm Black. We won our independence. We were the first nation to win the independence from the French's. We got our country back. Haiti have beautiful beaches. Jean-Baptiste Point du Sable was the founder of Chicago. In Haiti, we have a bus called, Tap Tap. The reason why it's called that because they tap to tell the driver to let me off. Dessalines was the king of Haiti. Toussaint was a man that was smart. When we won our independence, he rip the white out the flag that represent slavery. He ripped it out and put the red and blue and that's how we got our flag.

Manoucheca's page-long entry represents her expanded imagination of Haiti that is not solely constructed by images of poverty and need. She cites Haitian revolutionary lore, speaks of Haiti's founders, and connects this knowledge to everyday cultural references such as the Haitian city transportation. Most importantly, Manoucheca doesn't distance herself from Haiti in the same ways she did in her previous entry. Haiti is no longer a distant "them" to be pitied. Four weeks later, she actively uses the collective "we" to discuss Haitian Independence, its historical significance, and her connection to a new-found sense of Blackness.

The process of creating new narratives of Blackness is ongoing in the program. Nadège, Haitian-born rising ninth grader in her second and final summer in the program, articulated how the program functioned as a space for reinvigorating affirming Black identities. On June 22, 2015, Nadège responded to the perennial question of "Who am I?" with a wrenching description of her eighth grade year. She wrote, "Last year, I stood on stage and spoke to an audience about who I thought I was. I was filled to the brim with confidence about my identity. However, as I went through my eighth grade year, that solid image shattered. I came back to HELP to pick up the pieces and glue them back together." Nadège went on to describe herself as a Black scholar, a writer who "gets pulled into a reality that [she] created," and a Christian with a strong faith in God. Her narrative exemplifies why articulating who you are within a Black gendered body must be a continuous exercise performed in a supportive space.

As an IBI, HELP reconfigured learning spaces by creating multiple interactions for students to engage in intergenerational literacy practices with elders, academics, and artists from their communities. These actors, in turn, imparted to students literacies that disrupted harmful discourses and challenged engrained "mis-education" (Fisher 69) of Haitian and Haitian American students in Miami. Approximately once a week, a guest lecturer would facilitate a morning discussion with the students on a topic related to the weekly theme or their own work in the Haitian community. On June 19, 2015, Sokari Ekine facilitated the morning meeting during the week themed "Self (Duality)." After describing her ties to Africa as Nigerian-British woman, Ekine opened her talk with the question, "What is Vodou?" The students' responses announced the controlling discourses of Vodou in their communities. One boy responded, "dark magic," while one girl chimed in that Vodou is medicine, but people use it in the wrong way for other purposes. Another girl added, "originally used for healing, now something else, dark magic, bad stuff to kill people." One more girl added, "Ceremony that ancestors used to do to connect with magic." Ekine took the opportunity to unpack the word "magic" in the students' responses and queries by asking, "What is magic? What if I turn water into wine? Isn't that magic? They both require the power of a person. How do we use that power? Celebrating our ancestors, and drawing the spirit of ancestors, healing, communicating."

At this juncture of conversation, co-founder Charlene Désir put Vodou in conversation with Catholicism and Protestantism and asserted, "Vodou was a religion. It was the first religion, coming from Africa. Native Americans and [Africans] were not allowed to practice their religion. People vilified Vodou." She then connected the practices and products of Vodou to the everyday materials in their lives as Haitian youth. "Lwil mascriti," Haitian castor oil, and té, herbal tea remedies, came from Divine energy [and] connection to nature." Désir concluded by calling students to research and find out more about Vodou for themselves.

Ekine looped the conversation back to Vodou's connection to the African continent. She explained, "Look at Vodou as a historical and cultural tradition which draws connections to Ibo and Yoruba." She discussed how the names of the different Haitian Vodou traditions were the same names used in Yoruba and Ibo traditions, and that the ancestors "brought those together in Haiti. The history of Haiti is the bringing together of people." This portion of Ekine's presentation accomplished a range of things. With the assistance of Dr. Désir, she disrupted the vilification of Vodou and provided counternarratives to its epistemologies as a medium to connect to ancestors and nature and to bring people together. The conversation intertwined multiple discourses of Blackness, spirituality, and non-western epistemologies that drew explicit bonds between Haitian culture and the students' everyday cultural practices.

Centering Black Feminist Storytelling

HELP's curriculum supported Black feminist approaches to literacy instruction. The short stories of *Krik? Krak!* by Edwidge Danticat center Black female protagonists as mothers, daughters, elders, sex workers, and domestics. These short stories normalized Haitian women's voices driving the narrative perspectives. In summer of 2015, tensions around gender were most apparent in my eighth grade class' reading of "Night Women," a seven-page short story narrated by a sex worker. The reading of "Night Women" required pre-reading strategies to air out the discourses of women in the sex industry, as well as using supporting texts to contextualize the lived experiences of the girls and women who get pushed into the industry. I facilitated a pre-reading activity, an open word-association activity in which I asked students to generate words that came to mind with the phrase, "women of the night." Unsurprisingly, students tapped into the dehumanizing gendered discourses of women in sex work. Their responses included whore, demoralized, slut, desperate, nasty, prostitute, deviant, and THOT (that ho over there). From there, students unraveled the meanings behind these labels and why they get ascribed to women.

In reading "Night Women," I asked students to make note of all the things we learned of the nameless woman in the story. The majority of students highlighted that the woman is a loving mother and the notable absence of her child's father. They also wrote about her beliefs in God and her desire to want more for herself, feeling older than her twenty-five years. One girl asked poignant questions, such as "Will she teach her son to not be like the men that come to her? Was his father her pimp? Was she raped? Did he sell her?" While students did make critiques of the woman in the story, I observed that, for the most part, they tried to dig deeper with the text and extract as many meanings as they could from the seven pages detailing an evening in the character's life.

I further challenged students to think of other ways to frame women in sex work and brought in two media texts: a news report from the *The Washington Post*, "Report: U.N. Peacekeepers in Haiti Had 'Transactional Sex' with Hundreds of Poor Women," and a publication from Black online media organization, *The Root*, titled "The Sex-Abuse-Prison Pipeline: How Girls of Color Are Unjustly Arrested and Incarcerated." These texts were used to shift perceptions and allow students to think of women in humanizing frameworks that explored patriarchal social structures that pushed some Black women and girls into vulnerable situations. As part of the reading, students were tasked with annotating the texts with questions and responses. A handful of students took to the inquiry process and annotated a series of thought-provoking comments to the text. In *The Washington Post* report, one girl gravitated to the following passage: "For rural women, hunger, lack of shelter, baby care items, medication and household items were frequently cited as the 'triggering need,' the report said. In exchange for sex, women got 'church shoes, cell phones, laptops, and perfume as well as money' from peacekeepers" (Moyer). She wrote in response, "If woman [sic] were in need why would they exchange sex? Wouldn't they go to the government are [sic] family members?" Two other girls made note of the report's finding that "most [Haitian women] were unaware the United Nations prohibited sexual exploitation and has a hotline to report it" and "only seven interviewees knew about the United Nations policy prohibiting sexual exploitation and abuse" (Moyer). Some girls speculated whether the women were too scared to report, and why so many to did not know how. One eighth grade girl, Venus, lodged a critique of the UN, and stated, "they're being very quiet and slow about what is happening... if the UN was more together maybe this might not happen." Malika Saada Saar's piece on the sex-abuse-prison pipeline elicited the most poignant responses in student annotations. Saar made the case that girls who run away from abusive environments or are forced into sex traffic are often criminalized for running away or jailed for prostitution. One girl angrily wrote, "why does no one arrest the men that buy and sell them? It's not their fault that they're being trafficked." Venus added, "that seems stupid to me. They're being locked up while the real bad people get to live their lives :/."

Our eighth grade class' reading of "Night Women" and the two accompanying media texts facilitated an exercise in humanizing Black women's experiences. We accomplished this by revealing the patriarchal structures that hypersexualize Black Caribbean women and perpetuate the colonial legacies of exploitation which continue to ravage Haiti's most vulnerable communities. All three texts assisted students in recognizing the humanity in sex work and thus breaking down the binary of us/them, especially considering the US contexts in which Black girls are sexually abused into the prison pipeline. Centering Black transnational women's experiences gave students an entry point into understanding the precarity of Black girls in the United States.

Developing Spiritual Consciousness

HELP's curriculum encouraged students to develop spiritual consciousness that encompassed both Haitian Vodou principles and Judeo-Christian traditions. While trying to develop spiritual consciousness, the program did not explicitly promote any particular religion or its specific practices. Instead, the curriculum engaged in developing spiritual epistemologies, meaning, "how individuals know the transcendent and how they use and disseminate this knowledge in their lives and communities" (Désir et al. 336). The most commonly practiced religions in Haiti are Catholicism, Protestantism, and Vodou. Scholars have paid little attention to the spiritual development of Haitian and Haitian American young people, despite "religion being a complex phenomenon in the Haitian tradition" (344). As a program geared towards providing students the opportunity to explore their identities, HELP deliberately includes spiritual activities in the curriculum. Instead of instilling students with "traditional beliefs, behaviors, and rituals to participate in and perpetuate the institution and religious community" (Désir et al. 341), spirituality manifested "as both the search for meaning and life's purpose and the practices that deepen one's experience of transcendence" (342).

Haitian Vodou is an African cosmology that functions as a comprehensive religious system that "ties together the visible and invisible, material and spiritual, secular and scared" (Michel 282). Vodou grew in response to Haiti's brutally violent colonial history. Newly enslaved Africans from various regions created new collective communities anchored in shared spiritual ancestry and a quest for freedom. European colonial logics, 'til this day, demonized African spiritual ways of knowing and embedded Catholicism within the institution of slavery on the island. Haitian Vodou scholar Claudine Michel notes this repression of Vodou "forced the Africans to hide allegiance to their ancestral religions and stimulated them to develop innovative forms of worshiping African deities....Thus, Vodou became not only the means for revitalization through ancestral traditions but also the channel par excellence to organization and to resistance" (281).

Haitian Vodou principles manifested in HELP's curriculum as the weekly themes. These themes are represented in Table 1.

Table 1.

Lwas/Haitian Principle	Meaning of Principle	Weekly Themes
Gede	Life/Death	Self
Marasa	Duality	Self
Simbi	Healing	Interpersonal
Legba	Crossroads	Interpersonal
Jeni	Psychosocial Spiritual Intelligence/Awareness	Community (Internal)
Ezili	Love	Community (External)
Azaka	New Beginnings	Integration

Within each week, students participated in a series of reflective writing in their journals, meditations during morning meetings, and various activities with guest lecturers from the community. For the scope of this case study, I will focus specifically on the activities generated in week three of the program. The writing genre for this week consisted of prayer writing. Students participated in scaffolded reflective writing activities that culminated in constructing individual and co-constructed classroom prayers centered around the Haitian *lwa*, or spirit, Simbi. Within the Vodou tradition, Simbi represents a water spirit. The element of water occupies a central space in Afro-Haitian cosmology and represents "life-giving and purifying energy… A body of water is said to divide the ordinary world of humans and the invisible world of the spirits and the ancestors" (McAlister 261). Spirits that dwell within the waters, such as Simbi, contain energies that "can be 'worked' by humans for healing treatments" (261). As a *lwa*, Simbi represents "a type of reconfigured ancestor spirit" and is believed to be derived from the basimbi spirits from the Kongo region (261). As a water spirit, Simbi possess the power to offer healing and "purify what is soiled" (260).

Given the nature of Simbi, the reflections and eventual construction of prayers were anchored in ameliorating our collective relationships with each other and requesting healing and peace for others. Early in the week, I prompted students to define prayer, its purpose, and the multiple contexts in which someone may turn to prayer. Although students were well-versed in participating in prayer, the Simbi *lwa* principle facilitated conversations around trauma, healing, and the necessary actions to mend broken relationships and societal ills. In the final reflective activity, students created heart maps to articulate their desires and guide their prayers. Students were instructed to trace a large outline of a heart in their composition journals. From there, they were advised to chart out all the things they wanted for themselves in order to practice voicing what was in their hearts. From there, the students used the heart maps as a framework for their individual prayers. This guiding principle was also tightly aligned with the reading activities for the week. The sixth graders in the program were assigned to read Edwidge Danticat's *Behind the Mountains*, a Scholastic "First Person Fiction" that tells the story of a young Haitian girl's migration narrative from Haiti to New York. Because the story grounds Haitian cultural references and practices, the main character, Celiane, takes up prayer during especially tense moments in the story. To connect the prayer writing genre to the text, students wrote prayers from the perspective of the main character and decided which of her experiences warranted prayer. In this activity, sixth grader Lucy in summer 2013 makes the choice to pray about the political tensions described in the story. She writes, "Dear Heavenly Father, thank you for keeping my family safe from the pipe bombs that were thrown at the camion. Help those who throw bombs realize they are hurting us and killing the souls of young children." Here, Lucy applies our classroom discussions of the Simbi principal of communal healing. Voiced as Celiane, Lucy recognizes an important part of ending the political violence occurring in the story involves appealing to the humanity of the instigators rather than condemning them as monsters.

Lucy's prayer at the end of the week incorporated a host of cultural and linguistic resources. Her prayer was written in both English and Haitian Creole, and she seamlessly oscillates between both languages to articulate her prayer. Lucy's prayer asks God to "let us build a foundation in our country" and for "people not to see us as boat people [but as] people of change." In Haitian Creole, Lucy thanks God for "all the children that survived the earthquake" and in English she expresses being "thankful for this country, a strong country." In this example, Lucy participates in writing as a spiritual reflective practice (Dillard 38) to make meaning of a Haitian canonical text centering a Black girl her age, while also engaging in the extensive anticolonial practice of translanguaging. Her prayer privileges her multilingual resources to process the text (Cushman 235) and spiritual consciousness.

Exploring Multimodalities of Haitian Visual and Performance Arts

Students' learning contexts at HELP took on multiple modalities throughout the duration of the program, which reflects the holistic approach to empowering Black transnational students with rich cultural backgrounds. HELP's curriculum created a cultural bridge for students to participate in literary experiences directly connected to Haitian visual and performance arts. The enrichment learning blocks were facilitated by community members from a range of creative disciplines. The objectives of the enrichment learning activities were for students to engage in multiple forms of expression to develop affirming identities. Incorporating the body, movement, and music were major parts of the enrichment experience. Students also participated in week-long Haitian folk dance and capoeira workshops with local dancers and capoeira masters.

The highlight of the enrichment experience was the filmmaking workshop conducted by Rachelle Salnave, an Emmy-nominated filmmaker, creator of Ayiti Images Film Series, and adjunct Film Professor at Miami Dade College. Students had the opportunity to write and direct their own film produced by Salnave. In the film, Salnave inquired, "What do you see in the mirror?" The film is a compilation of footage shot by students responding to Salvnave's question and capturing candid moments in the program. Students had a chance to use filming equipment and learned the ropes of capturing video, recording audio, and staging participants in the interviews. They were also responsible for writing the script to go along with the film. Students who volunteered to be interviewed also took the liberty to speak in two languages, both English and Creole, to detail their aspirations. The film premiered at the end-of-summer celebration during the last week of the summer institute, which is attended by parents, community stakeholders, and supporters of the program. The showcase was the high-point of the summer. Students highlighted what they had learned in their chosen medium of spoken word poetry, dance, singing, instrumentation, or art. Students played a significant role in developing the programming and crafting the narrative of the summer.

Concluding Thoughts and Implications for the Year 2020

The HELP program functioned as an independent Black institution exercising transnational feminist and anticolonial pedagogy congruent with the African Diaspora's long traditions of literacy as liberation. Using Black literacy traditions, transnational feminist praxis, and anticolonial perspectives, I was able to interpret the ways its curriculum facilitated emancipatory approaches towards literacy instruction for Black transnational children. HELP's curriculum strived to disrupt the colonial discourses of Haiti and provided students with an epistemological framework of the home island rooted in agency and liberation. Community activists and artists heartened students to connect Haiti's legacy to solidarity movements across the African Diaspora. The HELP curriculum, rooted in Haitian feminist canonical texts of Edwidge Danticat, gave students access to themselves in a literacy classroom that is often missing in their traditional schooling experiences. In addition, the program emphasized developing spiritual consciousness to support students' meaning-making processes and expand their conceptualization of spirituality to include Haiti's Afro-cosmology of Vodou. Overall, for curriculum to be emancipatory and serve culturally and linguistically diverse students, it must recognize and center the literacies embedded in their communities. Those literacies supply crucial frameworks in which to engage the lived experiences and intersectionality of student groups. Also, emancipatory curriculum is decidedly Black and gender inclusive. Transnational feminist praxis encapsulates the experiential knowledges of women of color and queer communities across the world. The most consequential critique of the program is that more work could have and should have been done around queering Black transnational epistemologies and experiences. Though we briefly discussed Caitlyn Jenner's transition in the summer of 2015, it was clear students did not have access to the same sorts of tools to discuss queer experiences as they had with Blackness, Haitianness, and gender. Lastly, people of color around the world are still deeply entrenched in colonial and imperial legacies. Therefore, emancipatory curriculum must speak directly to those legacies and generate literacy experiences where students disrupt categories and learn histories rooted in anticolonial projects.

So, how does a literacy program that ended five years ago help us navigate our current realities of COVID-19 and white supremacy's hyper visible violence? To borrow from a ubiquitous Black adage, "if you stay ready, you ain't gotta get ready," meaning programs that are fundamentally designed to confront white supremacy and intentionally center epistemologies of communities of color are best prepared to take on the cyclical violence. COVID-19 has elevated public awareness around structural racism in ways that are both encouraging and frustrating. In our collective rush to honor the moment, and bring back some semblance of normalcy, we naively—or intentionally—overlook that "normal" for many communities has meant erasure, violence, and exploitation. As institutions dedicated to safeguarding the well-being and development of young people, especially young people of color, our work must be grounded in making sure that "normal" never comes back again.

A transformative community-based writing center recognizes our new realities and addresses them head on. This is done by connecting local experiences to communities around the world, centering the voices of women, and honoring diasporic sacred knowledges. When considering your context, in what ways can you practice deep listening and create spaces based on articulated needs of families? How can their cultural and spiritual epistemologies guide experiences within your centers? HELP's curriculum team consisted of Black female researchers; our academic expertise offered but one avenue for student engagement. Working closely with community organizers and artists, students had a wide selection of generational expertise to create rounded ideas themselves. Thus, are people at the decision-making level of your institution intimately connected to the experiences, scholarship, and communities of Black, Brown, or Indigenous people? If the answer is no, ask why; then do the work to find them. The pressure to "get it right" is a real one, and my intention is not to make light of this effort. However, interrupting generations of global anti-Black violence requires informed thoughtfulness, humility, and incredible visions for the future.

Works Cited

Alexander, M. Jacqui, and Chandra Talpade Mohanty. "Cartographies of Knowledge and Power: Transnational Feminism as Radical Praxis." *Critical Transnational Feminist Praxis*, edited by Amanda Lock Swarr and Richa Nagar, SUNY P, 2010, pp. 23–45.

Bellegarde-Smith, Patrick. "Resisting Freedom: Cultural Factors in Democracy—The Case for Haiti." *Vodou in Haitian Life and Culture: Invisible Powers*, edited by Claudine Michel and Patrick Bellegarde-Smith, Palgrave Macmillan, 2016, pp. 101–15.

Cushman, Ellen. "Translingual and Decolonial Approaches to Meaning Making." *College English*, vol. 78, no. 3, 2016, pp. 234–42.

Daniel, Jack L., and Geneva Smitherman. "How I Got Over: Communication Dynamics in the Black Community." *Quarterly Journal of Speech*, vol. 62, no. 1, 1976, p. 26-39, doi:10.1080/00335637609383315.

Danticat, Edwidge. *Behind the Mountains*. Scholastic, 2002.

—. *Krik? Krak!*. Soho Press, 2004.

Désir, Charlene, et al. "Discovering Haitian Youth's Spiritual Epistemology Through a Culturally Based Summer Program in Florida." *Les Jeunes Haïtiens Dans Les*

Amériques/Haitian Youth in the Americas, edited by Louis Herns Marcelin et al., Presses de l'Université du Québec, 2017, pp. 333–57.

Dillard, Cynthia B., and Chinwe Okpalaoka. "The Sacred and Spiritual Nature of Endarkened Transnational Feminist Praxis in Qualitative Research." *The SAGE Handbook of Qualitative Research*, edited by Norman K. Denzin and Yvonna S. Lincoln, SAGE, 2011, pp. 147-62.

Dillard, Cynthia B. ""*On Spiritual Strivings: Transforming an African American Woman's Academic Life*, SUNY P, 2006.

Ferreira da Silva, Denise. "Hacking the Subject: Black Feminism and Refusal beyond the Limits of Critique." *PhiloSOPHIA*, vol. 8, no. 1, 2018, pp. 19–41, doi:10.1353/phi.2018.0001.

—. "Toward a Black Feminist Poethics: The Quest(ion) of Blackness Toward the End of the World." *The Black Scholar*, vol. 44, no. 2, 2014, pp. 81–97, doi:10.1080/00064246.2014.11413690.Fisher, Maisha T. *Black Literate Lives: Historical and Contemporary Perspectives*. Routledge, 2008.

Grande, Sandy, and Lauren Anderson. "Un-Settling Multicultural Erasures." *Multicultural Perspectives*, vol. 19, no. 3, 2017, pp. 139–42., doi:10.1080/15210960.2017.1331742.

Grundy, Saida. "The False Promise of Anti-Racism Books." *The Atlantic*, Atlantic Media Company, 21 July 2020, www.theatlantic.com/culture/archive/2020/07/your-anti-racism-books-are-means-not-end/614281/.

Krueger-Henney, Patricia. "A Letter to Educators about Teaching toward Caribbean Decoloniality." *Transformations: The Journal of Inclusive Scholarship and Pedagogy*, vol. 27, no. 1, Sept. 2017, pp. 87–94. EBSCOhost, doi:10.1353/tnf.2017.0008.

Lewis, John. "Together, You Can Redeem the Soul of Our Nation." *The New York Times*, 30 July 2020, https://nyti.ms/2P6qaku.

McAlister, Elizabeth. "Sacred Waters of Haitian Vodou: The Pilgrimage of Sodo." *Sacred Waters: A Cross-Cultural Compendium of Hallowed Springs and Holy Wells*, edited by Celeste Ray, Routledge, 2020, pp. 259–65.

Michel, Claudine. "Of Worlds Seen and Unseen: The Educational Character of Haitian Vodou." *Comparative Education Review*, vol. 40, no. 3, 1996, pp. 280-94.

Moyer, Justin Wm. "Report: U.N. Peacekeepers in Haiti Had 'Transactional Sex' with Hundreds of Poor Women." *The Washington Post*, 11 June 2015, www.washingtonpost.com/news/morning-mix/wp/2015/06/11/report-u-n-peacekeepers-in-haiti-had-transactional-sex-with-hundreds-of-poor-women/.

Muhammad, Gholdy. *Cultivating Genius: An Equity Framework for Culturally and Historically Responsive Literacy*. Scholastic Teaching Resources (Teaching Strategies), 2020.

Nagar, Richa, and Amanda Lock Swarr. "Theorizing Transnational Feminist Praxis." *Critical Transnational Feminist Praxis*, edited by Amanda Lock Swarr and Richa Nagar, SUNY P, 2010, pp. 1–20.

"Pamela D. Hall, PhD." *Barry University*, 2020, www.barry.edu/psychology/psychology-bs/faculty/hall.html.

Patel, Lisa. "Countering Coloniality in Educational Research: From Ownership to Answerability." *Educational Studies*, vol. 50, no. 4, 2014, pp. 357-77, doi: 10.1080/00131946.2014.924942

Richardson, Elaine. *African American Literacies*. Routledge, 2003.

---. "Race, Class(es), Gender, and Age: The Making of Knowledge about Language Diversity." *Language Diversity in the Classroom: From Intention to Practice*, edited by Geneva Smitherman and Victor Villanueva, Southern Illinois UP, 2003, pp. 40–66.

Saar, Malika Saada. (2015). "The Sex-Abuse-to-Prison Pipeline: How Girls of Color are Unjustly Arrested and Incarcerated." *The Root*, 7 Sep. 2015, www.theroot.com/the-sex-abuse-to-prison-pipeline-how-girls-of-color-ar-1790860479

Salnave, Rachelle. "H.E.L.P. Summer Filmmaker Workshop 2015." *Vimeo*, July 2015, https://vimeo.com/133856345.

Smitherman, Geneva. "'Students' Right to Their Own Language': A Retrospective." *The English Journal*, vol. 84, no. 1, 1995, pp. 21–27, doi:10.2307/820470.

_____. "'The Chain Remain the Same': Communicative Practices in the Hip Hop Nation." *Journal of Black Studies*, vol. 28, no. 1, 1997, pp. 3–25., doi:10.1177/002193479702800101.

Subedi, Binaya, and Stephanie Lynn Daza. "The Possibilities of Postcolonial Praxis in Education." *Race Ethnicity and Education*, vol. 11, no. 1, 2008, pp. 1-10.

Tuck, Eve, and K. Wayne Yang. "Decolonization is Not a Metaphor." *Decolonization: Indigeneity, Education & Society*, vol. 1, no. 1, 2012, pp. 1-40.

Author Bio

Wideline Seraphin is an assistant professor of literacy in the department of Instruction and Curriculum Leadership at the University of Memphis. Her work centers the literacies of Black transnational girls, and engages Black Feminist Thought, Critical Media Literacies, and Black Geographies. She worked as a reading/language arts teacher in Miami, Florida before obtaining her PhD in Curriculum and Instruction at The Pennsylvania State University. Wideline's work is informed by her experiences as a second-generation Haitian American student and educator in urban schools.

You Can't Say Pupusa Without Saying Pupusa: Translanguaging in a Community-Based Writing Center

Stephanie Abraham and Kate Kedley

Abstract

In this article, we share our experiences with the ongoing language and literacy practices and pedagogies of a bilingual, community-based writing center located in South Philadelphia's Italian Market. This writing center - one in a network of sites across Philadelphia and southern New Jersey - targeted bilingual, Latinx children from ages seven to eighteen. For the past four years, we have partnered with the center to create a translanguaging space. Here, we reflect on the experience of offering translanguaging writing workshops.

Keywords

translanguaging; community based writing center; literacy; bilingualism; research partnerships

On a crisp, Saturday morning in October, five children and two teacher researchers were sitting around a large, rectangular table, located inside Autores Fuertes, a community-based writing center in Philadelphia. As part of a workshop on writing bilingual family stories, the children were busy writing and drawing, drafting revised versions of their stories. They were adding illustrations to a story board, stick figures for family members, and jotting down on yellow, sticky notes things that they wanted to add. The children checked their spelling using Google translate, and sometimes asked their peers how to say something in English or Spanish. Stephanie and Kate, the authors and teacher researchers, were checking in with each child, for more story details, complimenting their illustrations, and suggesting that they use more Spanish. When Stephanie sat down with Marcos (all participant names and sites are pseudonyms) he was revising his story, which centered around the things and people that he missed in El Salvador, and he had already listed his tíos, his primos, el calor, and now he had come to the word, pupusa, a popular food from El Salvador. He turned to Stephanie and asked, "How do you say pupusa in English?" Thus, Stephanie's response: "You can't say pupusa without saying pupusa." This short exchange illustrates the translanguaging nature of Autores Fuertes, as well as the unavoidable translanguaging of multilingual and transnational children who were in the workshop, whose lives are embedded in a translanguaging reality.

In this article, we explore this translanguaging reality and share our experiences with the ongoing language and literacy practices and pedagogies of Autores Fuertes.

Located in South Philadelphia's Italian Market, this community is a longtime receiving city for immigrants. Between 2000 and 2010 more recent immigrants began arriving in Philadelphia from Mexico, specifically the states of Puebla and Tlaxcala. Even more recently, immigrants from Central America, including Honduras and El Salvador, have found new homes in South Philadelphia. A new dual-language (English/Spanish) K-8 school opened a few blocks south of the center, in part to meet the linguistic and cultural needs of the community. The Italian Market has now become a new "Mexican Market" as proudly advertised by the Mexican American shop owners.

This community writing center—one in a network of sites across Philadelphia and southern New Jersey—targeted bilingual, Latinx children from ages seven to eighteen. The center itself is a bustling site, located amidst fish markets, produce stands, and tortillerías. It occupies about one thousand square feet of physical space, with an enormous Calendario Azteca in the front window display. Bookshelves line the dark pink walls, and there is row after row of high-quality children's literature, including bilingual books and Spanish language texts, free for the children and families to take home. There's a small kitchen area stocked with apple juice and bags of vegetable chips. Several areas in the center are designated as writing and learning spaces with long tables and chairs, and trays of markers, crayons, and pencils atop.

The center's central goal was "to teach children to write," and they offered services such as mentoring, homework help, evening and weekend writing workshops, summer camps, and a new Saturday morning toddler program. During the summer months when school was out of session, the center hosted daily writing camps where the children engaged in writing activities and participated in field trips to playgrounds and city museums. The center's afternoon academy ran from Mondays to Thursdays between 3:00 p.m. and 6:00 p.m. During academy time, children did homework and engaged in various writing activities with volunteers and staff teachers. Importantly, the center is not a grassroots organization or founded by the Latinx community; however, it did host workshops for families which focused on a variety of relevant and urgent issues to the Latinx community, including immigrant rights, applying for foreign passports, and presentations and exhibits featuring community immigrant rights activists.

In the fall of 2015, we approached the center to discuss a research partnership with our university. We sat down with Madison, the center's director at the time, to discuss what this partnership might look like and to express interest in learning about the language and literacy practices of the children who attended the center. Afterward, we observed the center to better understand their orientation to language and literacy and how the linguistic repertoires of the children were included in the center's practices. It was during those early observations that we noticed that though the site advertised itself as a *"bilingual"* space in Spanish and English, in practice, the language and literacy practices were overwhelmingly centered around English. The notable exception was when Madison spoke Spanish with the family members of the child attendees. After several weeks of observations, we asked Madison about this dynamic. Madison responded that she felt uncomfortable having the children read or write in

Spanish because she, as a non-native speaker of Spanish, was unable to correct the children's "mistakes" in Spanish.

We knew that hyper-focus on correctness and proficiency in language acquisition was a common language ideology for teachers, among others, to hold (Flores and Rosa 150). This language ideology is problematic in many ways, and in this instance, it positioned both the language and literacy practices of the teacher, Madison, and the children as deficit. However, we didn't want to correct or critique Madison or the center's efforts. Rather, we wanted to share a pedagogical model informed by a different language ideology known as translanguaging, which we believed would help Madison, and other volunteers and teachers, to think about and do language and literacy differently. Subsequently, we approached Madison about offering Saturday workshops, to be led by the two of us, that would model a translanguaging pedagogy focused on writing topics such as writing bilingual family stories, composing bilingual poetry, reading and creating graphica, and mapping community languages. These workshops began in the fall of 2017, and we have offered them each semester through the spring of 2020. All of the workshops that we sponsored were designed for children who were upper elementary or middle grades, or between eight and fourteen years old. Yet, every so often, younger siblings, as young as five years old, also attended workshop sessions. Attendance varied and was irregular, with as many as sixteen children attending some sessions, and as few as five in others. Several children attended multiple workshops.

Typically, our workshops ran from noon until 2:00 p.m. on Saturdays. As there were occasionally other workshops overlapping with our time frame, the center was a busy place on Saturdays. Upon our arrival, we spread out our books and supplies on an empty table. Some children always arrived early, while others wandered in throughout the two hours of the workshop. Because of this, we knew it wasn't beneficial to have a tightly timed lesson, so we took a more flexible approach, using the first twenty minutes or so visiting with the children and their families informally. Once we determined the direction of the session, the children spread out to begin the activities. At some point during the two hours, we offered snacks, while the children continued to work. The center offered many, diverse kinds of workshops, from dance to making alebrijes, yet the main difference in our workshops was the emphasis on highlighting the children's bilingualism. Specifically, through the books that we shared, our speech, and the writing that we prompted from the children.

In this project, we wanted to intentionally produce new practices of language and literacy that drew on the children's entire linguistic repertoire, which was embedded in their temporal and spatial realities. Thus, we wanted to examine how we, as authors and participants, produced, or could potentially produce a translanguaging space.

A Translanguaging Space

So then, what is translanguaging? Translanguaging is a theory of language, which frames language as something we *do*, rather than something we *have* (García and Li Wei 11). This framing is important because it departs from traditional and formalist views of language as something that is acquired individually through levels of proficiency (Li Wei 11). It eschews evaluations and assessments of language via terms such as native, first, second, home, and proficient. As well, it disrupts the easy naming of languages with terms such as Spanish or English, which are associated with the colonizing histories of their respective nation-states (Otheguy, García, and Reid 286). Instead of bounding languages in this manner, we thought of *"language"* as a verb enacted through our diverse linguistic repertoires. By taking up a translanguaging view of language, we also took a sociopolitical stance about the workings of power both behind and through language, which meant that we wanted to push back against monolingual language ideologies tied to nationalism, racism, classism, and post-colonialism.

Notably, we focused on both the language and *literacy* practices and pedagogies at the center. We believed the line between language and literacy is a blurry one and we viewed literacy as a multimodal social semiotic practice. In turn, our views and pedagogical design were heavily informed by scholarship stemming from New Literacy Studies (Gee 24; NLG 64; Street 77). While our views of literacy included the traditional notions of print, or reading and writing language, it also encompassed a range of modes in the social semiotic acts of meaning making (Street 78), such as images, sounds, and gestures. As well, just as language use is caught up in the systemic structures of power, we knew that literacy practices are also validated and invalidated based on similar power dynamics. Moreover, we needed to embrace this expanded definition of literacy so that more of the literate acts on the part of the children could be included or counted as literacy, such as their drawings or engagement with Pokémon.

Translanguaging Emerges from Authentic Community Language Practices

Rather than enforcing a language policy or practice *down* onto people, a translanguaging theory of language is built *up* from the authentic language practices of people in their respective homes and communities. For example, Creese, Blackledge, and Hu have documented the translanguaging nature of language practices across community food markets in England, noting that even those who are "supposedly" monolingual engage in translanguaging and transemiotic practices to negotiate transactions and communicate (841). Likewise, Canagarajah has shown the translanguaging natures of global workplaces, specifically showing the disconnect between schooled language learning pedagogies and the authentic language practices of workers (57). Thus, turning to this theory helped us account for and include the lived language practices of multilinguals or how the families and their children practiced language outside of the center, specifically in their homes and communities. At the same time, it disrupted some of the pedagogical practices that were excluding the translanguaging practices of the children.

Enacting Translanguaging Pedagogies in Community Literacy Spaces

While there is sufficient research that documents the practice of translanguaging pedagogies in K-12 schools, there is less work that has been done to examine these practices in community learning spaces (Creese and Blackledge 104; de los Rios and Seltzer 55; García and Kleyn 1). Alvarez's long-term research in an after-school, bilingual literacy program located in a Mexican neighborhood in New York City, showed the complex translanguaging practices and pedagogies of mothers and children, noting specifically how the children acted as language brokers, disrupting power dynamics between children, parents, and other official actors (1). Additionally, Alvarez and Alvarez showed how a translanguaging space in a public library located in a transnational, bilingual community was a safe space to leverage the language resources of the community (412). Kim and Song's recent project on creating a translanguaging space in a family literacy workshop showed how the workshop built upon the community translanguaging practices. More specifically, it allowed families to leverage their cultural and familial funds of knowledge while repositioning translanguaging from an individual competency to a collective practice (268). And in Axelrod and Cole's study, in a before-school program in the US South, they showed how translanguaging pedagogy allowed bilingual children to demonstrate their acute awareness of a writing audience and deploy their linguistic repertoires in nuanced ways to appeal to such audiences (146). Notably, there is also scholarship that shows some community-based "bilingual" programs advertise themselves as bilingual in name, but in practice, they may default to monolingualism in English in practice and pedagogy (Gast, Okamoto, and Feldman 96; Martínez-Roldán 55; Pastor 21).

In our translanguaging pedagogical approach, we intended to pull down the rigid walls between languages to allow the children to more flexibly draw on their linguistic repertoires in this space. To do this, instead of conceptualizing that the children spoke "English" and "Spanish" as two separate languages, we believed that the children had a linguistic repertoire that was rich and full for deployment through a translanguaging pedagogy. We also complicated what it meant to be proficient, correct, or standard in a language by resisting "*correction*" in our oral or written feedback to the children about their writing. Finally, we modeled in our speech what it meant to be "bilinguals" and "languagers," who were not two monolinguals in one person (Grosjean 3), so that the children, too, would take up "languaging" in their speech and writing acts (García 519). Ultimately, we hoped that enacting a translanguaging pedagogy in this manner would help us and the center to make larger pedagogical shifts to alter the deficit thinking around language and literacy.

Finally, as we moved forward in the project, it became pertinent to better account for how we shaped the language and literacy practices and pedagogies of the space itself. We knew, for instance, that this "bilingual" community engaged in translanguaging, both in their home lives and work lives (Creese, Blackledge, and Hu 843), and we wanted to draw those languaging and literacy practices into the community center through our practiced pedagogy (Mills and Comber 413). In this manner, we departed from documenting what *was*, and moved toward documenting what *could be* in this space. Specific to translanguaging pedagogies, Li Wei stressed that translanguaging spaces *must* be intentionally created due to the power relationships that undergird all language practices and values (23). In these translanguaging spaces, all actors must seek to disrupt boundaries between languages and the ideologies that position one language, or one form of language, as better or correct.

An Engaged Methodology

We framed this study as an ethnographic case study (Dyson and Genishi 1) that used a discourse analytical framework (Bloome et al. 1) and engaged methods (Kinloch 88) to document and analyze language and literacy events within this translanguaging space. With IRB approval, in April 2015, we began collecting data at Autores Fuertes through participant observations during the afternoon academy time, typically visiting weekly on Thursdays between 3:30 p.m. and 6:00 p.m. Beginning as participant observers, we sought to answer a generic question of what was happening in regards to the language and literacy practices of the teachers and children at the center. However, as this project progressed, and as previously described in our theoretical framework, we departed from this ethnographic stance of *collecting* data about the participants at the site and moved toward a view of *generating* data with our participants. For instance, as we began crafting and teaching Saturday workshops, we needed to account for and acknowledge how we were intentionally disrupting and changing the reality of the center. We embraced the notion that we were, and still are, co-creating the reality with the children and other actors at the center, even now as we write about it.

So far, the data corpus includes approximately twenty hours of participant observations of various aspects of the center, transcripts of approximately forty hours of audio and video recordings of Saturday workshops, and numerous writing samples from the children who participated in these workshops. We also have individual reflective field notes and our communication notes in the form of texts and emails throughout our planning and execution of the project. For the purpose of this article, we focus the findings around the data collected during four writing workshops: Writing Bilingual Family Stories, Writing Bilingual Poetry, Creating Graphica, and Community Language Mapping.

To analyze the data, we uploaded the field notes, transcripts, and writing samples into a shared Google Drive. We focused on identifying what Alvarez termed the "translanguaging event" (326). Building off previous constructs, such as the literacy event, Alvarez proposed the translanguaging event as a way to capture and bound the data around an instance where the translanguaging nature of language and literacy was highlighted. Then, using our theoretical framework as a guide, we developed analytical questions to ask of each of those translanguaging events:

- Where, when, and how did the children deploy an expanded linguistic repertoire?
- Where, when, and how did we prompt for this linguistic repertoire?
- Where, when, and how was space integral to this deployment?

Making a Translanguaging Space

When we first observed the center, we noted three pedagogical practices that we interpreted as limiting the inclusion of the children's entire linguistic repertoires in lessons and activities. First, although the center was designated as a bilingual space, there were clear demarcations as to when, where, and with whom Spanish was used, and thus English was the default language. For example, there were many bilingual and Spanish language books on the bookshelves; however, the books that the teachers and volunteers used with the children during the afternoon academy time were all in English, and children were encouraged to read books in English. As previously mentioned, the site's director spoke Spanish to parents, grandparents, and adult community members, but used English to speak with the children, and taught in English during the afternoon academy time.

Second, we noted the appropriation and recontextualization of "schooled" literacy practices in this space (McTavish 324), albeit not in a more agentive way. For instance, during the afternoon academy time at the center, the center director engaged the children in the reading of teacher-selected novels using the common "round-robin" styles of reading, where children read aloud one by one, taking turns, through the text. The literacy pedagogy, and specifically the writing pedagogy, was formed around "schooled" notions of informative, narrative, and persuasive writing genres. Although the children were bilingual, speaking and using both Spanish and English fluently inside and outside of the center, the language and literacy lessons required written responses only in English.

Third, other language and literacy spatial flows or translanguaging corrientes (García, Johnson, and Seltzer 21) were present and observed, especially when the children were considered "off-task" relevant to what the adults had asked them to do. However, their moments of being off-task were not capitalized on by the center's teachers, and were generally redirected or ignored. For instance, in one session during a round-robin reading of *Fantastic Mr. Fox*, Guadalupe sat at the table with a graphic novel in her lap, hidden from the view of Madison, silently reading and engaging with a text on her own, refusing to engage in the round-robin group reading. During a break from academy time, a group of four boys gathered around a laptop and searched for videos of Pokémon, listening to their video selections in Japanese, reading the subtitles in English, and chatting amongst each other in Spanish about the inner workings and nuances of the world of Pokémon.

We knew that schooled pedagogical practices, such as round-robin reading, are difficult to disrupt and change in classroom spaces, as they are practices that are deeply ingrained in the culture of schooling and education. However, we believed that because this space was not "school," there was more freedom to shape the pedagogical practices and to be informed by a translanguaging framework of language and literacy. Thus, our intentions were twofold: first, that our deliberate use of a translanguaging pedagogy would disrupt some of the "schooled" language and literacy practices, such as round-robin reading and homework that the children were typically engaged in at the center. Specifically, we wanted to redirect literacy flows to and from home and community, among other lived experiences. Second, we hoped that by actively challenging monolingualism and modeling translanguaging in this space, we could contribute to a ripple effect across the center. This, we hoped, would create a space where more of the children's linguistic repertoire would be engaged and deployed. In the following sections, we describe each workshop, including an example of a translanguaging event within each workshop, and follow it with a collective analysis.

Escribiendo Historias Bilingües Familiares/Writing Bilingual Family Stories

We have long used the collecting and writing of family stories as a way for children to draw upon their familial and linguistic funds of knowledge. Previous research has shown that writing family stories is a way to pedagogically leverage the familial and linguistic funds of knowledge of young children, especially those of emergent bilingual children (Abraham 410; Dworin 518; Flores 62). We intended for the writing of family stories to be a departure from some of the traditional and "schooled" writing pedagogies that we had documented at the center, such as assigning the children a specified and narrow writing prompt or genre. Instead, we encouraged the children to inquire into their lives and bring forth a story that they would like to tell us and others.

For this project, we defined family stories as those stories that are told, over and over again, within a family. We prompted family stories by asking the children: Do you have any stories in your family that you tell over and over again? These types of stories usually start with "Oh, do you remember when so and so did . . . ?" During the first session of this Saturday workshop, we posed these questions to the five children who attended. We also read them an example of a bilingual family story from children's literature, Juan Felipe Herrera's *Calling the Doves/El Canto de las Palomas*, and we shared an example of our own family's stories. At the end of the session, we sent the children home with a bilingual family story questionnaire that prompted the children to ask their family members questions about their lives such as:

- ¿Quién fue importante para ti cuando eras un niño o una niña?
- Who was important to you when you were a kid?
- What type of stories did they tell you when you were a kid?
- ¿Qué tipo de cuentas te contaron cuando eras una niña o un niño?

We hoped these prompts would help the children collect stories that captured their family's lived experiences, along with the translanguaging reality embedded in those experiences.

The following excerpt illustrates a translanguaging event during the first session of this workshop. In this event, we, the authors, are reviewing the family story questionnaire.

1 Stephanie: Alright, in Spanish. Okay, look where it says memory questions.

2 Put your finger on two there, where it says memory questions. Alright,

3 let's read them all in

4 Spanish. Can we do it?

6 Children: (Whining)

7 Stephanie: I know we can! Okay, memorias. So, we are going to read the

8 first one that starts with "que." Alright, you all have to read along with me.

9 All: ¿Qué es algo gracioso, qué te ha pasado?

10 Stephanie: Okay, the next one.

11 All: ¿Qué es algo aterrador que te ha pasado?

12 Damian: So, something scary?

13 Stephanie: Something scary.

14 Damian: Ooo! I think I know!

15 Stephanie: Okay. But, you have to ask your mom or your dad or your grandma.

16 Remember? Thirteen. Okay, la próxima. La tercera.

17 All: ¿Qué es algo triste, qué te ha pasado?

18 Daniel: I know this.

19 Stephanie: You do! Did you ask your mom or dad? You gotta ask them. Maybe

20 they'll tell you more. Okay, la ultima. Juanito, ready? ¿La ultima?

21 All: ¿Cuáles fueron tus sueños cuando era una niña o niño?

22 Children: (chatting about possible answers)

During this session, there was some notable discomfort on the part of the children when asked to read aloud in Spanish, indicated in line 4 of this transcript with their "whining." As well, in this excerpt, in line 7, Stephanie and Kate began to choral read the questionnaire with the children to relieve some pressure on the individual child to "read" aloud in Spanish, but also offering a way to scaffold the children's decoding of Spanish print. The children's responses to the questions, albeit in English, indicated that they fully understood the questions as posed in Spanish. For example, in response to the question posed in line 9, "what is something scary that happened to you?" Damian responded in English, in line 10 asking a clarifying question, "So, something scary?" and states that he already has an example for this in line 12.

In the subsequent session, the children returned with the completed questionnaires containing answers to many of these questions, thus demonstrating the effectiveness of offering flexible translanguaging approaches to creating the questionnaire, reviewing it, and allowing answers in any language. Building on the collected answers, during the rest of the workshop sessions, the children chose one story to more fully develop, draft, revise, and illustrate into one complete "published" family story. And many types of family stories were generated— they were sad, funny, and everything in-between. The children wrote stories of emigration from El Salvador and Mexico to the United States, una mama being attacked by a gallina in Mexico, and a papi's bicycle, which had two lights and a bell, that he rode to and from work every day at a restaurant in Philadelphia's Center City. Figure 1 contains Marco's entire family story, whose storytelling and translanguaging inspired the title for this article.

Figure 1: Marco's Family Story

In his family story, Marco described how he immigrated to the United States. He came in an airplane, he ate Popeye's in the airport, and he missed everything about El Salvador, including las pupusas. Flores, referencing Eve Tuck, claimed that these kinds of stories disrupt "stories of damage" about minoritized families, and instead Marco's story highlighted how his family "thrive[d] and sobrevivi[ó]" (68). Marco did this by disrupting one-dimensional stories about El Salvador, specifically that it is a violent place, full of gangs, where no one wants to live. In Marco's story, he construed El Salvador as his home, a place of family, warm weather, and great food.

Cruzando Fronteras con la Poesía Bilingüe/Crossing Borders with Bilingual Poetry

In the spring of 2018, we offered a workshop focused on writing bilingual poetry. We turned to bilingual poetry because we knew the condensed wording, flexible structure, and malleable grammatical rules could scaffold the children's biliteracy development, as well as their translingual writing (Cahnmann-Taylor and Preston 235). Previous research has shown that young emergent bilinguals, especially those educated in a US English-only school context, may experience stress or frustration when asked to write in a first or home language, in which they have not been schooled (Abraham). Thus, we relied heavily on bilingual poetry written and published by Latinx, bilingual poets as mentor texts as a way to relieve some of this stress and model translingual writing for the children (Flores 59). Specifically, we turned to collections of bilingual poems published by Francisco Alarcón and Jane Medina to guide each session. At the beginning of each session, we read and modeled examples of a variety of bilingual poems for the children, including "Soy de/I Am" poems, found poems, shape poems, and parallel poems.

Transcript

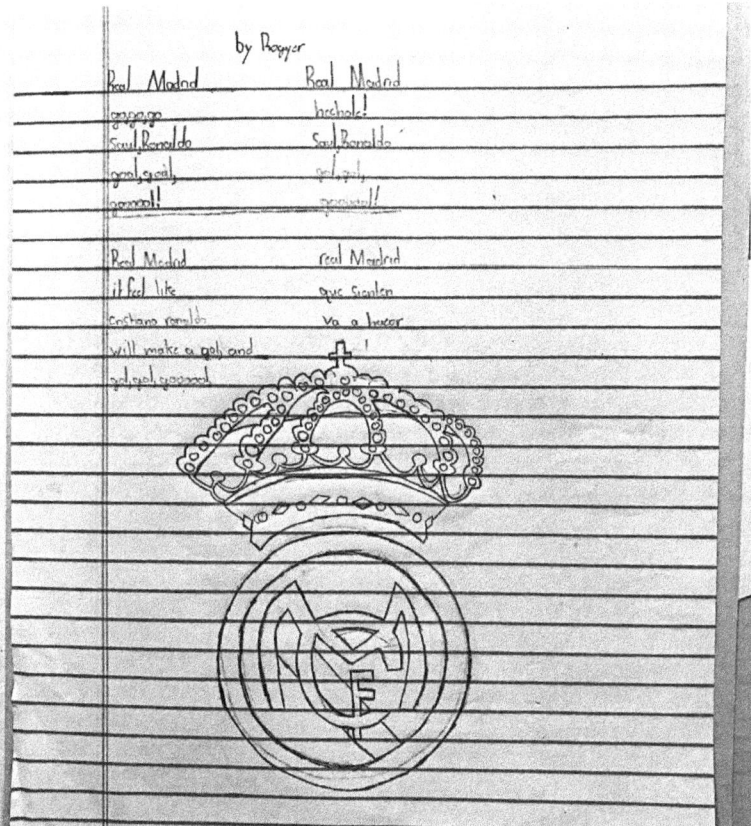

Figure 2: Raul's Real Madrid Poem

Real Madrid

go, go, go
Saul, Ronaldo
goal, goal,
goooool!

Real Madrid
it feel like
Cristiano Ronaldo
will make a gol, and
gol, gol, gooool,

Real Madrid
Hechale!
Saul, Ronaldo
gol, gol,
gooool!

Real Madrid
que sienten
va a hacer

    The children were prolific poets, producing dozens of poems in this eight-week workshop. They wrote poetry about everything from pizza to futból, as seen in the above poem. In this poem, in Figure 2, Raul wrote about his favorite futból team, Real Madrid, and favorite player, Cristiano Ronaldo. Raul's translanguaging skills were advanced, as he captured many words that *trans* English and Spanish, such as Real Madrid, Saul, and Ronaldo which are spelled the same across English and Spanish, with differences in pronunciation. As well, in lines 5, 9, 10, 14 and 15, his spelling of gol conforms to Spanish orthography and by not using the letter "a" he captured the subtle differences between the English and Spanish pronunciations. Notably, his spelling of goal, with multiple "o's" in lines 5, 10, and 14 was meant to index the iconic elongated "goooool" that is yelled out by the announcer just after a goal is scored. In this manner, his poem captured his translanguaging aural reality perfectly, demonstrating his transnational knowledge of Spanish, English, and the intricacies of futból.

Novelas Graficas and Cómicas/Graphic Novels and Comics

We imagined graphic novels and comics as a way for the children to engage in multimodal acts of reading and writing, and coupling translanguaging and graphica would allow the children to engage more freely with their linguistic, or communicative, repertoires. We did not intend for graphica to be simply a bridge to "more literary" or "difficult" texts; rather these texts were meant to help the children to engage with the dynamics of language, disrupting the idea that language is print alone (Dallacqua 365;

Schwartz 262). In one way, graphica already challenges notions of literacy as restricted to only print, by showing how print, image, and space can better construct a narrative than print alone. Finally, reading comic books or graphic novels allows children to engage with words and drawings, the use of speech and thought bubbles, shifts in perspective or point of view, and unique arrangements on each page of the text (Kedley, McCloud).

Thus, in this workshop, the children evaluated these elements in *El Deafo* (Bell), *American Born Chinese* (Luen Yang), and *Lowriders in Space* (Camper and Raul the Third). They also participated in activities where language, gestures, and visuals were used to share ideas, including looking at art, watching videos, or acting out charades that led to brainstorming for graphica writing activities and stories.

The following excerpt comes from the fourth session of this eight-week workshop.

In this transcript, Kelly, an adult volunteer and researcher, and twelve-year-old Dina act out a short improvisational skit they wrote together. Their only prompt was that the skit should involve two people using all their languages, and that it should show the opportunities or challenges that might come with people whose linguistic repertoires differ.

1 Dina: [talking very fast] OK, vamos hacer galletas.

2 Kelly: What's a kai-etta?

3 Dina: [pronouncing the word carefully and slowly] Ga-llet-a

4 Kelly: [repeating slowly] Ga-llet-a… is that like… cake?

5 Dina: Kind of…

6 Kelly: Like a big cake?

7 Dina: It's a cookie…

8 Kelly: A cookie! Ok, what are we going to do?

9 Dina: First we are going to start with flour.

10 Kelly: [to the other children] Como se dice flour…?

11 Children: Flor…? Flower???

12 Kate: [laughing] It's harina…[The children groan and laugh]

Dina, who frequently talked about baking cakes, pies, and cookies at home and one day owning a bakery, started the skit by speaking in Spanish very quickly to Kelly. Dina intended for Kelly to not understand the quick pacing of the Spanish. Outside of the skit, Kelly speaks Spanish, but because they were acting, Kelly pretended not to understand Dina's quick and fluent comment in Spanish. In line 9, Dina switched to English, and said they would start with baking flour. In line 10, Kelly "broke the fourth wall," so to speak, and spoke directly with the rest of the children, asking them how to say flour in Spanish. Because these words are homophones, the children responded with flor, the Spanish translation for the English flower, but not for flour. The children all laughed when they realized that Kelly was asking how to translate flour, and not flower.

After the skit ended, the children were to draw, in the style of comics, what they thought would happen next if the skit were to continue (See Figure 3).

Figure 3: Comic Panels of Dina, Julio, Edwin, and Marx

Dina, as shown in the upper left panel of Figure 3, drew the two characters of Kelly and Dina continuing to confuse ingredients. Julio, in the upper right panel, omitted captions, thought bubbles, and talk bubbles entirely, and drew only a smoking kitchen with one of the characters calling on a phone for help. Presumably, the inability to communicate well between the two characters led to the burning cookies and smoke-filled kitchen. Edwin, in the bottom left panel, noted that the character Kelly played didn't seem to understand Spanish or English. This was an astute observation; in line 2 of the previous transcript, Kelly acted as if she didn't know "galleta" in Spanish, but in line 10, Kelly acted as if she didn't know "flour" in English. Finally, Marx, in the bottom right panel, also thought miscommunication would lead to disaster, as he drew a mess, with Kelly not understanding in English what the meaning of mess was. The children's skilled acting, appropriate laughter at a translation "error," and their panel drawings all index their acute senses surrounding communication across languages, the acknowledgement of "mis"communication, and the subtlety of linguistic negotiation.

Mapeando los Idiomas de la Comunidad/Community Language Mapping

We chose to design a workshop around community language mapping (Dunsmore, Ordoñez-Jasis, & Herrer 327) as a way for the children to explore, document, and build upon the language practices in their communities. Just as a translanguaging theory of language eschews top-down policies and practices of language, we also wanted to do this pedagogically by actively asking and encouraging the children to think deeply about their language practices, as well as to document those practices in their community. To help the children do this, we purchased eight iPods for the children to use to film and document the language and literacy practices in the neighborhood surrounding the community writing center.

We began our first session of the workshop by having the children draw a personalized language map. Language maps are meant to help children document their language practices, as well as associate those practices to specific places and contexts. This kind of pedagogical practice was a way to push back against traditional vocabulary activities, such as assigning a list of specific, decontextualized vocabulary words that the children *must* learn. Instead, the language map was meant to build up from the children's everyday experiences of language, actively encouraging them to share their words with us and their peers.

To begin, we asked the children to think about how they used languages in their everyday lives, and what words and phrases they used with their family. In subsequent sessions, we shifted the focus to how spaces dictated different kinds of talk. We prompted the children to discuss how they talked on the playground as opposed to how they talked in the classroom. The children noted how they used specific phrases when playing video games, such as Fortnite, that they probably wouldn't use with a grandparent or a teacher. Figure 4 is a photograph of Marco's language map.

Figure 4: Marco's Language Map

In Marco's map, he identified eight different contexts for his language use, showing examples of the language he would use in each one. In his context of "angry," he humorously wrote, "*?:+" to represent the expletives he uses when angry, yet his orthographic choices on his language map indicate his understanding of his current context and audience at the community writing center, a place where writing curse words might not be appropriate.

Near the end of the workshop, the children used the iPods to document and film a walk around the community surrounding the writing center with the entire group. The children focused on capturing evidence of language in use such as signs in store windows or transactions in stores. Afterward, using the video and images they captured on their walk through the community, the children created a short film using the iMovie application to represent this language experience.

Discussion

In these Saturday workshops, we set out to disrupt some "schooled" pedagogies by intentionally using a translanguaging pedagogy, in turn redirecting pedagogical practices to follow the spatial and temporal flows of language in the lives of the children. We found that across all of the workshops, by eliciting writing that stemmed from the lived experiences of the children, we could leverage the children's transnational funds of knowledge, along with the translanguaging practices that were embedded in such experiences. More specifically, translanguaging pedagogical strategies, such as the bilingual family story questionnaires and the language map, helped shift the space from "standardized" English dominance to a flexible practice of both English and Spanish during all the speech and writing acts in the workshop. As well, intentionally forefronting and sharing children's literature, written by Latinx, bilingual authors who visibly translanguaged in their publications, modeled for the children how to deploy more of their linguistic repertoires in their own writing. Another vital practice was the visible and active use of all of our languages, specifically noting aloud when we didn't know a word in English or Spanish and using other resources such as peers and Google Translate to help us locate, discuss, and decide on terms.

Our first analytical question pertained to where, when, and how the children deployed an expanded linguistic repertoire during these translanguaging workshops. As an answer to this question, we noted that in the final "published" family stories, the children used complex and specific language to construct their narratives. For instance, they used words related to specific places, formatted in both English and Spanish orthographies, written about places such as El Salvador, Mexico, the United States, and Filadelfia. In the language maps, the children demonstrated a wide linguistic range of words coming from English and Spanish, including words associated with videogames, that even we, Stephanie and Kate, did not know their meaning.

Our second analytical question led us to look for times when we prompted the use of an expanded linguistic repertoire. This happened specifically through the creation and distribution of the bilingual family story questionnaire given at the beginning of the workshop, which helped shape the translanguaging nature of subsequent workshop sessions. Also, using bilingual parallel poems as mentor texts for the children appeared to target the use of an expanded linguistic repertoire, when composing poetry. The language map activity was a way to capture English and Spanish across a variety of contexts, from schools to videogames. The charades activities during the graphica workshops prompted children to think of times where language could be confusing or offer opportunities, depending on each individual's language repertoire. Finally, during writing conference times that focused on the children's drafting and revising of the family stories, we intentionally prompted the children to think about how the dialogue should be captured. For example, if something had been spoken in Spanish as it happened, we discussed whether or not it should be written in Spanish within the story. Importantly, translanguaging pedagogies and related bilingual education have been critiqued when only used as a scaffold for learning English (de los Rios et al.; Palmer), yet we found that translanguaging, rather than a scaffold for English, was a way to scaffold Spanish language and literacy development.

Our final analytical question asked how space influenced our work and the subsequent translanguaging opportunities within the space. In terms of prompting translanguaging shifts across the center, we offered these workshops in an open physical space, where families, teachers, and volunteers could observe and even participate, which prompted even more inclusion of translanguaging practices. We also intentionally expanded the space we used, for instance, by engaging with and walking around the neighborhood around the community writing center, documenting signs in the street and in storefronts, and video recording the street scenes. As well, at the end of each workshop, we set aside time to invite the community, the children's families, and other actors at the center to view the child-created literacy products. This intentional probing into the spaces that the children visited or even knew about was vital to creating this translanguaging space.

Implications

In terms of implications for other community-based writing sites, there are many to extract from this current project and we continue analyzing the data and looking for new ways to translanguage with the children. Here, we offer four implications to think about as we move forward which may be of interest to other researchers and teachers.

First, it is imperative to examine these sites for the reinforcement of "schooled" pedagogies. These traditional pedagogies, stemming from school culture, are often restrictive and not culturally responsive. This can lead to the exclusion of community and family language and literacy practices. To disrupt these, a researcher or teacher might intentionally examine the site, asking: Are all the languages of the attendees being included? How can more languages be included? What language and literacy ideologies appear to be reinforced or disrupted in this space?

Second, if it is determined that traditional and schooled pedagogies are present, teachers and researchers must act to intentionally disrupt them. This can be done in a number of ways and methods, but ultimately, a focus should be on redirecting writing pedagogies to build off the spatial and temporal flows that the children live in. Based on what we've found, we suggest creating workshops or sessions that have translanguaging as a focal goal, meaning that while the objective of a workshop may be to write a family story, the main goal must be to highlight the translanguaging practices of the children.

Third, translanguaging is a normal and authentic practice of multilinguals. To include translanguaging in pedagogical practice, teachers, directors, and volunteers must recognize those practices as correct and brilliant, and not as deficit or problematic. Then, they should work to build off the authentic language practices of these multilinguals who attend community-based writing centers. If the center's actors are not multilingual, then they must learn about translanguaging practices; reading about translanguaging is one way to do this, but the best way is to participate with community members doing language every day, from shopping at stores to attending local religious services, tuning in their ears to the language practices happening there. If the center's actors are multilingual, specifically in the languages of the local community, still they must rethink the standardized language ideologies that translanguaging tries to disrupt, which often exist across and within all language groups.

Fourth, and finally, community-based writing centers have great potential to be sites of pedagogical resistance and validation for many communities that have been minoritized and marginalized in US society and "formal" schools. However, to do so, centers must intentionally establish and develop relationships with each community, and not simply exist as a space. The relationship building must be intentional and based on community values and norms. Developing confianza with families and the community can be done in a variety of ways. For example, a center may create an open-door policy that allows families to attend workshops with their children. As well, the center's teachers must know the needs of the community and respond to them. For instance, at this center, many parents have lamented the lack of formal bilingual education and worry about their children's Spanish proficiency; thus, a response may be to specifically develop workshops and activities that foster Spanish learning in authentic ways.

Concluding Thoughts

Overwhelmingly, all of our workshops have received praise from the center and families, and we are often called on by the center to host more workshops or be a teaching assistant in a current workshop. Although we cannot credit this entirely to the implementation of the workshops we designed and led, a translanguaging shift has become evident in the center's overall approach, including bilingual advertisements of workshop offerings for the community, the hiring of a new bilingual and bicultural director and assistant teacher, and the more prominent use of bilingual or Spanish language materials in the afternoon academy, as well as workshops that are offered in "Spanish" to directly support the children's Spanish language development.

Our work is ongoing. Reviewers of this article asked us to think about and detail what we would do differently as we move forward with the project and research. Notably, we are focused on the translanguaging nature and prioritizing the translanguaging pedagogies of this center. Sometimes, it seems, the center has prioritized homework completion during after-school time and "accurate" writing in either English or Spanish during writing workshops. As well, we have a clear goal of encouraging the children at the center to become bilingual and biliterate, while the center doesn't clearly articulate this goal in any official way, although their actions appear to support this.

Moving forward, we plan to continue each of these workshops just as they are because they were successful in accomplishing their intended goal of bringing the translanguaging reality into the children's writing at the center. However, our pedagogical practices are intentionally flexible and responsive to the children who enroll, and we react in the moment to the children's needs, wants, and interests. Thus, if the children decide that they do not want to make a language map or write poetry, then we will find something else that leverages more of their linguistic repertoire.

On the other hand, there are ways our plan does differ and change moving forward. As we noted above about differing goals, we want to more explicitly engage translanguaging pedagogies with the center's directors and teachers, so that this process isn't so dependent on us. This has been an ongoing and difficult task due to the high turnover of paid staff and volunteers. For instance, since the first author began a partnership with the center, she has seen three different center directors and five different assistant directors/teachers, along with numerous volunteers changing and dropping in every week and into various workshops across the center. One way we plan to do that is partnering with the organization's curriculum director, who doesn't work directly at our site, but can initiate more systemic changes in the curriculum. In turn, we also plan to develop a series of collaborative inquiry discussions with the current director, teachers, and volunteers around the topic of translanguaging and translanguaging pedagogies.

Works Cited

Abraham, Stephanie. "A Critical Discourse Analysis of Gisela's Family Story: A Construal of Deportation, Illegal immigrants, and Literacy." *Discourse: Studies in the Cultural Politics of Education,* vol. 91, no.3, 2015, pp. 409-423.

Alvarez, Steven. "Translanguaging Tareas: Emergent Bilingual Youth as Language Brokers for Homework in Immigrant Families." *Language Arts,* vol. 91, no. 5, 2014, pp. 326-339.

Alvarez, Steven. "Brokering Literacies: Child Language Brokering in Mexican Immigrant Families." *Community Literacy Journal,* vol. 11, no. 2, 2017, pp. 1-15. doi:10.1353/clj.2017.0000.

Alvarez, Steven, and Sara P. Alvarez. ""La Biblioteca es Importante": A Case Study of an Emergent Bilingual Public Library in the Nuevo US South." *Equity & Excellence in Education,* vol. 49, no. 4, 2016, pp. 403-413.

Axelrod, Ysaaca, and Mikel W. Cole. "'The Pumpkins are Coming... Vienen Las Calabazas... That Sounds Funny': Translanguaging Practices of Young Emergent Bilinguals." *Journal of Early Childhood Literacy,* vol. 18, no.1, 2018, pp. 129-153.

Bell, Cece. *El deafo.* Abrams, 2014.

Bloome, David, et al. *Discourse Analysis and the Study of Classroom Language and Literacy Events: A Microethnographic Perspective.* Routledge, 2004.

Camper, Cathy, and the Third, Raul. *Lowriders in Space.* Chronicle Books, 2014.

Canagarajah, Suresh. *Translingual Practices and Neoliberal Policies: Attitudes and Strategies of African Skilled Migrants in Anglophone Workplaces.* Springer, 2016.

Creese, Angela, and Adrian Blackledge. "Translanguaging in the Bilingual Classroom: A Pedagogy for Learning and Teaching?." *The Modern Language Journal,* vol. 94, no. 1, 2 010, pp. 103-115.

Creese, Angela, Adrian Blackledge, and Rachel Hu. "Translanguaging and Translation: The Construction of Social Difference Across City Spaces." *International Journal of Bilingual Education and Bilingualism,* vol. 21, no. 7, 2018, pp. 841-852.

Dahl, Roald. *Fantastic Mr. Fox.* Penguin, 2016.

Dallacqua, Ashley. "Exploring Literary Devices in Graphic Novels." *Language Arts*, vol. 89, no. 6, 2012, pp. 365-378.

de Los Ríos, Cati V., and Kate Seltzer. "Translanguaging, Coloniality, and English Classrooms: An Exploration of Two Bicoastal Urban Classrooms." *Research in the Teaching of English*, vol. 52, no. 1, 2017, pp. 55-76.

Dworin, Joel E. "The Family Stories Project: Using Funds of Knowledge for Writing." *The Reading Teacher*, vol. 59, no. 6, 2006, pp. 510-520.

Dyson, Anne Hass and Celia Genishi. *On the Case*: *Approaches to Language and Literacy Research*. Teachers College Press, 2015.

Dunsmore, KaiLonnie, Rosario Ordoñez-Jasis, and George Herrera. "Welcoming Their Worlds: Rethinking Literacy Instruction through Community Mapping." *Language Arts*, vol. 90, no. 5, 2013, pp. 327-338

Flores, Nelson, and Jonathan Rosa. "Undoing Appropriateness: Raciolinguistic Ideologies and Language Diversity in Education." *Harvard Educational Review*, vol. 85, no. 2, 2015, pp. 149-171. https://doi.org/10.17763/0017-8055.85.2.149

Flores, Tracy. "The Family Writing Workshop: Latinx Families Cultivando Comunidad through Stories." *Language Arts*, vol. 97, no. 2, 2019, pp. 59-71.

García, Ofelia. "Languaging and Ethnifying." *Handbook of Language and Ethnic Identity: Disciplinary and Regional Perspectives*, edited by Joshua Fishman and Ofelia García, Oxford, Oxford University Press, 2010, pp. 519-534.

García, Ofelia, Susana Ibarra Johnson, and Kate Seltzer. *The Translanguaging Classroom: Leveraging Student Bilingualism for Learning*. Caslon, 2017.

García, Ofelia, and Tatyana Kleyn, eds. *Translanguaging with Multilingual Students: Learning from Classroom Moments*. Routledge, 2016.

García, Ofelia, and Li Wei. "Translanguaging and Education." *Translanguaging: Language, Bilingualism and Education*. Palgrave Macmillan, 2014, pp. 63-77.

Gast, Melanie Jones, Dina G. Okamoto, and Valerie Feldman. "We Only Speak English Here: English Dominance in Language Diverse, Immigrant After-School Programs." *Journal of Adolescent Research*, vol. 32, no. 1, 2017, pp. 94-121.

Gee, James. *Social Linguistics and Literacies: Ideology in Discourses*. Routledge, 2015.

Grosjean, François. "Neurolinguists, Beware! The Bilingual is Not Two Monolinguals in One Person." *Brain and Language*, vol. 36, no. 1, 1989, pp. 3-15.

Gutiérrez, Kris D. "Developing a Sociocritical Literacy in the Third Space." *Reading Research Quarterly*, vol. 43, no. 2, 2008, pp. 148-164.

Kedley, Kate E., and Jenna Spiering. "Using LGBTQ Graphic Novels to Dispel Myths about Gender and Sexuality in ELA Classrooms." *English Journal*, vol. 107, no. 1, 2017, pp. 54-60.

Kinloch, Valerie, et al. "Literacy, Equity, and Imagination: Researching with/in Communities." *Literacy Research: Theory, Method, and Practice*, vol. 65, no. 1, 2016, pp. 94-112.

Kim, Sujin, and Kim H. Song. "Designing a Community Translanguaging Space Within a Family Literacy Project." *The Reading Teacher*, vol. 73, no. 3, 2019, pp. 267-279.

Leander, Kevin M., and Margaret Sheehy, editors. *Spatializing Literacy Research and Practice*. Peter Lang, 2004.

Martínez-Roldán, Carmen María. "Translanguaging Practices as Mobilization of Linguistic Resources in a Spanish/English Bilingual After-School Program: An Analysis of Contradictions." *International Multilingual Research Journal*, vol. 9, no. 1, 2015, pp. 43- 58.

McCloud, Scott. *Understanding Comics: The Invisible Art*. William Morrow Paperbacks, 1994.

McTavish, Marianne. ""I'll Do it My Own Way!": A Young Child's Appropriation and Recontextualization of School Literacy Practices in Out-of-School Spaces." *Journal of Early Childhood Literacy*, vol. 14, no. 3, 2014, pp. 319-344. https://doi.org/10.1177/1468798413494919

Mills, Kathy A., and Barbara Comber. "Space, Place, and Power." *International Handbook of Research on Children's Literacy, Learning, and Culture*. John Wiley & Sons, 2013.

Otheguy, Ricardo, Ofelia García, and Wallis Reid. "Clarifying Translanguaging and Deconstructing Named Languages: A Perspective from Linguistics." *Applied Linguistics Review*, vol. 6, no. 3, 2015, pp. 281-307.

Pastor, Ana María Relaño. "Competing Language Ideologies in a Bilingual/Bicultural After- School Program in Southern California." *Journal of Latinos and Education*, vol. 7, no. 1, 2007, pp. 4-24.

Rogers, Rebecca. *An Introduction to Critical Discourse Analysis in Education*. Routledge, 2011.

Schwarz, Gretchen. "Graphic Novels for Multiple Literacies." *Journal of Adolescent & Adult Literacy*, vol. 46, no. 3, 2002, pp. 262-65.

Soja, Edward W. "Thirdspace: Toward a New Consciousness of Space and Spatiality." *Communicating in the Third Space*, edited by Karin Ikas and Gerhad Wagner, Routledge, 2009, pp. 49-61.

Street, Brian. "What's "New" in New Literacy Studies? Critical Approaches to Literacy in Theory and Practice." *Current Issues in Comparative Education*, vol. 5, no. 2, 2003, pp. 77-91.

The New London Group. "A Pedagogy of Multiliteracies: Designing Social Futures." *Harvard Educational Review*, vol. 66, no. 1, 1996, pp. 60-93.

Wei, Li. "Translanguaging as a Practical Theory of Language." *Applied Linguistics*, vol. 39, no. 1, 2018, pp. 9-30.

Zapata, Angie, and Tasha Tropp Laman. "I Write to Show How Beautiful My Languages Are: Translingual Writing Instruction in English-Dominant Classrooms." *Language Arts*, vol. 93, no. 5, 2016, pp. 366-378.

Author Bios

Stephanie is an Associate Professor of Language and Literacy Education at Rowan University. She studies the language and literacy practices of emergent bilinguals, both in and outside of schools. She has published in the *Journal of Educational Policy*,

Equity and Excellence in Education, and *Discourse: Cultural Studies in the Politics of Education*. Her work has been funded by the Spender Foundation, the National Endowment for the Humanities, and the Fulbright Organization.

Kate is an assistant professor in the Department of Language, Literacy, and Sociocultural Education at Rowan University. Kate's research centers around critical literacy and education, public engagement, LGBTQ and young adult literature, language education, and social and educational movements in Honduras. Kate has published work in various journals such as the *English Journal, Sex Education*, the *eJournal of Public Affairs*.d work in various journals such as the *English Journal, Sex Education*, the *eJournal of Public Affairs*.

Beyond 'Literacy Crusading': Neocolonialism, the Nonprofit Industrial Complex, and Possibilities of Divestment

Anna Zeemont

Abstract

This article highlights how contemporary structural forces—the intertwined systems of racism, xenophobia, gentrification, and capitalism—have material consequences for the nature of community literacy education. As a case study, I interrogate the rhetoric and infrastructure of a San Francisco K-12 literacy nonprofit in the context of tech-boom gentrification, triggering the mass displacement of Latinx residents. I locate the nonprofit in longer histories of settler colonialism and migration in the Bay Area to analyze how the organization's rhetoric—the founder's TED talk, its website, the mural on the building's façade—are structured by racist logics that devalue and homogenize the literacy and agency of the local community, perpetuating white "possessive investments" (Lipsitz) in land, literacy, and education. Drawing on abolitionist and decolonial education theory, I prose a praxis encouraging literacy scholar-practitioners to question and ultimately divest from institutional rhetorics and funding sources that continue to forward racism, xenophobia, imperialism, and raciolinguistic supremacy built upon them.

Keywords

non-profits, divestment, technoimperialism, neoliberalism, urban education, activist literacy

In a May 2020 *San Francisco Chronicle* article highlighting the work of the literacy non-profit she directs, educator-administrator Bita Nazarian asserts, "We know we have a health crisis and a financial crisis . . . But I would put an educational crisis right next to that" (Anderson). As the article's author Scott Thomas Anderson concurs, COVID-19 has given "a greater sense of urgency" for community literacy centers like 826 Valencia—where Nazarian works—to intervene in the poor education of "underserved students," particularly given "concerns around American students' reading skills." In fact, Anderson continues, "data shows that literacy levels among young people are troublingly low," but "826 Valencia has been one of the few bright spots" through its work "help[ing] kids complete homework, learn English as a second language and turn their daydreams into stories on the page." The article's title, "826 Valencia's Literacy Crusaders Are on the Front Lines of COVID-19's Education

Crisis," reinforces what Anderson underscores as literacy centers and tutors' critical, powerful role to this end.

As many literacy theory scholars have pointed out, the rhetoric of education crisis—often centered on the assumed "poor literacy skills" of students coded as Black, brown, and/or multilingual—is astoundingly commonplace in our cultural imaginary, and, of course, preceded the COVID-19 crisis by decades (Rosa and Flores; Kynard "This Bridge"; Alvarez). So too is the related rhetoric of what Amy J. Wan calls "literacy hope," a trope that improving individuals' literacy skills will result in the alleviation of other barriers they face: poverty, oppression, or, in this case, vulnerability to a deeply racialized pandemic. As are discourses of literacy education as paternalistic saviorism by teachers and intuitions (Kynard "This Bridge"; Hernandez-Zamora), acting as literacy sponsors, or "agents who enable, support, teach, model . . . recruit, regulate, suppress, or withhold literacy," via their relative financial and/or cultural capital (Brandt 166-7).

What may be less apparent to a reader unfamiliar with the Bay Area are the specific connotations of the article's language given the historical context of the non-profit's location in San Francisco's Mission District. Though likely unintentional, the article's rhetoric, particularly its use of the phrase "literacy crusaders," blatantly harkens back to the neighborhood's namesake: Mission Dolores (located just two blocks from 826 Valencia). This mission was established in the mid-1700s by Spanish colonizers amidst a genocidal colonial land grab with the express purpose of evangelizing—in a sense educating—the indigenous Ohlone about their religious, linguistic, and ontological inferiority. These missionaries may too have perceived their role as "crusaders," "urgently" needed to attend to the "crisis" of evangelizing the "troublingly" "underserved" local Black and Indigenous people of color (BIPOC).

Though today's city certainly looks different than that of the eighteenth century, critical-race and Indigenous studies scholars underscore that legacies of imperial, white supremacist dispossession maintain a felt presence (Cushman; Tuck; INCITE!; Grande). Since the late twentieth century, new manifestations of coloniality and racism have emerged under neoliberalism, a pervasive set of policies and ideologies promoting "self-interest" and the "withdrawal of government from provision for social welfare on the premise that competitive markets are more effective" (Lipman 6). Neoliberalism operates through the trickling upwards and privatization of material goods and land to a corporate elite, accomplished by seizing public resources from the poor—a process historically rooted in anti-Blackness and settler colonialism (Au and Ferrare; Patel). In San Francisco, this dynamic may be most visible as gentrification: so-called urban renewal geared toward a white wealthy class, coupled with mass displacement, typically of low-income BIPOC residents. At the same time, areas targeted by dispossession are particularly vulnerable to the invasion of privatized, sometimes minimally regulated measures to "reform" racialized inequality caused by divestment from public services, such as schooling (Aggarwal and Mayorga). In education, this dynamic has been bolstered by policy trends toward "shifting the implementation" of education "programs from the public sector to the private and nonprofit sectors"— which certainly includes community literacy centers (Patterson and Silverman 2).

As educators, scholars, and practitioners of community literacy, then, we need to be attuned to how colonialism and its neoliberal iterations are transforming our contemporary educational landscape. As Gregorio Hernandez-Zamora asserts, "Poor literacy and school failure are not individual phenomena in the ex-colonial world, but rather the historical and pervasive result of invasions, slavery, and modern 'development policies'" (3). Yet, Leigh Patel cautions, if scholars fail to attend to the histories and material ramifications of literacy education, as is too often the case, then "longer standing patterns of coloniality and oppression can be easily invisibilized and reseated" (2). In this light, I explore how community literacy education, though often unintentionally and with positive motives, can remain ideologically, rhetorically, *and* materially invested in colonial and white supremacist logics and tactics.

Why This *Case Study?*

In this article, I use the remarkable rise of one non-profit, 826 Valencia, as a case study exploring the challenges and complexities of community literacy education within a San Francisco that has been rapidly gentrified by tech capital. The center was established in 2002 in the predominantly Latinx[1] Mission District by literary celebrity Dave Eggers, a white, Midwestern, acclaimed writer and publisher. Since then, "it has blossomed from a noble experiment into one of the top innovators and influencers in the education field" (Ralston). The nonprofit, which offers local K–12 students free, one-on-one tutoring and classes in expository and creative writing, took off to the extent that it has now established eight affiliated locations across the country and inspired similar sites worldwide (Anderson; Ralston).

826 Valencia and Eggers himself have received acclaim in mainstream media and some education circles, including being featured at the 2005 CCCC (Hesse 374). But as a Bay Area native, I heard about 826 Valencia in high school because I had a few acquaintances—who mostly shared my positionality as a white teen with financial privilege and graduate-educated parents—who'd taken creative writing or publishing workshops there or at McSweeney's (Eggers' adjacent publishing house). I didn't get involved with the organization myself until after I left California: in 2010, on break from my Midwest liberal arts college, I participated in a month-long, unpaid internship at 826 Valencia for school credit. Although this was only my second-ever teaching experience, I recall that I received only a few hours of training before diving into working with students. My main task was providing K–12 attendees with one-on-one tutoring in any subject that they had homework in—not just English and literacy, as I had expected. I also occasionally helped set up writing and publishing activities for classes visiting on fieldtrips. My memories from this short time are mostly positive: I enjoyed getting to know the students, though I remember feeling at a loss when tutoring students in areas I had no expertise in (by that point, I'd forgotten all my high school math), and occasionally bored because there were sometimes more volunteers present than students and little to do. Still, I liked the organization's atmosphere—its shabby-chic hipster aesthetic, its vibrant location—and I liked working with the young people when I got the chance.

That said, while in some ways my time with 826 Valencia was personally gratifying, I didn't think critically about my role or the center's work in the context of racial, linguistic, economic, or "spatial justice," or "the fair and equitable distribution in space of socially valued resources and opportunities to use them" (Soja 2). Indeed, as I recall, the organization did not directly foster this kind of thinking either: on top of receiving little pedagogical training, I certainly received no information about the history of the neighborhood and its residents; no trainings around educator positionality; no suggestions for working with multilingual students, given that many of the students and family members the center works with are Spanish speakers. In the years since, even after many other teaching experiences and moving across the country, I've continued to linger on my short time at 826 Valencia. Despite my complicated experience there, 826 Valencia has continued to expand, garner acclaim, and secure donations, even as racialized inequality—in terms of access to quality jobs, housing, and education—has skyrocketed in a San Francisco that looks less and less as the one I remember from growing up, one that is increasingly colonized by the tech industry.

Beginning with the organization's rhetoric but expanding to interrogate the geographic history and funding structure of 826 Valencia, this article examines literacy sponsorship in the context of gentrification and privatization under urban neoliberalism. After providing additional context, I discuss 826 Valencia's founding in the Mission by a white, Midwestern, non-educator, and examine the organization's rhetoric at this point, particularly its invocation of deficit rhetorics and tropes of white liberal saviorism and investment in literacy and real estate as "white property" (Ladson-Billings; Harris). I then move to the present to think through 826's rapid, nationwide spread coupled with the financial support of massive for-profit companies, including major tech firms, coinciding with the Bay Area's intensifying gentrification under dot-com boom "technoimperialism" (McElroy). In doing so, I argue that on top of an organization's rhetoric and intentions, we must consider the material and economic consequences of their presence as it affects a larger community. Ultimately, drawing on critical scholarship in decolonial and abolitionist education and literacy, I think through possibilities for divestment—financially, ideologically, and spatially—as an educational praxis.

My project centers on rhetorical and material features of educational institutions as they intersect with issues of coloniality, race, and justice, rather than on specific decolonial instructional practices, about which there is substantial scholarship.[2] In doing so, this article is by no means intended to be a sweeping critique of *all* education or literacy nonprofits, nor all educational public-private partnerships. Community literacy organizations vary widely in terms of funding, scope, and approach. Many offer amazing, critical resources; some too draw on radical, activist pedagogical frameworks. Yet, all institutions and organizations are embedded within particular geographic, economic, and historical contexts, which I believe merit interrogation.

Given that neoliberalism is marked by embedded "relationships between restructuring in education, the increasingly explicit role of market forces that permeate state-driven education reforms, and the gentrification of urban neighborhoods," 826 Valencia felt to me to be a salient example of how literacy education is changing in our contemporary climate (Aggarwal and Mayorga). I also selected 826 Valencia given its fame, public availability of media and promotional material, specific geographic location, rhetorical features, and funding structure—not to mention my personal relationship with the Bay Area—but these conversations certainly exceed this organization and city. My intention here isn't critique for critique's sake, but rather to attempt a methodology interrogating how structural forces—the intertwined systems of racism, xenophobia, gentrification, and capitalism—have consequences for the nature of community literacy education, and to illuminate the specific ways these consequences play out in a particular geographic context.

Education, Privatization, and the Non-Profit Industrial Complex

In a neoliberal landscape where public education is rapidly defunded along deeply classed and raced lines, financial support from the corporate sector and their investment in particular privatized "reform" measures are increasingly seen as the solution to crumbling or shuttered city schools and "failing" students, and is increasingly expected to pick up where public services inevitably fall short. Indeed, low-income Black and Latinx students living in areas experiencing uneven development, often triggered by gentrification, are typically subjected to the most intensely neoliberal approaches to education, given how "neighborhood decline and the demise of public education often occur in conjunction" (Patterson and Silverman 1). Such measures, often sponsored not by education experts but by individuals with economic and/or social capital, include the expanding presence of charter schools, high-stakes testing (Au and Ferrare), "(corporate) managerialis[t]" structures in public education (Lipman 46), and "school-adjacent" institutions (Patterson and Silverman).

The rise of educational but out-of-school nonprofits is particularly relevant to the context of community literacy. A vital concept here is what grassroots activist coalitions like INCITE! call the nonprofit-industrial complex (NPIC), "a system of relationships between the State (or local and federal governments), the owning classes, foundations, and non-profit/NGO social service and social justice organizations" (xiii). Coinciding with intensifying divestment under neoliberalism and a broader state of economic turmoil triggered by the Great Recession, "school-supporting nonprofits" under the 501(c)(3) model rose astronomically in number from 1995 to 2010 (Nelson and Gazley). It is therefore surprising that research directly interrogating the NPIC remains scant in community literacy—and even writing studies more broadly. In a key exception, Cherish Smith and Vani Kannan point to "the material reality we were inhabiting as mentor/mentee" at their community literacy center: "the non-profit's need to raise money, the coded fundraising language, and by extension, larger trends in public education" (68).

As a concept developed by on-the-ground activists, the NPIC asks us to not just consider the goals or ideologies of community organizations, but their infrastructure, emphasizing that our community work is inextricably tied to political economy and demography. Inspired by this heuristic, I argue that our understanding of community literacy education should be explicitly attuned to the geographic and material specificity of our own sites, that we think through "the specific locale" of community literacy centers as they intersect with the "larger environment" (Rousculp xx). Drawing on scholars who see literacy as material and as inherently shaped by local and transnational geographies and literal and/or figurative mobilities (Wan; Lorimer Leonard), I hope to trace the evolving spatial politics that foreground this case study.

The Mission District and San Francisco: Some Brief Context

San Francisco—and the Mission District in particular—has a long history as a locus of immigration and colonialism; of negotiated ownership over its space. For thousands of years, a cluster of distinct indigenous communities now collectively called the Ohlone lived in the area eventually named "San Francisco" by colonizers (Alejandrino; Kamalakanthan; Spencer). During the 1700s period of ecological destruction and imperial genocide by Spanish missionaries, the Ohlone population rapidly dwindled, either due to diseases carried over by or being murdered by colonists; while before colonization the Ohlone population was in the thousands, between 1833 to 1841, it plummeted from four hundred to just fifty individuals (Spencer; Alejandrino). Though they have constantly had to combat disenfranchisement since colonization, the Bay Area maintains a vital Ohlone presence, who continue to fight for the return of their land (Kamalakanthan).

By the mid–1800s, working-class migrant settlers were flooding into the Mission, and continued to make up the majority of the neighborhood until the 2000s; though the races and nationalities of these residents shifted with movement into and out of the neighborhood, what remained consistent was the city's remarkably segregated geography by class and race (Williamson et al.; Shange). Initially, these Mission residents were white Europeans, whose population continued to rise in the neighborhood until the 1960s, when many left due to white flight out of the neighborhood, in part triggered by government divestment, compounded with mass migration from essentially every country across Central and (to a lesser extent) South America (Alejandrino). These residents—many of whom migrated due to instability in their home country resulting from US imperialism—soon came to make up the majority of the neighborhood (Cordova; Sandoval).

Although the Mission's Latinx population was extremely heterogenous in terms of race, language, ethnicity, and more, the neighborhood became generally associated with Latinidad, and remained so for more than 25 years (Cordova; Mirabal). However, the late 1990s/early 2000s dot-com boom and local politics spurred "dramatic economic and racial changes": as a result of "housing and rental policies" (notably the Ellis Act, which effectively gave landlords more leeway to evict), "real estate speculation" premised upon assumptions of continued technoimperial growth, and increased development, "thousands of Latin[x] families were displaced" from the Mission, in large part by white, wealthier gentrifiers working in tech (Mirabal 7; McElroy). These changes—especially massive rent increases and widespread evictions—spurred grassroots resistance from Mission residents that emerged in the form of protests, other actions, and political art (Maharawal).

As activists understood and continually fought against, San Francisco was transforming under a neoliberal technoimperialism that has made it increasingly unlivable for many BIPOC individuals (McElroy); yet, the city still maintained—and continues to maintain—a reputation as a hub of social progress and multiculturalism (Shange). For Savannah Shange, the association between San Francisco and inherent social justice bleeds into the education settings, where teachers, buoyed by presumptions of good intentions and appropriating the insurgent language of activist movements, see their work uncritically as progressive and just. However, this often obscures the ways in which San Francisco's "progressive" educational institutions—and individual actors within them—continued to perpetuate antiblackness and colonial violence, manifesting as a sort of well-intentioned "carceral progressivism" that polices and segregates BIPOC students, thereby contributing to racialized dispossession (Shange 14). In his study around decolonial composition instruction based out of his home university in the Silicon Valley, Cruz Medina relatedly observes the "enduring influence that colonialism maintains through monolingual ideology," contributes to non-whitestream English speakers' "isolation and insecurity"—"even in a geographical context as diverse as the Bay Area" (85).

"City" Students and "Trouble[d]" Teachers: Deficit Rhetoric and Literacy as White Property

Eggers established 826 Valencia in the Mission in 2002 during the height of these spatial and educational dynamics. In his massively popular 2008 TED Talk entitled "My Wish: Once Upon A School" (which currently has over 1.5 million views), Eggers begins by describing how he devised his idea for a literacy center prior to 2002, while he still lived in Brooklyn:

> my friends that were teaching in city schools were having trouble with their students keeping up at grade level, in their reading and writing in particular. Now, so many of these students had come from households where English isn't spoken in the home, where a lot of them have different special needs, learning disabilities . . . in schools which sometimes and very often are under-funded. [These teachers would] say, 'You know, what we really need is just more people, more bodies . . . more hours, more expertise from people that have skills in English and can work with these students one-on-one . . . I thought about this massive group of people I knew: writers, editors, journalists, graduate students, assistant professors . . . that had sort of flexible daily hours and an interest in the English word . . . in the primacy of the written word in terms of nurturing a democracy, nurturing an enlightened life. ("My Wish")

This talk may seem heartwarming and inspiring, but also might function within what Sujatha Fernandes calls an "economy of storytelling" weaponized by the for- and nonprofit industries alike, which rely on "curated stories"—palatable anecdotes and soundbites—as self-promotion. Curated stories are rich with pathos, but strategically portray philanthropy as *the* project that will save and liberate the oppressed, and to do so covers up the complex networks of racism, colonialism, and capitalism that foreground structural inequality in education and elsewhere. In this case, Eggers' story leverages rhetorical tropes such as raciolinguistic supremacy, white saviorism/paternalism, and valorization of the written word to establish the efficacy of his project, even as in key ways he evades or minimizes crucial context around political economy, migration, coloniality, race, and place—a typical feature of neoliberal education rhetoric (Patel; Leonardo).[3] The talk rhetorically functions through perpetuating a binary between educators and students, aligning the former with competent writing skills, education credentials, English monolingualism, bourgeois socioeconomic status, democratic citizenship, altruism, and whiteness; the latter with illiteracy, limited or poor education, multilingualism (especially speaking Spanish), poverty, inability to assimilate, neediness, and Blackness/brownness. This rhetoric is especially effective in the context of the Mission because of the flexibility of Latinx racialization: current scholarly and political rhetorics, leveraged by colonialist tropes in the US cultural imaginary based on "the perspective of hegemonically positioned white perceiving subjects," strategically collapse Latinx identity with brownness and/or proximity to Blackness—contingent on colorism—immigrant and/or undocumented status, poverty, and difficulty in school and speaking English (Rosa 6; Ribero; Alvarez).

Eggers solicits empathy, then, in part by centering "hegemonically positioned" white bodies and simultaneously othering and homogenizing Mission youth. In detailing his decision to start the organizing, Eggers discusses his friends far more than students themselves; in other words, Eggers' concept initially emerged not out of a desire to help youth, but rather "trouble[d]" teachers, painting them as subjects worthy of empathy. His imagined solution to their struggle was simply to leverage his peers in a new, adjacent institution while failing to name the root problem itself: the systemic issues triggering the mass, if uneven, educational divestment and teacher shortages, with schools serving low-income Black and brown students. Eggers' vague description of these institutions as "city schools" has a racialized undertone; it evokes phrases such as "inner-city" or "urban schools" that have been more robustly critiqued as euphemisms to denote Black/brown youth through an assumed proximity to neighborhoods imagined as impoverished, violent, and/or gang-ridden, thus imagining the youth themselves as dangerous, criminal, and incompatible with normative schooling (Watson; see also Rosa; Kynard "This Bridge"; Wynter). For Eggers, the key was adding simply "more bodies," but very particular bodies: those of individuals with "skills in English," such as Eggers' fellow writer, editor, and academic friends.

Eggers explicitly cites his peers' "passion for the primacy of the written word in terms of nurturing a democracy" and "enlightened life" as characteristics that qualify them as tutors. Without providing much evidence, he also homogenizes "city" students as often coming "from households where English isn't spoken in the home, where a lot of them have different special needs, learning disabilities," and thus lacking access to or enthusiasm for the "written word." This language reflects what critical race theorists in education see as a deficit framework (Yosso, Ladson-Billings) or what Eve Tuck calls as a "damage-centered," pathologizing paradigm; both express a colonial "dualistic thinking" that pathologizes BIPOC students in reference to a white, middle-class norm (Cushman 239). In this case, Eggers rhetorically distinguishes himself/his peers from the Mission community, implying that the former have something to give (expertise in monolingual written English) that the latter clearly lacks. It is precisely this "damage"—marked by raciolinguistic inferiority ("English isn't spoken in the home") and disability ("special needs")—that makes the community a fitting target for the nonprofit. Eggers too implies that students *need* their help to cultivate an "enlightened life," thus not only imagining their deficits, but also their desire to be aided through writing pedagogies possessed by (white) people whom he deems appropriate (see Kynard "This Bridge"). Such rhetoric plays into presumptions of the efficacy and universality of ableist, Western epistemologies of learning/writing (Wynter), which by definition downplay "knowledge bases of [BIPOC] communities" and "societal forces gripping [BIPOC] students, in an effort to find quick solutions" or maybe just explanations as "to why they cannot do as well" (Carey 7–8).

Yet Eggers directly states that "there was no stigma [toward students]. Kids weren't going into the 'Center-for-Kids-That-Need-More-Help.'" However, Eggers' defense here is not, for instance, that they applied a particular antiracist pedagogical model, but simply that the center shared its space with McSweeney's, whose "interns were actually working at the same tables very often, and shoulder-to-shoulder" with students. This language suggests that physical or imagined proximity to the book publishing industry and to "real" writers could in and of itself alleviate stigma against students. Yet Eggers' allusion to an egalitarian writing center directly contradicts discourses he relies on elsewhere repeatedly distinguishing students (coded as Black/brown novice writers) from the "professional" tutors, interns, and publishers (coded as white writing experts). This is reinforced by Eggers' anecdote that he and his colleagues call 826 Valencia a "publishing center" rather than a tutoring or writing center, a framing that also contrasts with tenets of process-oriented composition pedagogy, and translingual/languaging approaches where actively "negotiating assumptions about language is more important than the product" (Matsuda 481; Alvarez and Alvarez).

To exemplify the organization's success, Eggers again harnesses deficit rhetorics to tell the story of a student previously "addicted to video games and TV," unable to "concentrate at home." Such language evokes the racist, xenophobic stereotype that "immigrant parents don't care about their kids in school" and/or have home lives that are antithetical to mainstream/ whitestream education (Alvarez 25). But upon coming to the center, the student received "concentrated attention," and "soon enough, he was writing . . . [H]e's now been published in five books." Eggers here alludes to normative literacy acquisition—in fact, mainstream corporate publishing, the industry that he and his colleagues make their living in, throughout collapsed with bourgeois whiteness—as the end point for students, not, say, cultivating critical or coalitional consciousness. This rhetoric praises one student painted as exemplary within a neoliberal progress narrative, implying that the student had to depart from an impoverished, unruly home life and language to get there.

In doing so, Eggers' talk tacitly invokes the pervasive association between normative literacy and liberal citizenship (Wan), both as inherently white property (Ladson-Billings). Although rooted in earlier settler colonialism, during which indigenous languages were intentionally eradicated (Grande), and chattel slavery, as slaves were barred from learning to read and write (Ladson-Billings), literacy as white property has been cemented under neoliberalism, which underpins both the mainstream rise of deficit/damage rhetorics and meritocratic logics blaming inequality on individual failure rather than systemic racism (Au and Ferrare; Leonardo). Leveraging this ideology, Eggers' rhetoric valorizes tutors' literacies as linked to their "enlightenment" and "democra[tic]" citizenship, racializing and homogenizing students as not only illiterate, but un-enlightened and non-citizens, questioning not only their writing abilities but their personhood (Ladson-Billings; Ribero; Wynter).

The "Printed Word" of the "Human Race": Murals, Whitewashing, and Liberal Humanism

The TED talk's dehumanizing rhetoric goes hand in hand with Eggers' implicit erasure of the neighborhood's identity. In discussing 826 Valencia's origins, Egger offers so little contextual specificity that the talk could be about basically anywhere, nor much explanation as to why he chose to establish the center in the Mission (except that his landlord was pleased and the building was convenient). Yet, Eggers opted to name the organization after its street address, perhaps to suggest to locals a sense of its belonging—while also alluding to an inherent *right* to possess this address and this building. If, following Katherine McKittrick, "naming place is also an act of naming the self and self-histories," then in naming this site after its address, Eggers and his cofounders were inserting themselves and "self-histories" into a neighborhood and building that had only just become "theirs" (xxiii). Yet despite the name, upon opening the center, "we waited" for "weeks and weeks," but "nobody came in." Eggers and his colleagues "never put it together" that there might be a "trust gap," which he attributes to the fact that 826 Valencia had a storefront on the outside, not that it was started by a gentrifier; it was only then that Eggers brought in a co-director with more experience and ties to the Bay Area.

Perhaps to blend in further with the neighborhood (or as a nod to the Mission's cultural heritage) Eggers hired the white, Chicago-based artist Chris Ware to paint the building's façade. One of the Mission's most renowned cultural sites are its alleys lined with murals, including Clarion Alley just a couple blocks from 826 Valencia. As Cary Cordova describes, these murals represent powerful legacies of Latinx aesthetic practices—what I would call literacies—rooted in cultural, political expression that has long existed in the neighborhood. And as Mirabal notes, members of the Mission community often view murals as an element of their ties to the Mission and a site of Latinx advocacy. Many recent murals protest raising rents and eviction caused by gentrification, while centering Latinx art and life (see Fig. 1 and 2, both from Clarion Alley).

Fig. 1 Artist Carina Goldblatt's mural shows a magenta-haired, Brown woman, whose facial features evoke calavera iconography, in a pink maid's outfit holding two pink dog-like pets. She seems to be trying to run but is constrained by a rope wrapped around her right ankle. Above her head are the words "evict," its letters dripping and red like blood, and "Google," in in blue, red, yellow, and green letters like Google's logo.

Fig 2: A mural with "Bomb Condos! Not Murals!" in red letters; a bomb with a face replaces the first O. Below this is a row of gray buildings bordered by dollar signs. On each side of the buildings is a blue, personified spray paint can: one sprays the phrase "crush buses, not art!"; the other, "smash the system instead of our paintings." The mural's lower edge has the tag "respect your wallz | respect cups" atop red flames.

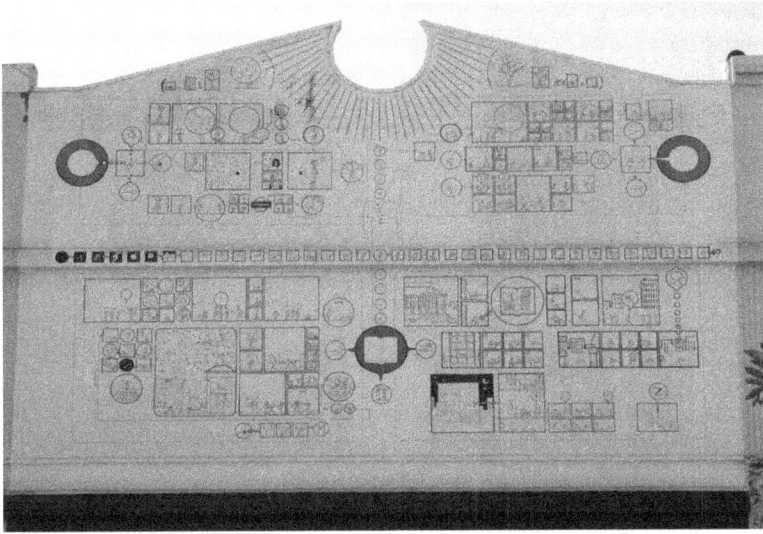

Fig. 3: Ware's mural on a building's white upper façade, above a dark awning (labeled "826 Valencia" in large letters, cropped out). Composed of fine, black pigment, its foreground is separated into quadrants, each containing wordless, cartoon-like sequences of small squares and bubbles with small scenes of people interacting with various objects and settings. Standing out are three, larger bronze circles on the left (enclosing a thought bubble), right (enclosing a speech bubble), and center-bottom (enclosing an open book).

At first glance, 826 Valencia's mural (Fig. 3) has few visual similarities to neighboring ones. It is geometric, linear, and painted solely in black and white. It contains no tags or signifiers pointing to its artist's identity or artistic lineage, nor an insurgent political message speaking to the perspective of Mission residents. Visually, this is both a literal and figurative white-washing of the neighborhood's literate, sociopolitical legacies. Indeed, locals have protested developers painting over or destroying murals in the redevelopment process, "symboliz[ing] for many Latin[x] [residents] the white-washing of Latin[x] culture in the Mission" and the "usurpation of [its] history and public culture" by gentrifiers (Mirabal 24). In this sense, Ware's mural plays into Erin McElroy's observation that the area's gentrification was "correlative to a real estate marketing strategy that preys upon Mission Latinx culture" and literacies "to boost property value" (827).

According to Ware, the mural portrays "the development of the human race, along with its efforts at, and motivations for, communication" (Thompson) or, in Eggers' words, "basically explains the entire history of the printed word." It thus depicts a very traditional type of textual literacy—book-based and embedded within a publishing cycle—which fails to center what Tara J. Yosso calls "community cultural wealth." In this sense, and also by aligning with a sort of hipster/bourgeois aesthetic (Ware's work may be most recognizable from the cover of many *New Yorker* issues), the mural is inherently biased toward what Jonathan Rosa and Nelson Flores call a "white listening subject," suggesting that this mural—and literacy itself—is by and for white people. Indeed, Ware explicitly aligns his depiction of "communication" with the "human race" itself, conflating humanity itself with white liberal humanism and normative literacy, both coded as white, while evoking progress narratives of neoliberal "development" (Wynter). Though 826 Valencia may have been attempting to signal openness, its mural also invokes "possessive investments" in both land and literacy, a neocolonial manifestation of "whiteness as property" that is simultaneously ideological and material (Lipsitz; Harris).

826 Valencia Today: Now Sponsored by Tech Capital

In today's San Francisco, eighteen years since 826 Valencia was founded, gentrification has continued to surge, the tech industry has continued to expand beyond levels many could have imagined, and additional start-ups have moved into San Francisco and the neighboring Silicon Valley. As detailed in numerous studies, the Mission has gotten both whiter and pricier—phenomena that are, of course, intimately linked (Garofoli and Said; McElroy). The neighborhood's rent prices and eviction rates have skyrocketed—predominantly along racial lines. As one result, between 2009 and 2013, the Mission's Latinx population decreased by 27% (Maharawal 31).

Concurrently, 826 Valencia has expanded across the country, including sites in Brooklyn, Detroit, and Chicago, as well as two new San Francisco locations, one in the Tenderloin and its newest in Mission Bay; both are neighborhoods, like the Mission, that until recently were largely low-income and predominantly Black/brown but now are less so as they undergo "urban renewal" facilitated by the city in tandem with the real estate sector. Besides its expansion, what's most apparently different about 826 today is its branding. Its website got a major image makeover sometime between 2016 and 2018 (indeed, the long-time chair of 826's board was an advertising executive for BBDO); the new site is minimalist yet whimsical, littered with small animated drawings and bold infographics quantifying the organization's "impact."

At the same time, in line with shifts in mainstream education discourses, 826 Valencia seems to rely less on overtly deficit/damage-centered rhetoric, typically describing the students and communities it engages as "under-served" and "under-resourced" (*Annual Report 2015-16*; "About"). Crucially, this updated rhetoric has shifted away from blaming students' educational struggles on their attitudes, behaviors, or home lives. Yet, it still fails to account for other modes of being "served" in one's education besides in a typical K–12 school setting through community cultural wealth (Yosso). The phrase "under-resourced students" is also quite individualistic in its emphasis on students rather than systems; it describes youth using an adjective typically ascribed to institutions or infrastructures.

For literacy scholars, such as Rousculp and Linda Flower, interrogating and shifting the rhetoric of sponsoring institutions are key ways to encourage more fruitful community projects. Flower proposes we embrace a "rhetoric of engagement," of "making a difference within an intercultural community," which "shifts the locus of agency from the program to the young people" and their community to confront the unequal power relations undergirding many community literacy programs; I agree that this is vital (228, 149). However, in the context of profound and violent racio-economic inequality, simply shifting away from deficit frameworks—or, per Flowers, coming to view students as agentic—is crucial but may not be sufficient if institutions remain invested in neoliberal spatial and economic (dis)possession, even if these investments are not immediately discernable (Paris and Alim).

Indeed, even as 826 Valencia's discourses have shifted to more closely align with rhetorics of reciprocity, it has increasingly fostered intimate ties to large corporations. For instance, 826 Valencia and its sister sites' current Boards of Directors are made up largely by employers of for-profit companies that benefit from mechanisms of neoliberal accumulation and wealth hoarding, in fields like banking/investment, real estate development, venture capitalism, advertising/branding, and, of course, tech, with Board and Associate Board Members employed by Bay Area-based tech companies like Lyft, Microsoft, Google, Dropbox, Facebook, and Twitter ("Staff "; "The 826 National Team"). Beginning in 2014, 826 Valencia broadened its volunteer force through official "corporate partnerships"; its first was with Twitter; Adobe, Apple, Dropbox, LinkedIn, and Salesforce have now joined ("A Huge Thank You to Our Partners"; *Annual Report 2018-19*). And major donors to 826 Valencia include local tech companies such as Yelp, Cisco, Twitter, and Microsoft (*Annual Report 2018-19*). Google seems to be an especially significant sponsor: 826 Valencia was able to open its second San Francisco site thanks to a $500,000 grant from them ("About").

This arrangement not especially unique. That 826 Valencia has sustained itself and expanded significantly in substantial part through corporate partnerships is the norm for many nonprofits and NGOs (INCITE!; Au and Ferrare). But I cite these affiliations explicitly to name and question aspects of nonprofits that have become so naturalized that they're often not mentioned at all: 1) their deep ties to corporations, including those with stances that lie directly at odds with the community they are supposedly "engaging" with, and 2) the idea that an organization's continued expansion (inevitably through such partnerships) is equivalent to its success. The NPIC isn't simply corporate altruism: companies reap significant tax benefits through their sponsorship. It also facilitates corporate image boosts: through philanthropy work with local organizations, companies appear generous, responsible, and connected with neighborhood residents that they are simultaneously displacing, a sort of band-aid that then enables such companies to proceed with violent capitalist accumulation as usual. This too aligns with neoliberalism's broader project to obscure or justify dispossession of public resources under free-market logics; Ruth Wilson Gilmore in fact refers to philanthropy as "the private allocation of stolen social wages" (Keynote Conversation).

What I think this particular case makes especially clear, though, is that an organization's material infrastructure can actively contradict or negate its espoused goals. As one example, 826 Valencia started building its Google-sponsored Mission Bay around the time the tech firm began building a controversial "mega campus" in nearby San Jose, which has been critiqued for its potential to further displace Bay Area residents (Elias). Yet, though 826 Valencia's rhetoric has shifted in recent years, one thing that has remained consistent is that it frequently cites supporting "overburdened teachers" as a key objective ("My Wish"; "History"). However, San Francisco is currently undergoing a severe teacher shortage—no doubt spurred by the tech boom and resulting rises in rent (Lambert and Willis; Williamson et al.). This suggests that the nonprofit to some degree relies on the expansion of tech—and by proxy, the pushing out of low-income BIPOC, including students as well as public-school teachers—in its ongoing expansion.

McElroy sees the tech industry's enthusiasm to partner with organizations like 826 Valencia as a trend to mask the "malevolent effects" of the neocolonial "extractive technologies" they rely on, including both gentrification-fueled displacement *and* "data colonialism"—the surveillance, extraction, and commodification of internet users' online data (827). We might see these tech corporations, then, as literacy sponsors in another sense aside from their philanthropic partnerships: they also foster and finance new forms of technological literacy, the authoring of codes and algorithms that promote digital surveillance and extraction. The consequences of literate and "technoimperial" (McElroy) mechanisms are, again, highly racialized and classed, since they too are justified by logics of white supremacist coloniality. But their digital nature underscores that these consequences are not restricted to one city, but circulate transnationally, across networks of neocolonial domination. This project, then, could never really be about 826 Valencia as an individual organization, but rather, per Gilmore, "an entire realm of social policy and social investment" made up of "dense and intricate connections" between many institutional actors—connections and investments that were actively made, and thus are *not* foreclosed ("In the Shadow" 42, 47).

Divestment as Educational Praxis

As INCITE! acknowledges, the NPIC operates in complex, paradoxical ways contingent on geographies, histories, and economies. There is no doubt that many nonprofits and/or out-of-school educational organizations do vital work and have the potential to create transformative and liberatory spaces for community members (Alvarez; Alvarez & Alvarez). Thus, as Gilmore posits, "it's not the fact of being a nonprofit, it's rather the *relationship* that the institution has to the institutions of racial capitalism as it is destroying us" (Keynote Conversation, my emphasis). For Nan Alamilla Boyd and Jillian Sandell, who taught a San Francisco State class placing students into nonprofit internships, examining this relationship head-on and interrogating spaces of complicity "in the contradictions of global capitalism" often evokes tension and unease, yet is pedagogically and theoretically useful, perhaps necessary. Their teaching incorporates overt discussions around the contradictions of "service" learning: in interrogating the geopolitical context, aim, and "function of nonprofit organizations," students and professors together "grapple with and confront our own participation" (257).

Informed by Boyd and Sandell's assertion that we examine the "troubling histories and structures" of the community sites in which we work, we might consider what I am calling *divestment as an educational praxis*.[4] My understanding of divestment draws on education scholarship pertaining to both decolonization and abolition. I am inspired here by Eve Tuck and K. Wayne Yang, whose vision of education justice draws on Indigenous and Black studies, simultaneously mobilizing abolition and decolonization as frameworks "to contest the violence and legitimacy of the nation-state and its apparatuses, and to refuse routes to justice which require us to appeal for our humanity" (9). I am drawn to Linda Tuhiwai Smith's understanding of decolonization in part "as a long-term process involving the bureaucratic, cultural, linguistic and psychological *divesting* of colonial power" (101, my emphasis). I also draw on abolitionist, critical-race education theorists, such as Shange and the coauthors of "Abolitionist University Studies: An Invitation." The latter project points to the "proliferation of divestment movements" in campus-based organization—organizing that interrogates educational institutions' economic investments in corporations/institutions that promote national and/or transnational militarized violence, inhumane labor practices, environmental destruction, and more.

Drawing on these scholars, then, I see divestment as both material and ideological, a refusal of both "colonial power" foregrounded in indigenous dispossession (Smith; Grande) and the abolition of "institutions of unfreedom" foregrounded in antiblackness, both of which underly neoliberalism (Tuck and Yang 9). In the context of community literacy, as I envision it, divestment as an educational praxis foremost requires us to rigorously understand and attend to the geographic, historical, cultural, racial, and economic specificity of our own sites, which are often hidden or naturalized as inevitable. In writing this article, I've attempted this sort of methodological approach, one built around interrogating educational investments—in particular rhetorics and ideologies that preserve literacy and space as white property, as well as investments in the local and global work of neocolonial capital. Because these investments spread far and wide, across multiple scales and structures, this work therefore requires an intentional interdisciplinarity.

This praxis also asks that we actually take seriously divestment—financial, ideological, and otherwise—as a legitimate political position and practical possibility. One of the challenges of neoliberal austerity logics, pervasive in education settings, is that they can convince us that, due to "limited resources" or assumptions of good intentions, we must accept all aspects of an institution wholesale and uncritically, perhaps because it has a "net positive" effect or "is better than nothing." However, leaning on positive intent, particularly when harnessed as a means to justify problematic associations, is empty "if we do not take responsibility and cannot be held accountable" for these associations and their material ramifications, and are thus not "answerable" to "genealogies of coloniality" (Castagno 43; Grande; Patel 68). In fact, rhetorics of intention echo paternalistic discourses around literacy and literacy education (discussed above in the context of 826 Valencia, but ubiquitous in similar settings) that center the desires, assumptions, and epistemologies of educators and administrators rather than those of students or communities, and thus often work to maintain status-quo investments in neocolonial capitalism.

An all-or-nothing mindset based around assumptions of scarcity and institutional loyalty, exacerbated by neoliberalism, also limits our ability to see alternative ways of teaching, knowing, and being. As scholars in decolonial and abolitionist rhetorics and literacies remind us, we do not have to accept institutionally sanctioned relationships or conditions, particularly those that pointedly reproduce racial and settler violence (Kynard; Rodríguez; Smith and Kannan). To loosely paraphrase Kynard during the Q&A of her CCW keynote, we all work within educational structures that to some degree perpetuate racist, classist, xenophobic and/or settler-colonial violence, not to mention compounding violence along the lines of gender, disability, and more. So, rather than "institutions or no institutions?" we have to ask ourselves and act on this question: what are we willing to accept and what must we refuse?

Tuck and Yang's barometers for divestment might serve as useful guidance: they refuse education/social justice projects that "rely upon the benevolence of the state or of the dominant in society" to enact change, "require us to prove humanity," center those "white settlers who are presumed to have agency," or "presume compromise as the main avenue for achieving solidarity" (8). However, Tuck and Yang are explicit that they "are not presenting this list as dogma" (8). In calling for divestment as an educational praxis, I'm also hesitant to provide a neat list of universally applicable "solutions" or "quick fixes" to complex, structural problems, which might have the risk of making a largely white, class-privileged audience of educators/administrators feel at ease. I also believe that what divestment looks like will vary significantly given the vastly different histories, geographies, and institutional networks of every community literacy site. What I do propose is that in our theorizing, pedagogical, and administrative work, we follow Tuck and Yang's lead to explicitly interrogate and clarify "the whys and why nots of our own participation," recognizing that in all institutional partnerships, funding sources or educational discourses are sites of *active* investment and divestment (8).

My ideas here are also deeply inspired by the work of on-the-ground organizers for educational and spatial justice within and outside of academia, who have long been enacting and theorizing praxes of divestment. In San Francisco, we can see this through the unceasing work of grassroots activists in the Mission and beyond, who have fiercely called out "connections between inequality, wealth and evictions, and homelessness, and polic[ing], city policy," education, and "histories of colonialism" to refute their inevitability and demand an alternative (Maharawal 39). I see praxes of divestment and refusal in the literacies and actions of muralists who depict the city's neocolonial evolution while insistently taking up city space (Cordova); in the Ohlone's continued demands for the return of their land (Kamalakanthan); in anti-technoimperial actions such as physically blocking Google bus routes bisecting neighborhood streets (Maharawal); through the insurgency and "willful defiance" of Black and Latinx students and organizers to settle for an education where "the liberal eclipses the liberatory" (Shange 138); in collective movements and literacies insisting that a city and an education system divested from neoliberal coloniality are not only possible, but vital.

Notes

1. I use "Latinx" to denote people of Latin-American descent rather than Hispanic (which centers Spain) or Latino/a (which excludes nonbinary people) (Flores and Rosa; Rosa). I want to emphasize that "Latinx" doesn't index a static racial, ethnic, or national identity. Latinx racialization has been historically contingent, varying with evolving applications of anti-Black, settler-colonial logics/tactics locating Latinidad on imagined spectrums between phenotypic Blackness and Whiteness, and Spanish and English (Rosa). However, organizers in San Francisco and elsewhere have unified strategically, if across many differences, under the singular banner of Latinidad as an activist, solidarity-building praxis (Cordova; Sandoval).

2. For analyses of decolonial pedagogical practices by writing studies scholars (mostly in the context of college composition classes), see, for instance, Medina; King et al.; and Ruiz & Sánchez. For analyses of decolonial pedagogies in K-12 English or literacy education, see Paris & Alim; Kinloch et al.; de los Ríos et al.; and others.

3. Literary/cultural studies scholars note that Eggers' novels like *What Is the What* and *Zeitoun* draw on the same tropes: white paternalistic saviorism, individualism, capitalist assimilation, racial othering, speaking on behalf of those constructed as others, overemphasizing humanitarianism as the answer to systemic inequality, and underplaying racism's and colonialism's structural nature and ongoing ramifications. See, for instance, Goyal; Krishnan; and Hartnell.

4. Many thanks to Carmen Kynard for suggesting this phrasing.

Works Cited

"About – 826 Valencia." 826 Valencia, 826valencia.org/about.

Aggarwal, Ujju and Edwin Mayorga. "From Forgotten to Fought Over: Neoliberal Restructuring, Public Schools, and Urban Space." *Scholar & Feminist Online*, vol. 13, no. 2, 2016.

Alejandrino, Simon Velasquez. "Gentrification in San Francisco's Mission District: Indicators and Policy Recommendations." Mission Economic Development Association, 2000.

Alvarez, Steven. *Community Literacies en Confianza: Learning from Bilingual After-School Programs*. NCTE, 2017.

Alvarez, Steven, and Sara P. Alvarez. "'La Biblioteca es Importante': A Case Study of an Emergent Bilingual Public Library in the Nuevo US South." *Equity & Excellence in Education*, vol. 49, no. 4, 2016, pp. 403–13.

Anderson, Thomas Scott. "826 Valencia's Literacy Crusaders Are on the Front Lines of COVID-19's Education Crisis." *San Francisco Chronicle*, 5 May 2020.

Au, Wayne and Joseph J. Ferrare, editors. *Mapping Corporate Education Reform: Power and Policy Networks in the Neoliberal State*. Routledge, 2015.

Boggs, Abigail, Eli Meyerhoff, Nick Mitchell, and Zach Schwartz-Weinstein. "Abolitionist University Studies: An Invitation." *Abolition: A Journal of Insurgent Politics*, 2019. abolitionjournal.org/abolitionist-university-studies-an-invitation/.

Boyd, Nan Alamilla, and Jillian Sandell. "Unpaid and Critically Engaged: Feminist Interns in the Nonprofit Industrial Complex." *Feminist Teacher*, vol. 22, no. 3, 2012, pp. 251–65.

Brandt, Deborah. "Sponsors of Literacy." *College Composition & Communication*, vol. 49, no. 2, 1998, pp. 166-85.

Burke, Brandon. *Ware Detail*. 7 Oct. 2006. *Flickr*, flickr.com/photos/thejosephboys/278659562/.

Carey, Roderick L. "A Cultural Analysis of the Achievement Gap Discourse: Challenging the Language and Labels Used in the Work of School Reform." *Urban Education*, vol. 49, no. 4, 2014, pp. 440-68.

Castagno, Angelina E. *Educated in Whiteness: Good Intentions and Diversity in Schools*. University of Minnesota Press, 2014.

Cordova, Cary. *The Heart of the Mission: Latino Art and Politics in San Francisco*. U of Pennsylvania P, 2017.

Cushman, Ellen. "Translingual and Decolonial Approaches to Meaning Making." *College English*, vol. 78, no. 3, 2016, pp. 234-42.

de los Ríos, Cati V., Jorge López, and Ernest Morrell. "Toward a Critical Pedagogy of Race: Ethnic Studies and Literacies of Power in High School Classrooms." *Race and Social Problems*, vol. 7, 2015, pp. 84–96.

Eggers, Dave. "My Wish: Once Upon a School." *TED.com*. TED Conferences, LLC, Feb. 2008, ted.com/talks/dave_eggers_my_wish_once_upon_a_school.

826 Valencia Annual Report 2015-2016. 826 Valencia, 15 Nov. 2015, issuu. com/826valencia/docs/826_annualreport_2015_final_web.

826 Valencia Annual Report 2018-19. 826 Valencia, 2019, 826valencia.org/wordpress/wp-content/uploads/2019/11/AR_Spreads_F_low_res.pdf.

Elias, Jennifer. "Google's Plans for a Mega-Campus in San Jose Lurk Behind Its Recent $1 Billion Housing Pledge." *CNBC*, 11 Jul. 2019, cnbc.com/2019/07/11/google-san-jose-expansion-helped-drive-1-billion-housing-pledge.html.

Fernandes, Sujatha. *Curated Stories: The Uses and Misuses of Storytelling*. Oxford UP, 2017.

Flower, Linda. *Community Literacy and the Rhetoric of Public Engagement*. Southern Illinois UP, 2008.

Garofoli, Joe and Carolyn Said. "A Changing Mission." *San Francisco Chronicle*, 21 Dec. 2015.

Gilmore, Ruth Wilson. "In the Shadow of the Shadow State." *The Revolution Will Not Be Funded: Beyond the Non-Profit Industrial Complex*. Edited by INCITE! Women of Color Against Violence, South End Press, 2009, pp. 41–52.

Gilmore, Ruth Wilson. Keynote Conversation, Making and Unmaking Mass Incarceration Conference (MUMI), Oxford MS, 5 Dec. 2019, mumiconference.com/transcripts/.

Goyal, Yogita. "African Atrocity, American Humanity: Slavery and Its Transnational Afterlives." *Research in African Literatures*, vol. 45, no. 3, 2014, pp. 48–71.

Grande, Sandy. *Red Pedagogy*. Rowman & Littlefield, 2004.

Harris, Cheryl I. "Whiteness as Property." *Harvard Law Review*, vol. 106, no. 8, 1993, pp. 1707–91.

Hartnell, Anna. *After Katrina: Race, Neoliberalism, and the End of the American Century*. SUNY Press, 2017.

Hernandez-Zamora, Gregorio. *Decolonizing Literacy: Mexican Lives in the Era of Global Capitalism*. Channel View Publications, 2010

Hesse, Doug. "CCCC Chair's Letter." *College Composition & Communication*, vol. 57, no. 2, 2005, pp. 372–82.

Hilton, Tom. *Clarion Alley 05*. 13 Sep. 2014, *Flickr*, flickr.com/photos/tomhilton/15236342342/.

"History – 826 Valencia." 826 Valencia, 826valencia.org/history/.

"A Huge Thank You to Our Partners." *826 News*, 826 Valencia, 28 Nov. 2017., 826valencia.org/a-huge-thank-you-to-our-partners/.

INCITE! Women of Color Against Violence, editors. *The Revolution Will Not Be Funded: Beyond the Non-Profit Industrial Complex*. South End Press, 2009.

Kamalakanthan, Prashanth. "The Ohlone People Were Forced Out of San Francisco. Now They Want Part of Their Land Back." *Mother Jones*, 22 Nov. 2014, motherjones.com/politics/2014/11/ohlone-san-francisco-cultural-center.

King, Lisa, Rose Gubele, and Joyce Rain Anderson, editors. *Survivance, Sovereignty, and Story: Teaching American Indian Rhetorics*. Utah State UP, 2015.

Kinloch, Valerie, Tanja Burkhard and Carlotta Penn, editors. *Race, Justice, and Activism in Literacy Instruction*. Teachers College Press, 2019.

Krishnan, Madhu. "Affect, Empathy, and Engagement: Reading African Conflict in the Global Literary Marketplace." *Journal of Commonwealth Literature*, vol. 52, no. 2, 2015, pp. 212–30.

Kynard, Carmen. "'All I Need is One Mic': A Black Feminist Community Meditation on the Work, the Job, and the Hustle (& Why So Many of Yall Confuse This Stuff)." Conference on Community Writing, 18 Oct. 2019, Pittsburgh, PA. Keynote Address.

Kynard, Carmen. "This Bridge: The BlackFeministCompositionist's Guide to the Colonial and Imperial Violence of Schooling Today." *Feminist Teacher*, vol. 26, no. 2-3, 2016, pp. 126–41.

Ladson-Billings, Gloria. "Reading, Writing, and Race: Literacy Practices of Teachers in Diverse Classrooms." *Language, Literacy, and Power in Schooling*, edited by Teresa McCarty, Routledge, 2005, pp. 133–50.

Lambert, Diana and Daniel J. Willis. "California's Teacher Housing Crunch: More School Districts Building their Own." *San Francisco Chronicle*, 22 Apr. 2019.

Leonardo, Zeus. *Race, Whiteness, and Education*. Routledge, 2009.

Lipman, Pauline. *The New Political Economy of Urban Education: Neoliberalism, Race, and the Right to the City*. Taylor & Francis, 2013.

Lipsitz, George. *The Possessive Investment in Whiteness: How White People Profit from Identity Politics*. Temple UP, 1998.

Lorimer Leonard, Rebecca. *Writing on the Move: Migrant Women and the Value of Literacy*. U of Pittsburgh P, 2017.

Maharawal, Manissa M. "San Francisco's Tech-Led Gentrification Public Space, Protest, and the Urban Commons." *City Unsilenced: Urban Resistance and Public Space in the Age of Shrinking Democracy*, edited by Jeffrey Hou and Sabine Knierbein, Routledge, 2017, pp. 30–44.

Matsuda, Paul K. "The Lure of Translingual Writing." *PMLA*, vol. 129, no. 3, 2014, pp. 478–83.

McElroy, Erin. "Data, Dispossession, and Facebook: Technoimperialism and Toponymy in Gentrifying San Francisco." *Urban Geography*, vol. 40, no. 6, 2019, pp. 826–45.

Medina, Cruz. "Decolonial Potential in a Multilingual FYC." *Composition Studies*, vol. 47, no. 1, 2019, pp. 73–94.

McKittrick, Katherine. *Demonic Grounds: Black Women and the Cartographies of Struggle*. University of Minnesota Press, 2006.

Mirabal, Nancy Raquel. "Geographies of Displacement: Latina/os, Oral History, and the Politics of Gentrification in San Francisco's Mission District." *The Public Historian*, vol. 31, no. 2, 2009, pp. 7–31.

Nelson, Ashlyn Aiko, and Beth Gazley. "The Rise of School-Supporting Nonprofits." *Education Finance and Policy*, vol. 9, no. 4, 2014, pp. 541–66.

Paris, Django, and H. Samy Alim, editors. *Culturally Sustaining Pedagogies: Teaching and Learning for Justice in a Changing World*. Teachers College Press, 2017.

Patel, Leigh. *Decolonizing Educational Research: From Ownership to Answerability*. Routledge, 2015.

Patterson, Kelly L., and Robert Mark Silverman. "Urban Education and Neighborhood Revitalization." *Journal of Urban Affairs*, vol. 35, no. 1, 2013, pp. 1–5.

Ralston, Theresa. "826 Valencia: Transforming a Community, One Student at a Time." *Alternet*, 20 May 2012.

Ribero, Ana Maria. "Citizenship." *Decolonizing Rhetoric and Composition Studies: New Latinx Keywords for Theory and Pedagogy*, edited by Iris D. Ruiz and Raúl Sánchez, Palgrave Macmillan, 2016, pp. 31–45.

Rosa, Jonathan. *Looking like a Language, Sounding like a Race*. Oxford UP, 2018.

Rosa, Jonathan, and Nelson Flores. "Unsettling Race and Language: Toward a Raciolinguistic Perspective." *Language in Society*, vol. 46, no. 5, 2017, pp. 621-47.

Rodríguez, Yanira. "Pedagogies of Refusal: What it Means to (Un)teach a Student Like Me." *Radical Teacher*, vol. 115, 2019, 5–12.

Rousculp, Tiffany. *Rhetoric of Respect: Recognizing Change at a Community Writing Center*. National Council of Teachers of English, 2014.

Ruiz, Iris D. and Raúl Sánchez, editors. *Decolonizing Rhetoric and Composition Studies: New Latinx Keywords for Theory and Pedagogy*. Palgrave Macmillan, 2016.

Sandoval, Tomás Summers. *Latinos at the Golden Gate: Creating Community and Identity in San Francisco*. U of North Carolina P, 2013.

Spencer, Keith A. "Long Before Tech Bros, Silicon Valley Had a Highly Developed Society." *The Guardian*, 8 Jan. 2019, theguardian.com/technology/2019/jan/08/silicon-valley-history-society-book-ohlone-native-americans.

Shange, Savannah. *Progressive Dystopia: Abolition, Antiblackness, and Schooling in San Francisco*. Duke UP, 2019.
Smith, Cherish, and Vani Kannen. "'At Risk' of What?." *Reflections*, vol. 14, no. 2, 2015, pp. 51–77.
Smith, Linda Tuhiwai. *Decolonizing Methodologies: Research and Indigenous Peoples*. 2nd edition. Zed Books, 2012.
Soja, Edward W. *Seeking Spatial Justice*. U of Minnesota P, 2010.
"Staff—826 Valencia." 826 Valencia, 826valencia.org/staff/.
Utilizer. *"Evict Google" mural by Corrina Goldblatt, Clarion Alley, San Francisco, CA, 2016*. 19 Aug. 2016. Wikimedia Commons, commons.wikimedia.org/wiki/File:%22Evict_Google%22_mural_by_Corrina_Goldblatt,_Clarion_Alley,_San_Francisco,_CA,_2016.jpg.
"The 826 National Team—826 National." 826 National, 826national.org/about/the-826-national-team/.
Thompson, David. "826 Valencia." *Eye Magazine*. Issue 48, Summer 2003, eyemagazine.com/feature/article/826-valencia.
Tuck, Eve. "Suspending Damage: A Letter to Communities." *Harvard Educational Review*, vol. 79, no. 3, 2009, pp. 409–28.
Tuck, Eve and K. Wayne Yang. "Introduction: Born Under the Rising Sign of Social Justice." *Toward What Justice? Describing Diverse Dreams of Justice in Education*, edited by Eve Tuck and K. Wayne Yang, Routledge, 2018, pp. 1–18.
Wan, Amy J. *Producing Good Citizens: Literacy Training in Anxious Times*. U of Pittsburgh P, 2014.
Watson, Dyan. "What Do You Mean when You Say 'Urban'? Speaking Honestly about Race and Students." *Rethinking Schools*, vol. 26, no. 1, 2011, pp. 48–50.
Williamson, Peter, Xornam Apedoe, and Christopher Thomas. "Context as Content in Urban Teacher Education: Learning to Teach in and for San Francisco." *Urban Education*, vol. 51, no. 10, 2016, pp. 1170-97.
Wynter, Sylvia. "'No Humans Involved': An Open Letter to my Colleagues. *Forum N. H. I.: Knowledge for the 21st Century*, vol. 1 no. 1, 1994, pp. 42–73.
Yosso, Tara J. "Whose Culture Has Capital? A Critical Race Theory Discussion of Community Cultural Wealth." *Race, Ethnicity and Education*, vol. 8, no. 1, 2005, pp. 69–91.

Author Bio

Anna Zeemont is an English PhD candidate and Gittell Urban Studies Dissertation Fellow at the City University of New York (CUNY) Graduate Center, where she studies Composition-Rhetoric and American Studies. Across CUNY, she's served as a composition instructor, Writing Across the Curriculum Fellow, writing center consultant, and New Media Lab research fellow. Anna's research draws on queer-feminist, decolonial, and abolitionist frameworks to interrogate the politics, rhetorics, and movement of literacy across educational institutions and urban geographies. Before starting her PhD, Anna worked in secondary education in the Bay Area, where she grew up.

A Network Approach to Writing Center Outreach

Thomas Deans

When doing scholarship, we habitually work through overlapping networks: some are local, as when we consult with a colleague down the hall; some are national or global, as when we attend conferences and contribute to journals—or read them, as you're doing now. Derek Mueller helps us document and visualize such networks within writing studies. Researchers in other fields, most notably Bruno Latour, have adopted the notion of the network to trace relationships, both metaphorical and material, and make sense of complex phenomena. Networks are decentralized and distributed assemblages of elements acting and reacting to one another—interactions, both predictable and unpredictable, among multiple people, objects, events, and institutions. Few writing center outreach initiatives adopt the network as their signature identity, but the one that I describe here does.

In contrast, when college and university writing centers take up community engagement, most default to binary partnerships: a collaboration with a particular library or non-profit or school or neighborhood organization. These can be strategic collaborations between well-established institutions; they can be scrappy, grassroots efforts. They can be alliances designed to last; they can be initiatives pulled together to meet the exigencies of a particular moment. Either way, such partnerships rise or fall on the buy-in of each partner, and even the most well-planned partnerships can be difficult to sustain, though when they end that doesn't necessarily mean they have failed, as there are multiple ways to think about the lifecycles of community literacy projects (Restaino and Cella).

Networks and binary partnerships. Both have their merits and constraints, and one project can even pivot from one orientation to the other. This was the case with the University of Connecticut Writing Center's outreach efforts, which started fifteen years ago as a typical university-secondary school partnership—tutors from our university writing center started delivering writing tutoring to an urban school—but later shifted to developing a regional network that encourages middle and high schools to start and sustain their own peer writing centers. Our experience offers one model for imagining writing center outreach; it may likewise suggest the possibilities of network thinking for other kinds community literacy work.

The UConn Writing Center's Secondary School Outreach Program started in 2004, two years before I landed there, triggered by the actions of Nina Rivera, an undergraduate enrolled in a course on writing theory and practice taught by Laurie Cella, a doctoral student in English and director of the Writing Center. Rivera's final project for Cella's course was to plan and launch a partnership that brought several UConn Writing Center tutors to her old high school weekly to tutor. Rivera, Cella, and a colleague reflect on the rise and fall of this program in "Re-Assessing Sustainability: Leveraging Marginal Power for Service-Learning Programs," drawing on Paula Mathieu's notions of tactical and strategic modes of community engagement to affirm the program's tactical value despite its discontinuation after a few years. When that partnership ended for reasons typical in university/school initiatives—in this case the departure of key teachers and administrators—the Writing Center changed its outreach philosophy. We maintained our engagement with secondary schools but shifted focus from delivering tutoring at one school to building regional capacity for middle and high schools to start and sustain their own peer writing centers.

Ever since we made the shift from delivering tutoring to building regional capacity for peer tutoring, we have been growing a network whose main event is an annual Conference for Secondary Schools. More than 150 students and teachers gather in Storrs each fall to share strategies with UConn tutors, and especially with each other. Universities already have the infrastructure for conferences, and this half-day event serves as both a catalyst for new teachers and students to learn how good writing centers work and as a place for schools with established peer centers to train and re-energize their new cohorts of tutors. It is also a place for schools to connect with one another.

Figure 1. Students from Ellington High School present at the Twelfth Annual Secondary Schools Writing Centers Conference in September 2019.

Figure 2. Middle and high school students from different schools mix at a breakout session led by a UConn tutor

Meanwhile, across the academic year we work intensively with a different middle or high school in our region each year. A small group of experienced UConn tutors visits that school weekly to train a founding cohort of middle or high school tutors. Yes, this is a kind of binary partnership, but one that is term-limited to a year, although we hope to see that school the next year—and going forward—at our annual conference. In fact, every school we work with must commit to being a featured presenter at the next conference as a way of paying forward the professional development they received. This dual approach—a big annual conference for many schools, and weekly visits to one school to help them get a new center started—allows us to incrementally grow and sustain a network of relationships (see Deans & Courtmanche for a detailed account of how these processes work). You can track the cumulative reach of those efforts on a digital map of more than sixty schools that have attended our conference over the last dozen years (*Network Map*).

The regional infrastructure we have developed through the annual conference—and the range of relationships it has engendered—has reached an impressive stage of maturity: middle schoolers who have done peer tutoring in writing centers that we helped found now transition into high schools where we have helped found similar centers; student peer tutors trained by those high schools move on to UConn, where some now tutor at our center; each year an experienced UConn Writing Center tutor who is pursuing a degree in education becomes our graduate outreach coordinator, and the next year that person is typically hired by Connecticut middle or high school to teach English; some of those former UConn tutors and outreach coordinators have founded additional peer writing centers across the state and brought *their* students to our annual conference. Those homecomings are especially gratifying.

When compared to binary partnerships—even good, reciprocal ones—the webbed, flexible, dynamic relationships of a network can offer a wider range of ways to participate and different possibilities for growth. Networks need to be deliberately built and maintained—that is, they require some strategic and predictable infrastructure, like our annual conference—but their everyday functioning is tactical and protean. For example, the middle and high school teachers who work with us take several different pathways into our network and their relationships to the university range from one-time conference attendance, to a full year of weekly school visits by our tutors, to year-after-year conference attendance and presenting. Many of the connections run though UConn, but there are also more horizontal, school-to-school connections. There is no center of a network, yet there can be many writing centers in a network!

Some relationships within our network are thick; some are thin. Some relationships have been consistently active since we started; some have blinked on and off, or even permanently off, typically as a result of administrative changes or teacher turnover. We've accepted that about a quarter of the writing centers we help launch won't be operating five years later. It's tempting to view each those as a failed partnership, but instead we accept the pattern as natural to an evolving network, or at least characteristic of our network.

In our network ecology, teachers and schools toggle in and out of participation, or even drop out entirely, but the network continues. Many, many students churn through, most just for a year or two. The network offers multiple ways in, multiple levels of involvement, gentle ways out, and chances to re-enter. As the longtime director of the Writing Center, I know the teachers who have been our most reliable collaborators, but I don't personally know everyone involved, which from a partnership perspective might seem irresponsible, but from a network perspective is OK, even expected.

This kind of network could be developed from scratch, as we tried in our early days. We soon learned, however, that grafting our network to existing networks was a much better and more sustainable way to go. We collaborate with the local National Writing Project site, also housed at UConn, which does professional development for secondary teachers and shares our commitment to promoting writing as a social, iterative process for learning and doing. One might label the Connecticut Writing Project (CWP) our partner; however, what we really do is plug into their network, the relationships with teachers across the region that CWP has been cultivating for decades. CWP developed a network through its own distinctive infrastructure: the summer institute for teachers. When we mesh, we both become stronger.

We aspire to expand our network—this time beyond the thirty or so mile radius we now focus on. If this happens—and for May 2020 we had a new conference in the planning stages before it was cancelled due to coronavirus—it will involve another grafting of networks, this time with UConn's dual-enrollment program, which has many strong relationships with high schools across the state, and which shares a commitment to robust writing pedagogies that include peer-to-peer engagement.

The network approach often lacks the immediacy and intimacy of typical community writing center partnerships, yet we experience some such moments each year at our conference. We also trust that the network, and what teachers and student tutors have all learned through its connections and energy, have made possible many daily peer-to-peer tutorials, distributed across many middle and high schools, for more than a decade.

Works Cited

Cella, Laurie JC, Nina Rivera, and Melissa Rinaldo. "Re-Assessing Sustainability: Leveraging Marginal Power for Service-Learning Programs." *Reflections: A Journal of Public Rhetoric, Civic Writing, and Service Learning*, vol. 10, no. 2, 2011, pp.1–23. https://reflectionsjournal.net/wp-content/uploads/2011/04/Re-assessing-Sustainability.pdf

Deans, Thomas, and Jason Courtmanche. "How Developing a Network of Secondary School Writing Centers Can Enrich University Writing Programs." *WPA: Writing Program Administration*, vol. 42, no. 2, 2019, pp. 58-79.

Latour, Bruno. *Reassembling the Social: An Introduction to Actor-Network Theory*. Oxford UP, 2007.

Mueller, Derek. N. *Network Sense: Methods for Visualizing a Discipline*. University Press of Colorado and The WAC Clearinghouse, 2017. https://wac.colostate.edu/books/writing/network/

Network Map. University of Connecticut Writing Center, 2020, https://maphub.net/uconnWC/Outreach-Map. Accessed 10 Dec 2020.

Restaino, Jessica, and Laurie JC Cella, Editors. *Unsustainable: Re-imagining Community Literacy, Public Writing, Service-Learning, and the University*. Lexington Books/Rowman & Littlefield, 2013.

Author Bio

Thomas Deans is Professor of English and Director of the Writing Center at the University of Connecticut. His interests include writing across the curriculum, community engagement, writing centers, writing assessment, prose style, and representations of literacy in literary and sacred texts. He wrote *Writing Partnerships: Service-Learning in Composition* and *Writing and Community Engagement: A Service-Learning Rhetoric and Reader*, and he co-edits the *Oxford Brief Guides to Writing in the Disciplines* series.

Building a Community Literacy Network to Address Literacy Inequities: An Emergent Strategy Approach

Jeffrey Austin, Ann Blakeslee, Cathy Fleischer, and Christine Modey

Abstract

As a consortium of individuals, programs, and agencies that embrace the power of collaboration, the Washtenaw County Literacy Network works to shift conversations and practices surrounding literacy and literacy inequities. Using an emergent strategy lens, the authors describe the partnerships at the center of the network and the collaborative work that has emerged from these partnerships. The authors also analyze the adaptations recent events have generated in terms of the relationships and interactions that center the work, and they explore ways to rethink the idea of assessment for community literacy initiatives. Ultimately, the authors posit that emergent strategy helps networks like the WCLN navigate change in thoughtful and sustainable ways.

Keywords

emergent strategy, literacy networks, literacy inequities, collaboration, partnerships, social justice

Introduction: Five Scenarios

Fifteen middle and high school teachers—who are part of a county-wide Disciplinary Literacies team—spend a morning visiting classes on a university campus, then come together to talk with faculty about college writing. As the secondary teachers ask the college faculty—who are Writing Across the Curriculum Fellows—what they expect in terms of college readiness surrounding writing, one professor responds, "First, tell us more about you and the challenges you face. We need to learn from you."

Twelve writing consultants—from high school, university, and community-ty-based writing centers—gather together at one such community writing center, 826michigan, for the second in a series of *Dialogues* focused on "what counts as writing." Listening hard to each other, they share experiences and then thoughts on ways to help convey their values and beliefs to others. "Who else needs to know this?" they ask, as they decide on next steps to educate others.

Hundreds of children, teens, and adults flock to three branches of the Ypsilanti District Library to listen to local authors, try out writing activities, and share their own experiences with writing. Underneath signs proclaiming *Everyone's a Writer*, writers talk to other writers, whatever their ages and experiences, as volunteers from the community, faculty members and university writing consultants, and teachers and writing consultants from area high schools lead activities and cheer on the writers.

Thirty writing tutors meet for a morning of learning with each other. Soon-to-be seventh and eighth graders eager to become writing consultants emerge from an hour of talking with experienced high school consultants. As the experience comes to a close, students and teachers stand in a circle to share an "aha" moment from the day. Says one middle grader, "I really liked learning about funds of knowledge. Let me explain what that means." Gape-mouthed adults along with the students—of all ages—nod their heads in agreement.

Two secondary students—with enthusiasm and just a little trepidation—travel to a community center in a neighboring town to help lead a Family Fun Night with university faculty and volunteers. Children—with enthusiasm and just a little trepidation—come inside to try out different writing activities, alongside their parents, aunts or uncles, grandparents, and other interested adults. Everyone's voices fill the air as they all come together to share their writing at the end of the evening.

These five scenarios offer a window into some of the early activities of an emergent community literacy network—the Washtenaw County Literacy Network (WCLN)—that is being constructed through collaborative outreach across southeastern Michigan. The current network, emerging even as we, the authors of this article, write these words, includes a consortium of middle school, high school, and university writing centers (Washtenaw County Writing Centers Project); two groups devoted to community literacy (826michigan and YpsiWrites); a county-wide intermediate school district (Washtenaw ISD); a National Writing Project site (Eastern Michigan Writing Project); and a local library system with its three branches (Ypsilanti District Library). Numerous other partner groups contribute to and help form the network: an organization that provides free literacy support to adults (Washtenaw Literacy), an organization that runs an urban farm to support the local food system (Growing Hope), an organization that provides mentoring to at-risk youth (Mentor2Youth), and numerous others. (For a fuller view of this emergent network, see Figure 1 and the section describing the network below.)

In developing the WCLN, we, in collaboration with community literacy organizations and other community partners, have considered how to shift conversations and practices surrounding literacy in a diverse county with inequitable and uneven educational outcomes. The purpose of the network is to provide connection, mutual support, and reinforcement among local entities whose work not only supports school literacies, but also provides opportunities for students, teachers, parents, and community members to engage in meaningful writing activities and to engage in conversations about the importance and uses of writing and literacy for personal empowerment, education, and civic participation. The hope has been that, in some small ways, the Network might address literacy inequities through attentive listening and intentional engagement with, and not for, both our partner groups and the participants in these initiatives.

What it means to create and maintain this kind of network is something we think and talk about often. As four white authors who hold positions as secondary and university educators, we are aware of our privilege and the potential that privilege has for harm, especially when working with individuals, groups, and communities that are not similarly positioned. In contexts where asymmetries in power may well be present, we recognize and acknowledge the sustained attention required to work against social hierarchies that continually reinscribe differences in power between white high school and university faculty and communities of color, between speakers of "standardized English" and those who speak nonprivileged dialects, between "service providers" and "service recipients." As we connect with individuals, organizations, and communities in the hope of creating mutually beneficial partnerships, we endeavor to remain acutely aware of our own positionality and the tension inherent in the task of creating equitable working relationships in an educational ecosystem characterized by inequitable structures and outcomes.

The willingness to be reflexive about our identities and how they position us in community spaces is critical to the ability of the network to meet its mission. Without doing the prerequisite self-work, there is a danger of reproducing the same oppressive power structures inside the network that we are working against outside of it. The "twin pandemics" of COVID-19 and structural racism have laid bare the systemic inequities that make our advocacy and activism urgent. We hope that, like us, other white educators have felt the call to reflect, self-examine, and meet the historical moment. Our students' lives depend on it. The need for reflexivity and action are echoed, we believe, in the words of Nell Duke and Ernest Morrell (2020) when they argue:

> As is the case in policing, there are many well-intentioned educators—and some educators who go beyond good intentions to enact practices that research has found work toward equitable education and push back against educational oppression.

We foreground what "pushing back" means, looks like, and feels like in a networked community literacy context where good intentions are not enough. Within collectives of students, teachers, school administrators, community members, and non-profit organizations, we already have seen a shift in how we are doing our work. We find ourselves pushing to the surface what it means to purposefully decenter ourselves and to center the voices of students and others whose voices are often marginalized in educational space; to give up power so those with less acknowledged power can have more influence in the work; and to resist the white saviorism or colonialism that can damage collaborations between those with different levels of privilege. We also know that these relationships are only viable so long as we are willing to live the values expressed in this article in all aspects of our lives.

As we work with others to help move our community toward justice, we know, as the authors of this article, that we are not perfect and neither is our network; we've made mistakes and imagine that we will make more. This work is imperfect too. Despite the messiness and imperfection of the network, we continue to build durable relationships by being accountable and making our actions more aligned to justice each day. Thus, while the goal of this article is to describe this literacy network, we also understand that there are countless approaches and frameworks for both analyzing this work and navigating change. Many of them are rooted in structures of supremacy and hierarchy, which we are actively resisting. Thus, here we read our network through a lens of emergent strategy, a relational approach to social change we learned about through the writings of adrienne maree brown, a doula, women's rights activist, and Black feminist from Detroit. In the spirit of Christen Smith, a member of the Cite Black Women Collective, we believe, "We must reconfigure the politics of knowledge production by engaging in a radical praxis of citation that acknowledges and honors Black women's transnational intellectual production" (para.2). Smith reminds us that, given our positionality as authors of this article and as leaders within the network, decentering ourselves and centering marginalized voices is required. In this spirit, we use brown's work in adaptation, interdependence, and small group facilitation to analyze and reflect on the formation and development of this network, providing specific examples of how we see brown's ideas in the relationships and stories of network participants, especially amid the social shocks of the COVID-19 pandemic and the historical pandemic of police violence that killed Breonna Taylor, George Floyd, and countless others. We then consider how ideas for assessment drawn from emergent strategy may provide some frameworks for better understanding the health of the network and others like it and the movement of such networks toward the goal of collaboratively democratizing literacy practices and increasing educational equity.

Emergent Strategy and the Washtenaw County Literacy Network (WCLN)

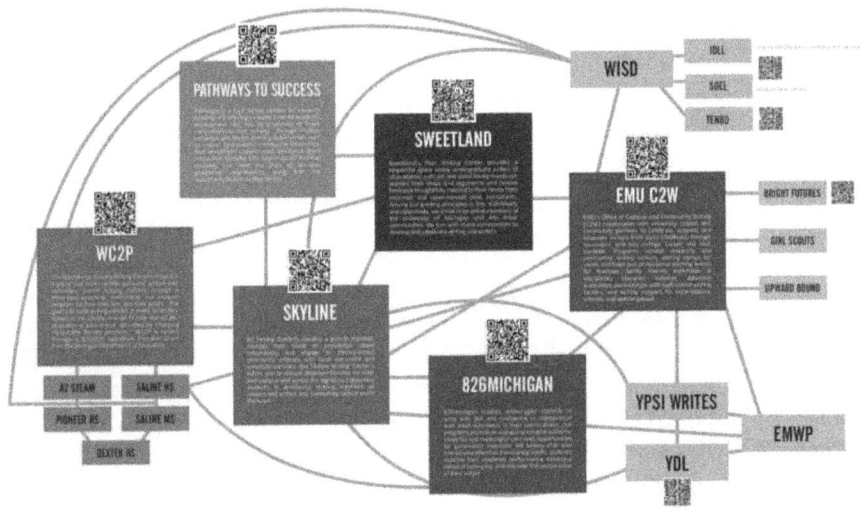

Figure 1: The Washtenaw County Literacy Network

Figure 1 shows the Washtenaw Community Literacy Network (WCLN) as it existed in fall 2019 and early 2020, prior to both COVID-19 and the police violence that killed Breonna Taylor and George Floyd. brown's emergent strategy characterizes networks as dynamic and adaptive, which certainly has been and continues to be the case for the WCLN, especially as the events of 2020 have unfolded. As noted already, being in a decentralized community network is messy and imperfect, but despite this, the WCLN continues to build relationships, be accountable, and strive to align its actions more to justice, acknowledging mistakes and then both working to repair those mistakes and working, within and with the network, to transform the root causes that may have allowed them to happen. This too is imperfect and requires trust, which needs to be built and rebuilt in each interaction. Additionally, the generative and evolving partnerships in the network have assisted with working within and through the inherent complexity, particularly throughout the twin pandemics.

The WCLN is a confluence of individuals, programs, and agencies that have eschewed institutional boundaries and embraced the power of collaboration to support literacy across a county. We would characterize it as an evolving grassroots network rooted in informal relationships and a do-it-ourselves ethos, and that, we recognize, requires a different strategy and approach than managing a hierarchical organization with clear central leadership. Instead, the WCLN relies on small, informal relationships and interactions between and among network members to achieve its ends. Indeed, the WCLN has been built small relationship by small relationship, often two or three people coming together to work on an initiative or project and slowly folding others into that project or expanding it to a different part of the network. The vignettes at the start of this essay demonstrate a variety of kairotic moments, as do the examples that follow of how nodes in the network have pivoted in response to COVID-19 and to the acts of police violence and institutionalized racism. While kairotic moments may happen by chance, being ready and able to seize them does not. Seizing kairotic moments leading to change requires remarkable presence and sustained, trusting relationships. brown's emergent strategy framework is one we found aligns with the WCLN's mission of transforming intent into organized impact to democratize literacy in communities.

brown's *Emergent Strategy*, published in 2017, is an outgrowth of her work as an organizer and facilitator in various activist organizations and networks that center the work of people of color, particularly queer and trans Black women, including Black Organizing for Leadership and Dignity, The Ruckus Society, and Allied Media Projects, among others. In the introduction to her book, brown notes that the notion of emergent strategy is one that she borrows from Nick Obolensky, the author of *Complex Adaptive Leadership: Embracing Paradox and Uncertainty*. *Emergent Strategy* is also heavily informed by the work in understanding organizational systems done by Margaret Wheatley and the speculative fiction of Octavia Butler; brown is the co-editor of *Octavia's Brood: Science Fiction Stories from Social Justice Movements*. brown's approach is also deeply influenced by the work and mentorship of the late longtime Detroit activist Grace Lee Boggs, to whom she dedicates the book. The humanistic vision brown lays out in the introduction is one that calls each of us to "align our behavior, our structures, and our movements with our visions of justice and liberation, and give those of us co-creating the future more options for working with each other and embodying the things we fight for: dignity, collective power, love, generative conflict, and community" (brown 6). Identifying herself as a "queer, Black, multiracial lover of life" (29), brown nevertheless calls her readers of a wide variety of identities into "collaborative ideation"—imagining a new future that offers freedom, justice, and joy for everyone. brown deliberately invites her readers into the work: "The more people that collaborate on that ideation, the more people will be liberated by the resulting world(s)" (7). In this spirit, the authors of this paper take up brown's invitation, to see how her ideas about emergent strategy allow us to theorize, enact, and assess a transformative literacy network.

brown describes emergent strategy as "relational, adaptive, fractal, interdependent, decentralized, and transformative" (56). Emergent strategy, according to brown, is centrally about building meaningful, sustainable relationships rooted in love and mutual understanding. brown emphasizes that emergent strategy is about being in healthy relationships with our work, our world, and our team to "grow our capacity to embody the just and liberated worlds we long for" (24). Emergent strategy is very much about a way of being and working in the world. It also is about the intention to embody in small interactions the larger aspirations of the institution, the group, or the network; it reminds us that attuning to others through interpersonal relationships allows nimble responses when conditions, such as COVID-19 and police violence, demand them (brown 71).

The WCLN

brown's analogies, such as fractals, provide helpful explanatory frameworks that begin to capture the complexity of a literacy network like the WCLN. According to brown, for example, "Fractals are infinitely complex patterns that are self-similar across different scales. They are created by repeating a simple process over and over in an ongoing feedback loop" (51). They also express relationships between small and large, which are depicted in Figure 1, above. The entities in the large boxes are those that functioned as initiators, anchors, and organizers as the network was being established. As such, these engaged in "binary partnerships," as described by Deans in his contribution to this volume (92). Such partnerships are often mutually beneficial, and, like Deans, we also see merit in their configuration into a network, whose resilience and adaptability exceeds that of any single partnership due to the distribution of responsibility. In the WCLN, the initiators and anchors include a university outreach office (Eastern Michigan University's Office of Campus & Community Writing); a literacy organization (826michigan, which is part of the national 826 initiative); a community writing center (YpsiWrites, which is a collaboration between EMU's C²W, 826michigan, and the Ypsilanti District Library); a university writing center (University of Michigan's Sweetland Center for Writing); a high school writing center (Ann Arbor Skyline High School); an alternative high school (Pathways, which collaborated with Sweetland and Skyline to support Pathways students); and a grant-funded project (the Washtenaw County Writing Center Project). All of these entities have functioned in the WCLN, even in the more recent times of crisis, as hubs for relationship-building and network expansion.

The mid-size boxes in the network rendering can be characterized best as collaborators—e.g., entities that work closely with the organizers and anchors. For example, the Ypsilanti District Library (YDL) had been, prior to COVID-19, sites for drop-in tutoring and workshops for YpsiWrites. Another collaborator, the Washtenaw Intermediate School District (WISD), an entity that encompasses all the school districts in the county, works with EMU's C²W as well as with Ann Arbor Skyline High School and the Washtenaw County Writing Centers Project. The WISD also has its own connections in the network: Inquiry into Disciplinary Literacy and Learning (IDLL), a secondary-level disciplinary literacies' group; Study of Early Literacy (SOEL), a group of elementary teachers interested in early literacy; and Ten80, a middle and secondary-level STEM initiative. EMU's C²W and YpsiWrites have connections with these programs as well. For example, YpsiWrites has provided writing workshops for the Ten80 initiative, and the C²W faculty associate helps organize and facilitate the IDLL group. The Eastern Michigan Writing Project (EMWP), a program within C²W and a site for the National Writing Project, provides teacher professional learning opportunities, student writing camps, and family literacy workshops.

The smallest boxes in Figure 1 include schools, groups, and community organizations that participate in programs offered by the other entities. YpsiWrites, for example, is partnering with a growing number of community organizations in Ypsilanti to provide literacy support for youth, teens, and adults. These include the Girl Scouts of Southeast Michigan, Washtenaw Literacy, Upward Bound, Bright Futures, Mentor2Youth, A2Ethics, and numerous other organizations.

Finally, also shown in the network rendering are schools participating in the Washtenaw County Writing Centers Project. Every one of these partnerships emerged from "a multiplicity of relatively simple interactions" (3) that brown says create complex systems and patterns. brown also emphasizes that these interactions are always intentional: "What we pay attention to grows" (brown 19). For example, it was through a request by the Ypsilanti District Library for coaching of its TEDx speakers that the seeds for YpsiWrites were originally sown. Interactions with 826michigan staff generated ideas for the *Dialogues* discussed in the opening vignettes for writing tutors across schools and contexts. A brief conversation after a meeting at a community center gave rise to two grant proposals for programs that would support at-risk youth in career and educational pursuits. Neither of these was funded due to the granting organizations reallocating their funding to relief projects connected to COVID; however, the conversations cultivated new partnerships, for example between EMU's C²W, the non-profit organization Mentor2Youth, and St. Joseph Mercy Hospital.

The lines connecting the entities in the WCLN network demonstrate their interdependence. No entity is or could be autonomous. brown talks about people coming together to accomplish more than they would accomplish individually, and the WCLN provides a living example of this. Over a short span of time, and even through crisis, it has expanded and gained momentum. YpsiWrites, for example, which is less than a year old, has multiple partners, more than sixty volunteers, and extensive community support. When the transition was made to offering virtual support during COVID, more than thirty volunteers offered to assist with the new initiatives. The Washtenaw County Writing Centers Project, in its second year, added four new middle and secondary schools interested in developing writing centers. A recent pivot to create the Washtenaw County Writing Center for Secondary Students (WCWC) further expands this initiative, responding to the reality that Washtenaw County, like most counties, has no monolithic literacy narrative. Ann Arbor Skyline's Writing Center, in collaboration with the University of Michigan Sweetland Center for Writing and EMU's C²W, continues to seek ways to normalize high expectations for all writers and to engage stakeholders in productive dialogues about equity and inclusion. All of these entities work with, for, and on behalf of each other in a distributed and decentralized, but interconnected manner. The network is thus also nonlinear and iterative, additional characteristics brown addresses. Each entity has its own mission and purpose, staff (volunteer and/or paid), and leadership, but each also values the network's shared vision for equity, transformative justice, and literacy.

brown's theory also stresses resilience, the creation of additional possibilities, and adaptability. Resilience, we believe, is achieved through the bonds and connections these entities form with each other; the lines in our network are solid and thick for a reason. But as in all relationships, this requires effort and intentionality, which in this case has been facilitated by each entity's willingness to engage in a truly reciprocal exchange. Adaptiveness and flexibility are at the heart of this reciprocity—as are, arguably, self-awareness and reflection. The network is continuously evolving, and this certainly has been the case since March 2020 when the world shifted in significant ways.

The Evolution of the WCLN in the Face of Change and Disruption

The significant shifts that occurred in March 2020, starting with COVID-19 and closely followed by the deaths of Breonna Taylor and George Floyd, threw the issues of equity that already marked our community literacy work into sharp relief. When the COVID-19 stay-at-home orders were issued in Michigan, for example, we watched many of our school partners struggle with helping their students through issues of food instability, equal access to technology and Internet connectivity, and family crises. We saw teacher partners shift to working at home, tasked with creating both digital and non-digital instruction for the variety of students they teach, all the while having to share computers, workspaces, and Internet access with other members of their families. We saw our libraries and community writing spaces close down for unforeseen lengths of time (they remain closed as of this writing). We, along with other members of our network, faced our own individual struggles. We saw our brave students organizing for social justice and marching in the streets even while COVID-19 cases were rising; their protests and efforts are ongoing today. In this environment, we knew that we could still be of use, even if, at first, we were immobilized by our own shock at the swift changes in circumstance. As we acclimated (as best we could), we wondered: How could we sustain a community literacy network—and still a new one at that—predicated on face-to-face interactions among our community partners, when the whole notion of community, and everyone's experiences as members of communities, were undergoing such radical change and disruption?

As we considered what to do—as individuals, educators, and participants in established partnerships in the network—we kept in mind adrienne maree brown's principle of *adaptation*. "Intentional adaptation," brown writes, "is at the heart of emergent strategy" (69). Such adaptation can be seen in the responses we made, both to COVID-19 and to the demonstrations and social movements that followed the murder of George Floyd in May 2020. These adaptations also demonstrate another hallmark of emergent strategy mentioned previously: *resilience*. Resilience, brown notes, is the capacity of a system to constantly "evolve while maintaining core practices" (9). In the case of the Washtenaw County Literacy Network, these core practices have included sustaining relationships and supporting teachers, writers, and their families. brown cites her mentor, Detroit activist Grace Lee Boggs' belief that times of crisis provide opportunities for those who are attentive and adaptable (44, 72). The ability to shift the activity of the network in response to crises while still maintaining the purpose and mission of the network is reflected in these words of scientist Margaret Wheatley: "Vision is an invisible field that binds us together, emerging from relationships and chaos and information" (qtd. in brown 27).

While we cannot report anything conclusive since we are composing this article while still in the midst of the disruption caused by these events, we can share some of the pivots that were made in response to changing conditions. We define pivots in this context as "collective real-time adaptations"—akin to brown's metaphors of flocks of starlings, schools of fish, and swarms of bees (71)—to address questions and needs. Whether the pivots we share become longer-term adaptations within the network remains to be seen, although we suspect that some, if not all of them will.

The pivots also illustrate the significance for the WCLN of the small, informal relationships and interactions between and among network members, with two or three people coming together to work on a project and slowly folding others into that project or expanding it to a different part of the network. When schools closed in response to the COVID stay-at-home orders, for example, two network members—826michigan and the Washtenaw Intermediate School District—were asked to help school districts by creating materials to support teachers and students. Seizing the opportunity for innovation, the two groups shared resources and ideas, considering each group's strengths as well as underlying values about writing and literacy. This kairotic moment led to these groups, along with EMU's Office of Campus & Community Writing, developing a survey for teachers, inviting them to tell us what we could best do to support them and their students during this time. The groups then worked together to create two outreach projects focused on providing timely literacy support: a series of videos for families, helping them understand ways to support writing at home, and mini virtual EdCamps, helping teachers connect with thought partners about specific issues of teaching writing online. By making these connections, the network adapted, expanded, and created new possibilities (brown 129).

Another pivot during COVID almost perfectly illustrates how a change in one part of the network can stimulate other parts of the network, much as when a flock of birds shifts direction in response to one bird's action (Pickett qtd. in brown 67). Mentor2Youth, whose outreach and programs that depended on in-person interactions had been halted by stay-at-home orders, saw the virtual adaptation of a proposed initiative as an opportunity to reboot its programming. In this case, the needs of one partner in the network sparked responses and new collaborations among other partners, thus strengthening ties and expanding the network. Additionally, responding to community needs and making adaptations requires trust; trusting relationships are durable and can survive changing and challenging conditions. Therefore, trust is critical to building the meaningful relationships required to sustain the network and achieve its vision, even, and perhaps especially, during times of disruption and crisis. For brown, being in trusting relationships requires group members to reduce their egos and reimagine where and how decisions are made. Indeed, emergent strategy reminds us that the funds of knowledge (Moll et al.) of every group member, another framework we have found helpful, are vital to the strength and growth of the network: Every individual, program, and agency provides something different and something vital to our efforts to democratize literacy.

Another example of such action during COVID occurred when the library that housed YpsiWrites closed and social distancing prohibited in-person tutoring. The YpsiWrites coordinators and volunteers quickly shifted to virtual tutoring so that teens and adults could continue to obtain writing support, either by submitting their writing for online feedback or by requesting a real-time consultation with a tutor (see www.ypsiwrites.com). Writers were also offered support through a collection of writing prompts, from journaling to make sense of this time to writing about nature; a list of curated writing resources; and activities, including a zine challenge, to supplant the scheduled workshops that had to be cancelled.

Adaptations like these illustrate the importance of sustained trusting relationships and the ways in which crisis can create opportunity. YpsiWrites volunteers rose to the occasion, responding in ways that reflected their own areas of expertise and comfort. Some became virtual consultants, others created writing prompts and materials, and some tested and provided feedback on activities. Although the loss of physical space and possibilities for in-person programming could have resulted in a complete shutdown of YpsiWrites, or certainly a significant loss of momentum, it instead created an opportunity to engage in creative problem solving and to innovate new ways to achieve organizational goals.

Creative problem solving also took place in the pivot that occurred with the Washtenaw County Writing Centers Project, which was grant funded. Leading up to March 2020, this project was helping four middle and secondary schools start new writing centers while also supporting five schools that had participated in the previous year's cohort. The stay-at-home order led to major events being canceled, including a workshop at the University of Michigan's Sweetland Center for Writing, which left fledgling programs without mentorship and support. As resilient and adaptable as other parts of the WCLN have been, these new writing centers became reminders of precarity. More established ones were able to carry on, but some of the newer, less rooted ones were put on hold, leaving students without an important resource at a time of need. These shifts also led to a reconfiguring of grant money and priorities. While this sounds dire, brown reminds us that, no matter what happens, "there is an opportunity to move with intention—toward growth, relationship, regeneration" (71).

The receding of one possibility sparked new adaptations in the network. In this case, thinking was furthered around a youth-driven, county-wide writing center. The idea of the Washtenaw County Writing Center for Secondary Students (WCWC) emerged with a mission of amplifying student voices; providing identity-affirming, justice-seeking, and equity-driven literacy support and events; and encouraging, mentoring, and supporting youth leaders and activists working for change. This vision was of an inclusive, youth-led space. brown argues that any structure that has those with marginalized identities performing actions without any role in leading or planning is a warning that our community-based work isn't as strong as we think (brown 65), and now, more than ever, a strong, youth-driven space centered on the needs, interests, and voices of youth is critical.

Throughout *Emergent Strategy*, brown references the science fiction writing of Octavia Butler regarding adaptation and reimagination, which, along with trust, which we addressed above, are critical factors for success and connection in emergent networks. While the work of the WCLN might not be the stuff of science fiction, the fractal relationships and grassroots organizing—and re-organizing—are helping achieve the network's vision of reimagining literacy across our county and certainly have aided in sustaining this vision during a time of significant disruption (brown 19). What remains stable and constant are the overarching vision of and hope for equity and transformative justice. This vision of literacy in Washtenaw County is more collective and compelling than the injustice of the present. brown presciently contends, "I suspect this is what many of you are up to, practicing futures together, practicing justice together, living into new stories. It is our right and responsibility to create a new world" (19).

Assessment

All of these ideas and possibilities surrounding emergent strategy lead us toward new thinking about how we assess the health of a network like the WCLN. While we certainly could focus on numbers—the number of partners, of individual programs, of students who attend a program, of volunteers who participate at particular sites—those numbers alone cannot adequately capture the story of the network and its goals, nor its strengths and its needs. In fact, a focus on numbers might lead us to false understandings of success: i.e., if we attract ten people to a program, is that successful? Does that number really help us understand the impact of the program on those attending? What else should we consider? As we think critically and deeply about this work, we wonder what other means of assessment might capture the essence of an emergent and evolving network in all its complexity.

One way into rethinking assessment practices emerges from our focus on one of brown's mantras: "What you pay attention to grows." What are we paying attention to? And what aren't we paying attention to? For us, this implies a shift in understanding: from a focus on using assessment as a way of proving something to using assessment as a way of paying attention to something. That shift in language seems vital for an emergent network with its integrated component parts. Indeed, our use of brown's framework invites us to pay attention to the network in new ways previously unavailable to us. We might, for example, pay attention to the ways in which the network sustains itself, thinking about the existing relationships. However, we might also pay attention to ways in which we develop and extend the network—to grow relationships with new people and programs. An ultimate goal might be to create, even to grow, change around literacy in the geographical area of the network, as we are seeking to do now with the WCWC. When we pay attention, we begin to see the integral components, which in turn help us see that the sustenance of an emergent network relies on strength and redundancy, with redundancy referring to multiple fail-safe measures: the bonds between nodes in the network must remain strong, and, when one connection fails or one node disappears, another connection or node must be formed or reinforced to sustain the activity of the system.

What might this "paying attention" approach to assessment look like in practice? A network might take a pause quarterly or even once a year to encourage its members to reflect and then come together in a retreat or other relaxed setting to talk about their individual insights and develop a shared understanding of the health of the network as a whole and its capacity for growth and change—considering the "next most elegant step" forward together (brown 220). Or different parts of the network might offer, as YpsiWrites has done, Town Hall meetings where volunteers come together to share their thoughts and ideas for moving forward. The health of our network might also be assessed by paying attention to how it represents the racial, cultural, and linguistic diversity of the communities it serves. brown argues that networks are healthiest when members of "impacted communities" have the opportunity to lead (63). The Skyline Writing Center, for example, actively recruits, admits, and trains a diverse, inclusive tutoring staff in an effort to center students of color, multilingual students, LGBTQ+ students, students experiencing material poverty, neurodivergent students, and students at the intersections of several of these identities in formal and informal leadership positions within the network. This will also be a priority as the Washtenaw County Writing Center for Secondary Students is formed and as students are recruited to serve as tutors, leaders, and board members.

In each of these approaches to assessment, we might consider some of brown's key areas that are particularly relevant to a community literacy network: assessment of fractals, adaptation, interdependence and decentralization, and assessment for creating more possibility. What an assessment model that addresses all of these areas looks like depends very much upon the kinds of questions being asked. And the answers to these questions give us so much more information than just numbers. As we ask these questions, and more, we can hopefully expand the story of how the WCLN is beginning to respond to literacy inequities in the local community, based on observations and on the reflections of participants. Along the same lines, stories of leadership within the network—such as those of high school peer tutors taking leadership roles in planning or presenting programming and in advocacy and social justice initiatives—help to demonstrate the strength of the network in deepening the number of relationships in the network and thereby increasing its resilience.

Conclusion

Throughout *Emergent Strategy*, brown reminds organizers that a vision for equity, inclusion, and democracy needs to be present before a network can truly effect change in a community. brown suggests that building fundamentally sound relationships rooted in mutual trust rather than performative "spectacle" is an important starting point (61). Our Washtenaw County Literacy Network is committed to building such relationships, and, in so doing, ensuring long-term sustainability even as the network undergoes constant and sometimes significant change, as COVID-19 and the acts of police violence have led to. Our efforts in this and our shared vision create stability in emergence, and even in uncertainty. brown also argues that reducing perceived hierarchy between organizational leadership and community partners is critical for an inclusive network to have long-term success. Thus, we are also working to ensure that those in the communities served by the network have engagement, ownership, and leadership in it. Equity work is never done, and we acknowledge that we still have much to learn and do to ensure that the WCLN fulfills its collective vision for democratizing literacy.

Finally, many of the feelings, thoughts, hopes, and fears that all of us have experienced during the pandemic and recent social protests responding to the police violence will likely inform the Washtenaw County Literacy Network in ways that are yet unknown. However, with emergent strategy, we hope to be able to continue pivoting to the "most elegant next step" (brown 220). Emergent strategy allows us to navigate change across individuals, institutions, and communities thoughtfully and sustainably; it allows us to organize for the long haul, not just the short sprint, by helping us to be in the "right relationships" with ourselves, our work, and one another.

We conclude these reflections with a quote from Sonia Renee Taylor, a poet, author, activist, and leader—someone who might be a kindred spirit to adrienne marie brown, whose ideas have been so helpful to us in describing and advancing the mission of the WCLN in these times. Taylor says:

> We will not go back to normal. Normal never was. Our pre-corona existence was not normal other than we normalized greed, inequity, exhaustion, depletion, extraction, disconnection, confusion, rage, hoarding, hate and lack. We should not long to return, my friends. We are being given an opportunity to stitch a new garment. One that fits all of humanity and nature. (@soniareneetaylor)

The evolution of the WCLN during the uncertain times of the COVID-19 pandemic and of the social unrest responding to present and historic anti-Black police violence provided opportunities to develop new approaches in our network, resulting in what, we suspect, will be a permanently altered and new network "garment," committed as ever to the goal of increasing literacy equity and social justice in schools and our communities.

Works Cited

brown, adrienne maree. *Emergent Strategy*. Chico, CA, AK Press, 2017.

Deans, Thomas. "A Network Approach to Writing Center Outreach." *Community Literacy Journal*, vol. 15, no. 1, 2020, pp. 92–96.

Duke, Nell K. and Ernest Morrell. "The Knee on the Neck of Children and Youth of Color in Schools," https://drive.google.com/file/d/10LbJwQ6A3Bqm8w5u-Js85qHrGb0CEAqUn/view. Accessed 14 October 2020.

Moll, Luis C., et al. "Funds of Knowledge for Teaching: Using a Qualitative Approach to Connect Homes and Classrooms." *Funds of Knowledge: Theorizing Practices in Households, Communities, and Classrooms*, edited by Norma González, Luis C. Moll, and Cathy Amanti, Abingdon, UK, Hillsdale, NJ, Lawrence Erlbaum, 2005, pp. 71-88.

@soniareneetaylor. "We will not go back to normal. Normal never was. Our pre-corona existence was never normal other than we normalized greed, inequity, exhaustion, depletion, extraction, disconnection, confusion, rage, hoarding, hate and lack. We should not long to return, my friends. We are being given the opportunity to stitch a new garment. One that fits all of humanity and nature." *Instagram*, 2 Apr. 2020, https://www.instagram.com/p/B-fc3ejAlvd/?hl=en.

Smith, Christen A. "Cite Black Women: A Critical Praxis." *Cite Black Women Collective*, 2018, https://www.citeblackwomencollective.org/our-praxis.html. Accessed 14 October 2020.

Author Bios:

Jeffrey Austin is the instructional coach, English Department Chair, and Writing Center Director at Skyline High School in Ann Arbor, Michigan. He was named one of the first members of the State of Michigan's Innovative Educator Corps in 2018 and helped expand secondary school writing centers in his community. His writing and advocacy focus on building humanized, student-centered spaces through culturally responsive curriculum and pedagogy, fair and equitable grading and assessment practices, and restorative justice.

Ann Blakeslee is a professor of written communication and director of the Office of Campus & Community Writing at Eastern Michigan University. She coordinates on-campus and community writing initiatives. She is the in-coming chair of the Association for Writing Across the Curriculum and serves on the executive committee for the Association of Teachers of Technical Writing. Her scholarship focuses on writing and learning to write in the disciplines, audience, qualitative research methods, writing in the workplace, writing pedagogy and transfer, and community literacy.

Cathy Fleischer is a professor of English education at Eastern Michigan University where she co-directs the Eastern Michigan Writing Project and serves as Faculty Associate for the Office of Campus & Community Writing. She publishes widely, leads professional learning experiences for teachers, and is committed to helping teachers raise their voices to change the public narrative about schooling.

Formerly the faculty director of the Peer Writing Consultant Program at the Sweetland Center for Writing at the University of Michigan, Christine Modey currently directs the Michigan Community Scholars Program, a residential learning community focused on social justice, community service, and intergroup dialogue. She has published articles about university-secondary school writing center partnerships, data visualization and corpus analysis of writing center session notes, and nineteenth-century literature, and has an abiding interest in networks, collaboration, and community building. She is the co-editor with David Schoem and Edward St. John of *Teaching the Whole Student: Engaged Learning with Heart, Mind, and Spirit*.

Write Here, Right Now: Shifting a Community Writing Center from a Place to a Practice

Christopher LeCluyse, Nkenna Onwuzuruoha, and Brandon Wilde

Abstract

In 2013, Westminster College in Salt Lake City, Utah, established Write Here: A Community Writing Center in collaboration with Promise South Salt Lake. In 2016 Write Here's operations shifted from a community center to the various spaces of Promise South Salt Lake after-school programs. The COVID-19 pandemic has further complicated this transition with the move to online workshops. The decentering of Write Here exposes the dynamics of place and practice inherent in both community literacy and writing centers. Occupying third space, Write Here consultants navigate changing locations, mentoring, and non-tutoring activities, challenging traditional writing center narratives. Accommodating community partners likewise requires dwelling in a rhetoric of respect. By remaining flexible and recognizing limitations, Write Here has opened channels of communication to reach shared understandings. This analysis models how other community literacy organizations can enter into more effective and meaningful partnerships and adapt to ongoing shifts of place and practice.

Keywords

community literacy, writing center, university-community partnerships, after-school program, space, place

In 2013, Westminster College in Salt Lake City, Utah, established Write Here: A Community Writing Center in collaboration with Promise South Salt Lake. This partnership among the South Salt Lake City Mayor's Office, the United Way, and other community partners supports fourteen after-school programs and community centers for K-12 students and their families, many of them immigrants and refugees. While Promise South Salt Lake's founding director was inspired by the example of 826 Valencia in San Francisco, we took more local inspiration from the Salt Lake Community College Community Writing Center (CWC), which has become a model for community writing centers nationwide since its establishment over fifteen years ago. Write Here was first established at the Historic Scott School Community Center, a complex of connected structures that includes a nineteenth-century school building. Since its inception, Write Here has offered individual and small-group writing consultations as well as writing workshops for community partners. Its original location limited access to services, however. Taking a cue from the University of Denver Writing Center, Write Here founder and director Chris LeCluyse decided to go where the writers were (Micke et al.). In 2016, Write Here left the Scott School in favor of placing consultants in Promise South Salt Lake after-school programs.

Write Here currently places a mixture of paid and volunteer writing consultants, all college students from Westminster and the University of Utah, in after-school programs at Cottonwood High School and Roosevelt Elementary School. A center liaison (Brandon Wilde) regularly contacts consultants and arranges occasional meetings while providing consultations himself. Meanwhile, an outreach coordinator (Nkenna Onwuzuruoha, hereafter Kenna) offers writing workshops for community partners, such as a senior center, a community mental health clinic, and a national girls' organization. Shifting from a place to a practice greatly expanded and diversified the range of writers we serve, as well as increased access to our services for K-12 students. Hard on these successes, however, the COVID-19 pandemic has further complicated this spatial transition. Since March 2020, Brandon and Kenna have offered online writing consultations and workshops to a significantly reduced number of writers. In this article, we consider what happens when a community writing center grows from being a place unto itself to a practice conducted in others' spaces and, most recently, an online practice in virtual space.

The decentering of Write Here has exposed the dynamics of place and practice inherent in both community literacy and writing center praxis. Nedra Reynolds promotes the use of geography and geographical metaphors to understand "writing as a set of practices more spatial than temporal" (3). These practices are "enacted not in stable, always-the-same places but within shifting senses of space, in the betweens, in thirdspace" (4). Parallel to Reynolds's focus on writing as a spatial practice is Julie Drew's consideration of the "politics of place" in writing instruction (57). As Drew explains, "Students pass through, and only pause briefly within, classrooms; they dwell within and visit various other locations . . ." (60). In Write Here's situation, consultants have joined the students they work with as travelers across various spaces.

While Reynolds and Drew present place and practice as commensurate, the two concepts have been in historical tension in writing center studies. Writing centers have two possible points of origin: as cocurricular spaces begun with the "writing laboratories" of the 1920s or as a practice developed in the "conference method of late nineteenth-century classrooms" (Boquet 455-456). How this history is told has ramifications for whether writing centers are seen as existing outside the hierarchy and control of traditional classrooms or as a means of controlling literacy (Boquet 466-467). Subscribing to the former perspective, several writing scholars have extended the concept of third space to writing center work. Nanci Effinger Wilson and Keri Fitzgerald frame the writing center as "a metacognitive, flexible third space—a part of the university but also apart from it" (11) while Cameron Mozafari advocates for "creating a 'third space' within the tutoring session" as a form of cultural mediation for multilingual writers (450).

Moving from place to practice, Write Here has occupied a range of third spaces in every sense of the term. As our analysis will show, these border-crossings have challenged the norms of writing center praxis as well as personal and professional boundaries. The ways in which community members perceive and interact with Write

Here practitioners in writing workshops also reveal that our practice has not fully abandoned the confines and expectations of classroom instruction. Moreover, the recent shift to online services in response to the COVID-19 pandemic has further revealed how systemic inequities and the digital divide can further complicate community literacy practices. As a result of these shifts, a change that we originally conceived as a one-time event has become an ongoing process.

Changes in Individual Tutoring

Write Here maintains its identity not by where it operates but by what it does and who does it. Operating in the spaces of various Promise South Salt Lake after-school programs provides Write Here with its primary purpose and identity. This community partnership also complicates Write Here's work, however, due to the schools' lack of dedicated space for after-school programs, which inhabit additional third spaces, such as libraries, cafeterias, outdoor portable classrooms, and gyms. As Write Here occupies changing places, its practice becomes much more dynamic. Personal space becomes more permeable, strengthening rapport between consultants and students but also blurring professional boundaries.

Under pre-pandemic circumstances, Write Here consultants visited schools at least once per week to conduct individual and small-group consultations. Many of the students attending Promise South Salt Lake programs are multilingual immigrants or children of immigrants, refugees, and at-risk youth. This context, however, challenges established understandings of what a writing consultant is—indeed pushing consultants' work beyond the narrow confines of writing, frequently to worksheets on anything from "Verb Forms of *Be*" to "Math Inequalities." Moreover, students may need the consultant to explain basic concepts and model solutions rather than engage in the nondirective methods traditionally espoused in writing center lore (see, for example, Thompson et al. 81-84). The focused conversation at the heart of writing center pedagogy can also be difficult to maintain amid distractions—other students, technologies, and food among them.

Further complicating Write Here relationships, students may want to approach consultants more as peers than as authority figures. While consultants maintain that they primarily help by tutoring, they often engage in vulnerable discourse with students and can easily be seen as "friends" rather than "friendly." What's more, students may negotiate with consultants to engage in a non-academic activity—for example, soccer or painting or sharing their weekend stories—which can make consultants feel as if they are being unprofessional and not doing "their job." And while Promise South Salt Lake after-school programs are supervised by staff members called prevention specialists, Write Here consultants are often asked to enforce behavioral rules and/or supervise other students when a prevention specialist cannot respond. Hannah Ashley traces similar conflations and uncertainties among college students working with high school students as writing mentors, "not teachers, not other students, but something else not quite fitting into the regular frames of the institution" (180). It is difficult to train consultants on the invisible geography of relationships with students just as much as on the unpredictability of the changing spaces they must occupy.

As a writing center operating in these varying and challenging third spaces, Write Here joins Jackie Grutsch McKinney in pushing against and pulling at what she calls the writing center grand narrative, that "writing centers are comfortable, iconoclastic places where all students go to get one-to-one tutoring on their writing" (3). As she observes, however, "[t]he effect of the writing center grand narrative can be a sort of collective tunnel vision. The story has focused our attention so narrowly that we already no longer see the range and variety of activities that make up writing center work or the potential ways in which writing center work could evolve" (McKinney 5-6). In the community spaces that Write Here inhabits, non-tutoring work—navigating changing places, mentoring, participating in non-academic activities—is paramount to the success of building sustainable relationships between consultants and writers, thereby challenging the traditional writing center narrative.

Write Here has especially seen how relationships need to be at the center of its practice when adapting to the changes brought by a pandemic. As schools in South Salt Lake halted in-class instruction mid-March 2020, their respective after-school programs followed. This challenged consultants to continue their work on digital platforms, which expose how rapport built with students beforehand is a prerequisite to effective and rewarding consultations. The few students at one after-school program that were able to attend live-video consultations were not the same students that Write Here consultants had built solid relationships with months before. In contrast, relationships Brandon nurtured with a ten-member refugee family over several pre-pandemic months yielded consistent and effective consultations through the end of the school year in spite of the technological hurdles. Even as COVID-19 disrupted in-person opportunities, a history of flexibility and social courage in third spaces has given Write Here the upper hand in continuing its practice amid a global health crisis.

Changes in Workshops with Other Community Partners

Write Here has similarly challenged writing center norms by offering literacy and skills-based workshops to marginalized populations in South Salt Lake. While community writing centers often provide workshops at their sites, Write Here staff ultimately decided to meet in spaces and at times that were the most convenient for participants. One such partnership was with a substance abuse treatment center in South Salt Lake. High turnover in staffing at the center created obstacles in maintaining a fruitful partnership, however. While the staff expressed that writing workshops would greatly assist clients in the writing-intensive assignments required to complete their treatment, they, like many social workers across the U.S., could not take much time out of their busy schedules to coordinate logistics: when workshops would take place, which rooms and technology would be available, and who would provide supplies and handouts to participants. Despite these communication gaps, Write Here continued to build relationships with the newly hired social workers, though accommodating the ever-changing staff meant accepting that programming could go dormant at any time.

Write Here was committed to hearing the needs of the clients at the treatment center whether articulated by the staff or by the clients themselves. It did not want to base its partnership on what Steve Parks disparagingly identifies as "a conception of hegemonic change that works by gaining the consent of those in local agencies to expand or broaden the service opportunities offered" (36). However, the nature of building partnerships—meeting with staff speaking on behalf of clients before meeting with the clients—meant that Write Here had to make assumptions based on its contacts' characterizations of clients' writing. Thus, the facilitators, Chris and Kenna, created workshops situated in generalizations about their participants' literacy levels and writing context. Later, the two would revise the workshops based on participant response, aligned more with Parks' model of partnership-building.

While some Write Here programming has been feasible during the COVID-19 pandemic, the center's experiences with two community partners—a national girls' empowerment organization and a substance abuse treatment center—reveal how access to technology and institutional norms can help or hinder online programming. For example, since writing workshops with the girls' organization occurred during the school year, the participants had access to computers. While gaps in digital literacy posed challenges, the girls had plenty of time and support to grapple with interfacing online through required virtual classrooms. The girls, though sometimes high-energy, were quick to correct their behavior during in-person workshops, and comportment issues were non-existent online. Participants in the outpatient treatment program, however, lacked such access to technology: many have experienced homelessness and do not have the luxury of a home computer and Internet connection. While all the participants at the treatment center are adults, the staff normalized rules for disciplining clients and maintaining decorum that cannot necessarily be enforced using video conferencing tools. Moreover, as the treatment center reconfigured programming, it could not prioritize "nonessential" services, a marker we understood would be rightfully placed on our workshops.

This reliance on channeling our programming through community partners' programs contrasts with the relative continuity the SLCC Community Writing Center (CWC) has experienced during the pandemic. Since the CWC has traditionally offered both stand-alone workshops in its own space at the Salt Lake City Main Library as well as programming for community partners, they have been able to shift online with the expectation that their established base of writers will come to them. Operating on a much more modest scale with more limited resources, Write Here does not have the infrastructure to draw writers to us and therefore must go to them. Here perhaps is the primary benefit of operating in a fixed space.

As Write Here's programming with almost all of its community partners has gone dormant, it has treated the pandemic as an invitation to envision what programming will look like in an ever-changing environment. While Kenna and Brandon have been quick enough on their feet to hold onto partnerships with the girls' empowerment group and after-school programs, reforming the relationship with the substance abuse center means starting anew when the time is right. Resuming the partnership will involve reaching out to new contacts, finding new ways to skirt foreseeable red tape, and figuring out how to tailor workshop presentation and content to meet the organization's expectations and its clients' needs as well as access to technology.

Dwelling in a Rhetoric of Respect

The factors complicating Write Here's writing tutoring in after-school programs as well as its writing workshops in the spaces of community partners underscore how community literacy work can challenge assumptions regarding what successful or sustainable partnerships look like. As Laurie Cella and her colleagues reflect on the themes they had previously raised in their collection *Unsustainable: Reimagining Community Literacy, Public Writing, Service-Learning and the University,* community "partnerships have the capacity to shift and change as we do, swerving with us through our evolving needs, interests, and resources. What we are guaranteed then is a story that is neither clean nor linear and that, to the extent it fosters true creativity and innovation, equally guarantees deep loss" (42). Central to negotiating the shift of Write Here from operating within its own space has been a reexamination of what we consider to be the work of a writing center. Comparing the issues raised by our individual tutoring on one hand and our writing workshops on the other, we are struck by two competing impulses. While placing consultants in after-school programs has at times led to frustration with work that falls outside the norms and practices of university writing centers, functioning effectively in the workshop spaces of community partners has led us to want to divest ourselves of that university baggage so that we may in Eli Goldblatt's terms "challenge the political limits inherent in literacy and language use" (Cella et al. 44).

In both cases, we find in community literacy scholarship a way of navigating these difficulties by focusing on relationships, both interpersonal and organizational. Crucial to this endeavor is Reynolds's notion of "dwelling":

> The concept of dwelling, then, is a third spatial practice I want to claim for geographies of writing: spatial practices related to dwelling have much in common with spatial practices related to textual production; texts, like dwellings, need to be planned, built, and then occupied, filled with meaning, significance, or history. They need to be arranged, and those arrangements are often enacted through memory. . . . Constructed as neither public nor private but somewhere in thirdspace, dwelling is a set of practices as well as a sense of place. (140)

The success of Write Here consultants is dependent on how they dwell and contour their practice to the syncopated rhythm of the places they engage with. Write Here praxis changes with its shifting context; the key is to find a threshold across which we can foster connections with community members free from the cognitive dissonance that we either are not "academic enough" or that we are in fact *too* closely associated with an academic institution. By dwelling and building rapport with writers and community partners, Write Here practitioners can allow room for surprise and develop transformative and meaningful relationships with writers.

Once established, these relationships can facilitate later interactions. This takes time, however. A first solution for Write Here consultants is building a culture of reliability and consistency. For consultants, this means working in their after-school programs week after week, moving among whatever third spaces are assigned to them, and being present for students in whatever professional capacity their needs require. In the case of working with community partners like Promise South Salt Lake or the substance abuse treatment center, this means opening and reopening channels of communication even as busyness and staff turnover may disrupt them. For example, we approached Promise South Salt Lake to jointly organize a training for both Write Here consultants and Promise prevention specialists on setting and respecting personal boundaries with students. This culture of reliability and consistency can reinvent the stability of a physical writing center while allowing for the diversity of praxis demanded in community literacy work.

At the same time, key to improving such communication is what Tiffany Rousculp terms a "rhetoric of respect" that frames the contributions of all participants from a strengths perspective. As Rousculp explains,

> Respect implies a . . . type of relationship . . . grounded in perception of worth, in esteem for another—as well as for the self. Even so, respect does not require agreement or conciliation—as "tolerance" suggests; rather, it entails recognition of multiple views, approaches, abilities, and, importantly, limitations (especially our own). In other words, respect needs flexibility and self-awareness. (24-25)

Rousculp's formulation of respect resonates with the work of many other community literacy practitioners, such as Paula Mathieu, who asserts, "Rather than sustainability, I think a key term in community writing should be relationships" (Cella et al. 44). By remaining flexible and recognizing both our limitations and those of our community partners, Write Here can continue its efforts to take discursive action by opening channels of communication and by reaching shared understandings of our mutual responsibilities, such as through joint trainings of Write Here and Promise South Salt Lake staff. In doing so, our fledgling community literacy organization can take a page from its larger and more established neighbor, the CWC, which Rousculp founded. Like the CWC, Write Here can "avoid falling into the stance that the [center], as an agent of higher education, 'knew better' than a partner" by "entering into relationships with 'blank' intentions, pushing our own ideas into the background unless circumstances might call them forth" and by "embrac[ing] the chaos and confusion of listening rather than taking comfort in directing the conversation" (Rousculp 27).

Engaging in this relationship-focused work with writers and community partners is a trade-off that requires an ongoing shift in perspective. As the previous analysis shows, effective community literacy work requires adjusting expectations and considerable trial and error. Like Mathieu, we have had to trade an absolute notion of success or performance in these partnerships for something more fluid, "as an action, not a thing—an act of questioning: What are we seeking to sustain? Why and how?" (qtd. in Cella et al. 46). In the case of Write Here, we have answered those questions by realizing that we seek to sustain these relationships to cultivate literacy in its broadest sense, even if this work requires us to leave our academic comfort zones. We hope that by learning from our experience, other community literacy organizations can enter into more effective and meaningful partnerships and weather the ongoing process of adapting to shifts of place and practice.

Works Cited

Ashley, Hanna. "The Idea of a Literacy Doula." *Unsustainable: Re-Imagining Community Literacy, Public Writing, Service-Learning and the University*, edited by Jessica Restaino and Laurie JC Cella, Lexington Books, 2012, pp. 160-175.

Boquet, Elizabeth. "'Our Little Secret': A History of Writing Centers, Pre- to Post-Open Admissions." *College Composition and Communication*, vol. 50, no. 3, 1999, pp. 463-482.

Cella, Laurie, et al. "The Powerful Potential of Relationships and Community Writing." *Community Literacy Journal*, vol. 11, no. 1, 2016, pp. 41-53, https://muse.jhu.edu/article/646981. Accessed 6 January 2020.

Drew, Julie. "The Politics of Place: Student Travelers and Pedagogical Maps." *Ecocomposition: Theoretical and Pedagogical Approaches*, edited by Christian R. Weisser and Sidney I. Dobrin, State U of New York P, 2001, pp. 57-68.

McKinney, Jackie Grutsch. *Peripheral Visions for Writing Centers*. Utah State UP, 2013.

Micke, Sarah Hart, et al. "On Community Literacy, Collaboration, and Change: A Conversation at a Community Writing Center." International Writing Centers Association Conference, 14 October 2016, Denver, CO. Special Interest Group.

Mozafari, Cameron. "Creating Third Space: ESL Tutoring as Cultural Mediation." *The Oxford Guide for Writing Tutors*, edited by Lauren Fitzgerald and Melissa Ianetta, Oxford UP, 2016, pp. 449-463.

Parks, Stephen. *Gravyland: Writing Beyond the Curriculum in the City of Brotherly Love*. Syracuse UP, 2010.

Reynolds, Nedra. *Geographies of Writing: Inhabiting Places and Encountering Difference*. Southern Illinois UP, 2004.

Rousculp, Tiffany. *A Rhetoric of Respect: Recognizing Change at a Community Writing Center*. National Council of Teachers of English, 2014.

Thompson, Isabelle, et al. "Examining Our Lore: A Survey of Students' and Tutors' Satisfaction with Writing Center Conferences." *The Writing Center Journal*, vol. 29, no. 1, 2009, pp. 78-105.

Wilson, Nancy Effinger and Keri Fitzgerald. "Empathic Tutoring in the Third Space." *The Writing Lab Newsletter*, vol. 37, nos. 3-4, 2012, pp. 11-13.

Author Bios

Christopher LeCluyse is the founder and director of Write Here and directs the Westminster College Writing Center in Salt Lake City, where he is also a professor of English and associate provost for curriculum and assessment. He served as president of the Rocky Mountain Writing Centers Association and co-chaired the 2015 National Conference on Peer Tutoring in Writing and the 2017 International Writing Center Association Summer Institute. His scholarship focuses on language, identity, and performance and draws on both his background as a medievalist and his recent engagement in game studies.

Nkenna Onwuzuruoha is Write Here's outreach coordinator. She previously served as an AmeriCorps VISTA at the Salt Lake Community College Community Writing Center. Nkenna also has facilitated workshops for Woke Words, YWCA Utah's multi-genre creative writing and reading series for young women of color, since its founding in 2019. She is currently a Ph.D. student in Writing and Rhetoric Studies and a member of the African American Doctoral Scholars Initiative at the University of Utah. Her research interests include first-year composition, community literacy practices, revisionist historiography, and activist methodologies.

Brandon Wilde was the center liaison for Write Here after working as a Write Here writing consultant. He is currently a medical student at the University of Utah School of Medicine. Within the medical school, he co-leads the RealMD program—a professional development initiative at UUSOM that connects students with their higher purpose in medicine through contemplative writing workshops and guest speakers.

Whose House? A Dual Profile of Two Spaces for Writers in Camden, New Jersey

Catherine Buck and Leah Falk

Abstract

The leaders of two Writers Houses in Camden, New Jersey, examine the intersections and divergences of their programming philosophies and practices, as well as their spaces' identities as rooted in, and in collaboration with, the communities they serve and the institutions they are part of. In light of the COVID-19 pandemic, they also explore what distanced programming has meant for the accessibility of their programs and strategic planning of their organizations.

Keywords

writers house; new jersey, neighborhoods, accessibility, generative writing

Creo que el mundo es bello,
que la poesía es como el pan, de todos.
Y que mis venas no terminan en mí
sino en la sangre unánime
de los que luchan por la vida,
el amor,
las cosas,
el paisaje y el pan,
la poesía de todos.

I believe the world is beautiful
and that poetry, like bread, is for everyone.
And that my veins don't end in me
but in the unanimous blood
of those who struggle for life,
love,
little things,
landscape and bread,
the poetry of everyone.

— "Como Tú" ["Like You"] by Roque Dalton, trans. Jack Hirschman

Introduction: What Is a Writers House for?

Camden, New Jersey boasts a unique and strange literary distinction: not one, but two Writers Houses. Before looking at the shared and divergent philosophies of the two houses, we'd like to ask: what is a Writers House for, anyway? It is not, in either Camden case, a writing center; though one House is located on the Rutgers University—Camden campus and one is on the corner of a residential neighborhood in south Camden, neither students nor residents drop in or make appointments explicitly for writing assistance. Neither is a Writers House a presenting organization alone, although both houses offer calendars of readings and workshops by published authors. When we examine the intertwining history of these two spaces, we find a hybrid architecture: one that inherits ideas from the academic writing center model, from the evolution of civic engagement on college campuses, from community organizing and from models of writing generatively and creatively together as a group. In their first years, we've seen these models adapt and transpose to meet the needs of their most ardent participants and to reflect the training and influences of the teams that lead them. Both houses have also been challenged to adapt their missions and programming models to the needs of their constituencies in response to the multiple community crises springing from the COVID-19 pandemic.

The Writers House at Rutgers—Camden: From a Legacy of Faculty Literary Events to Programs Rooted in Community Interest and Partnership

Director introduction: I'm Leah Falk, and I direct the Rutgers—Camden Writers House. My academic background is in English literature and creative writing, linguistics, and Spanish language and literature. My work has found me teaching in the university classroom; supporting staff building literacy programs in out-of-school-time contexts; implementing an urban environmental studies curriculum; developing poetry curriculum for in-school programs; and managing programs and volunteers in a variety of nonprofit contexts. At the Writers House, I develop and sustain programs and partnerships, communications, and funding strategies, within the campus and externally. I work closely with the English department and Creative Writing program but also partner across the campus with faculty, staff, and students from Biology, Africana Studies, History, Psychology, Robeson Library, Veterans Affairs, and Civic Engagement, to name just a few. I also collaborate with community partners ranging from Camden after-school programs to informal coalitions of nonprofit directors.

The Writers House at Rutgers—Camden, located in a refurbished Queen Anne home in Camden's historic downtown, began as a faculty dream of a campus and community space, modeled on joint university-community spaces like the Kelly Writers House at the University of Pennsylvania and growing out of decades of English department programming that brought novelists, memoirists, and poets to campus for talks and conferences. At the beginning of its life in 2015, the Writers House housed the Writing and Design Lab, the campus writing center, but since that center moved in fall of 2018, the house has offered no one-on-one writing consultancy model. Instead, its programming has centered on workshops that introduce participants to fiction writing, political poetry, business writing, and other topics, often as requested by participants; public readings and discussions; and multi-format programs that call attention to the role of writing and storytelling in particular communities, such as veterans and LGBTQIA people. The House also runs two youth programs: one on-site, the High School Writers Conference, dedicated to introducing high school students to the ways writing plays a role in a range of professional careers; and Growing Great Writers, an off-site program that gives elementary and middle school students in Camden dedicated, guided time for creative writing during after-school programs. For the above programs, the Writers House has established partnerships with Warrior Writers, a national nonprofit dedicated to veterans' creative expression; the Salvation Army Kroc Center; and the after-school program affiliated with Camden-based Catholic Schools Partnerships.

Although the Writers House's four classrooms—converted from their residential use with historic details preserved—are used for university classes, they are not in constant scheduled use, and increasingly, students can be found in an empty classroom or lounge space, taking advantage of the quiet atmosphere to study. Attendees of community workshops, which often occur on weekends, are invited to make themselves at home in the historic space. Impromptu library spaces on the first and second floors are stocked with books, periodicals, a computer, typewriter, and coffeepot, inviting un-programmed engagement on an individual or group basis.

Nevertheless, it usually takes intensive stewardship and design to promote the kind of engagement we would most like to see, and to make the space central to the mission of the center. This stewardship comes in the form of in-person greetings, whiteboard messaging, and events that may be less structured than a class and that embrace a spirit of improvisation, but still have a set time, place, and theme. We've seen participants take ownership of these events in small ways: at a recent tribute to the work of Toni Morrison, participants were invited to bring and read their favorite passages from the Nobel Laureate's work; when we ran out of chairs, guests helped remove the cushions from the lobby sofas so people could sit comfortably on the floor. With the Free Library of Philadelphia, we hosted a book discussion of Tommy Orange's debut novel *There There*; a small group, made up of residents of Camden and surrounding suburbs as well as Rutgers staff and students, moved from reading passages from the novel to discussing whether an author has a responsibility to write representations of his community in a positive light. Even when programming is more audience-oriented, most important to the Writers House identity is that participants have their own motivation for being there, and that moments of collaborations and discovery, such as the ones described above, are possible.

Our programming philosophy began with an informal assessment of which populations on campus and in the community might be receptive to programming that invited them to use writing to reflect upon their identities, experiences, and interests. Early on, veterans were an obvious choice for pilot programming. Rutgers has seen an increase in student veterans, active duty military, or dependents every year since tracking began in 2008, and Rutgers has the distinction of being named a Purple Heart University, noting its support of student veterans and active duty service members. New Jersey has close to half a million veterans, with many concentrated in nearby Cape May County.

As a programming curator and leader approaching the new project of the Writers House in 2016, I also tried to understand the legacy of faculty programming that inspired the space. I brought with me influences from the worlds of generative community creative writing workshops and museums: specifically, the work of Nina Simon, author of *The Participatory Museum* and CEO of OF/BY/FOR ALL, and Pat Schneider, author of *Writing Alone and With Others*. I learned about Ms. Simon's work and influence on the museum world while employed at the YIVO Institute for Jewish Research, and about Ms. Schneider's while I was a volunteer workshop leader for NY Writers Coalition.

Simon envisions museums as not merely cultural institutions to experience passively, but rather places where people can actively connect to culture and other people, often across social differences. As director of the Santa Cruz Museum of Art and History, Simon and her team examined ways people participated in cultural activities outside of institutions, and imagined ways for institutions to reclaim that participation: for example, inviting amateur artists to paint together on weekends, using the museum's collection as inspiration. In this way, she writes, the community becomes a "co-creator" of the significance of the museum's collection.

Simon's idea of the community as co-creator was an essential pivot in my thinking as a program curator. I had long looked for ways to position reading, especially the reading of complex literary works, as a creative act. In my workshop facilitation and teaching at the high school and university levels, I have seen participants and students become more empowered as readers and writers when they feel invited to create original interpretations of the work, rather than seek a supposedly hidden, single meaning of a text. For example, at our 2017 panel discussion highlighting the narratives of medical professionals in the military, audience members waited for the invited speakers to finish, then during the question and answer session stood up to give testimony about their own service, often at length. Simon might refer to a discussion that prompted such a response as a "social object," a concept she discusses in *The Participatory Museum* (ch.4, "Social Objects.") Social objects are cultural touchstones that makes participants feel invited to share their own reflections and make new connections.

Simon stresses that this fruitful community collaboration doesn't come out of nowhere: institutions must create well-designed opportunities that facilitate meaningful, creative participation. "If you give someone a special tool…it transforms what they do in return," she says in her TED talk "Opening Up the Museum" (Simon 05:45-05:53). Although Writers House programs began with a legacy of traditional author talks, readings, and workshops, we've expanded our programming to try to honor this principle of quality participatory design, especially through our veterans' programs and our High School Writers Conference.

Pat Schneider, who founded and helped to spread the Amherst Writers and Artists workshop method, has been a more indirect influence on the way I've gone about seeking partners for Writers House programs and looking to create an environment of trust and cross-community participation. In her book *Writing Alone and With Others,* Schneider lays out a set of values for community writing workshops. I've taken to heart two in particular: that of eliminating the hierarchical structure or spirit of writing workshops and other programming, and that of encouraging facilitators of writing programming to generate work alongside participants in order to build a trusting environment where everyone, including the "leader," has something at stake (Schneider x).

I consider these two philosophies as I conduct evaluations and needs assessments, as I assemble speakers and workshop leaders for multi-format programs, and as I develop partnerships with departments and individual faculty members on campus as well as community members. The questions I try to keep front of mind include: does this program have a barrier to entry, in the form of physical spaces that are not universally accessible, inconsistent transportation, unexpected/inflexible/inaccessible costs, or technology that not everyone may be practiced in using? Does this program center perspectives that matter to audiences that may or may not be fluent in the shorthand of academic research, storytelling, and work products? Does this program allow participants the chance to give testimony about their own relationship to the kind of writing, reading, and/or storytelling being discussed? Do the speakers and workshop leaders I invite or hire understand that they are working in a context where all of the above is important?

Who Participates and How – Cultural Differences and Identifying Expertise

In a survey of a representative sample of participants taken in spring 2020, we found that students make up about twenty percent of Writers House program participants, but the majority of participants are not Rutgers affiliated, and live in Camden or other South Jersey communities. They are primarily young, between ages twenty-five to thirty-four, though these respondents may be the ones most comfortable with online surveys. Some participants are veterans who do not primarily see themselves as writers, but who crave a safe and like-minded community to reflect on and share their experiences of service, post-traumatic stress, and transitioning back to civilian life. Others have careers as healthcare professionals, early childhood educators, or entrepreneurs, but write novels and poetry after the workday is done. Still others may be college students—no less part of our "community-based" model for being degree-seeking—who show up to workshops to practice the storytelling skills to turn their knowledge of biology, public policy, or environmental studies into advocacy campaigns, grant proposals, or opinion-editorials.

Often, the above participants may share space without explicit acknowledgment of the different cultural values and experiences they arrive with, or without discussing the a priori assumptions they may have of a university space, or that the university may have of them. What does this look like? A middle-aged man who owns a small contracting company, attending our email and business writing workshop a couple years ago, apologized for his lack of facility in "writing," by which he might have meant crafting a fluid argument or an aesthetically beautiful sentence. This apology might reflect his perception that the university holds those values as the principal hallmarks of good writing. But when a facilitator asked about the kind of communication that was important to his business, he shared a few oral techniques he had for assuring prospective clients that he was experienced and trustworthy; the facilitator encouraged him to make these the foundation of a writing exercise that would provide copy for his business's Facebook page. This example embodies Pat Schneider's anti-hierarchical workshop value. When participants look to a facilitator for expertise or the guiding values of the institution, the facilitator's first technique can be to flip the request and ask for participants' expertise. In future programs, we hope to encourage participants to reflect on and identify their expertise and values as a first step in any workshop.

With staff at Mighty Writers Camden, the organization that operates out of the other Camden writers' house, we've discussed the value of different programming models for our overlapping but distinct constituencies. Should a Writers House that aims at value for a community with wide variation in experience and cultural values be approaching programs with a curatorial or responsive eye? That is, should we be creating offerings that seem relevant and exciting to us, given our understanding of our participants; or should we be asking participants explicitly what they want at every turn? Is there a middle road between these programming philosophies that can offer participants valuable experiences that may be unexpected, but still respond to expressed need and interest? The key to identifying this middle road, I believe, is constantly reiterating the model in the example above: by asking participants about their values and experiences, and assessing together the relevance of what we have to offer, we can fulfill their needs and interests while participating in a more equitable community exchange.

Forthcoming Challenges: Remote Programming and Equitable Accessibility During the COVID-19 Pandemic

During regular programming seasons, the Writers House faces challenges familiar to many joint campus-community spaces, including infrastructural barriers, such as limited public transportation; lack of universally accessible physical spaces; and limited opportunity for reflection on and discussion of cultural differences between participants and the institution that hosts them. We've also experienced the challenges of asserting a community identity in the context of a university whose campus has a mixed imprint on public memory in Camden. In the midst of the COVID-19 pandemic, however, these challenges have changed shape, and in the immediate future we'll be focusing on addressing new questions of accessibility and equity.

Our historic building is not universally physically accessible – a chair lift brings participants with accessibility needs up to the first floor level, but not beyond, posing limitations for programs based in the Writers House, such as workshops. Additionally, some participants coming from Philadelphia or from elsewhere in New Jersey find the financial and time burdens of a toll bridge and parking to be a deterrent. In the spring, we piloted online workshops for our veterans program, in collaboration with partner Warrior Writers, and saw a dramatic uptick in participation, not only from our local participants but from all over the country. We were encouraged by the idea that remote programming might decrease the barrier to entry for public programs.

Planning for an all-remote fall season, however, I worry that the absence of in-person programming will limit access for the part of our constituency that lacks reliable internet and/or device access, or for whom in-person events are the best way to build connections and trust with an institution that can feel distant and inscrutable. Also, of concern to me is the elimination of the "browsing" element for our participants, which the pandemic has eliminated elsewhere. By "browsing" I mean the opportunity for someone to happen upon a discussion or reading because they are nearby, to drop in to the house and look around, to make a commitment to a workshop because they have talked casually with a workshop instructor or with me at a festival or other neighborhood event. Browsing makes it possible to bypass the many steps—or "conversions," in advertising language—between a participant's learning about a program and making a plan to attend it. Prior to spring of 2020, I could expect a community member or student to wander into the House once a week or so, allowing us this opportunity. Other times, a phone call occasioned this kind of impromptu connection, often accompanied by an exchange of ideas about possible programs or a participant's needs. As with the leaps in ideas that often come about in workplaces because of casual hallway or water cooler discussion, I believe that this browsing element helps form stronger and more enduring connections between the house and students, community participants, and others.

Two Houses, Both Alike In…?

The creative energy that made the Rutgers Writers House possible can be found in abundance elsewhere in the city. After an initial plan to collaborate with the campus on a single Writers House structure, the Nick Virgilio Haiku Association instead put down roots in the Waterfront South neighborhood, just two miles south of Rutgers–Camden. Early cross-pollination between the people responsible for the acquisition and refurbishment of both spaces still engenders fruitful relationships: former Rutgers faculty sit on the board of the Virgilio House, an annual Rutgers event celebrating contemporary practitioners of haiku attracts members of the Virgilio association, and program directors at the two houses have ongoing conversations about the overlap between their respective programs and constituencies. The geographic and institutional divide between downtown Camden, where Rutgers resides, and Waterfront South, a primarily residential neighborhood, means that the two houses serve somewhat different populations and operate with distinct pressures and concerns, despite intertwined missions. Since 2018, Philadelphia-based nonprofit Mighty Writers has operated the principal programming at the Virgilio house, which is discussed more below.

Mighty Writers at the Nick Virgilio Writers House: Haiku House to Community Resource Hub

Director Introduction: My name is Catherine Buck, and I work as the Program Director of Mighty Writers Camden. Our youth writing programs are located in the Nick Virgilio Writers House, as described earlier. I run Mighty Writers' Camden-based programming and collaborate with seven other MW locations across Philadelphia. From 2016-2018, I was part of the creative writing MFA program at Rutgers—Camden and found a home in their Writers House as a student and teacher. There, I organized the Growing Great Writers After School Program that pairs MFA students as teaching artists in Camden elementary schools. Outside of writing, I have led youth volunteer initiatives in El Paso, Texas, and Leon, Nicaragua. My BA is from La Salle University, where I studied English with a multidisciplinary social justice and international studies minor. This background serves as a foundation for my current work with Mighty Writers.

Like the Rutgers—Camden Writers House, the Nick Virgilio House serves as a 'third space' for the Camden community. For its founders, the house upholds the legacy of Virgilio with a small museum alongside a living room, kitchen, and library space. For many local residents, the house is just now fully opening up to community-driven possibilities. Since summer 2018, adults have sought out programming based around haiku and personal writing, and students ages five to seventeen have participated in Mighty Writers' creative writing workshops, mindfulness programs, tutoring, and mentorship. For young students, our writing programs also functioned as a social hub with peers as much as a site of academic enrichment.

During the COVID-19 pandemic, the space has evolved to be a major distribution site for meals, diapers, and literacy resources for the Waterfront South community. Beginning in spring 2020, Mighty Writers has used this house to distribute weekly supplies of five thousand diapers, six hundred lunches, 210 boxes of produce, face masks, and baby formula, and a constant stream of books. Considering this year's changing demands on education, all writing workshops have moved online, and the 'lunch and literacy' distribution will be operational for the duration of the school year.

Mighty Writers' mission is to ensure students "think and write with clarity." In our current moment, this is understood with the premise that children can't do either if they're hungry. So, we've pivoted, and as a result, have seen a huge influx of new visitors to the site, including a marked increase from a Spanish-speaking immigrant community. While one primary motivation for guests is the diaper and food distribution, we're also focusing on our core value of literacy education by ensuring that books and learning packets are readily available. We've been able to do this with the support of strong community partners, like the Camden County Pop Up Library and Book Smiles NJ, both of which 'redistribute book wealth' with donations from neighboring suburbs and bring gently used children's books for us to share at the Writers

House. We also create in-house activity packets and have a full roster of free online workshops readily available to students, along with writing contests and one-on-one mentoring.

These online offerings are possible only through the robust network of staff and partnerships developed over Mighty Writers' eleven year history as a major metropolitan-area non-profit. Before the pandemic, there were seven youth writing centers across the greater Philadelphia region, each operating relatively independently. Camden had its own standalone programming and creative direction, which continues now at the Writers House through food and diaper distribution, while the writing programs themselves operate mostly merged with other sites.

There are two notable exceptions of Camden-specific programming. In our Camden site, we were particularly concerned about regular students who may not have reliable internet access when we closed in-person programs. We had until that point been building a robust sense of community among these young writers and did not want to lose that momentum. To create some measure of continuity, we developed Mighty by Mail, a themed box of books and writing exercises sent to this group of forty students each month. Along with personalized notes from their instructors, these boxes included fun an useful materials, including candy, art supplies, and MW-branded face masks. One of our most consistent goals is in meeting students where they are, and at this time, that's at home.

The other initiative comes through a partnership with a local cornerstone, the Heart of Camden. Primarily an affordable housing non-profit, this organization has close ties to the Catholic church and school which many of our regular students attend. With their support, we brought on five teenage summer interns to assist in running distribution efforts. Along with sorting thousands of diapers and walking the neighborhood to spread the word, these students are also now engaged in an intentional reflective writing practice. Each afternoon, they journal about their experience and goals for community growth, which we then share as a small team. They've also penned their own notes of encouragement for younger Camden students in the Mighty by Mail boxes.

I came into the position of Program Director at Mighty Writers Camden in the fall of 2019. Before then, this location had only part-time staff and limited after school programs. The majority of students came directly after school, walking over together as a group. Many students did not live in the immediate neighborhood and travelled due to the school's high reputation. One of my primary goals from the beginning was to reach local kids who lived on our block, which we've now accomplished in this twist of circumstance. When we switched to offering distribution of goods and resources, a neighborhood parent joined our efforts as a community liaison. He's been able to spread the word effectively, reaching far more local residents through social media and long-established connections than any other communications initiative. When families arrive for food and diapers, they're also handed books and stacks of flyers about online classes and writing contests. There's an explicit focus on making the experience of picking up resources a positive one, attempting to limit the stigma often attached with receiving free meals. When needed, we engage visitors in Spanish. By pairing writing education along with food, we can concentrate on helping make the kids excited to pick out a book and emphasize a future-focused vision for parents. We want to celebrate the active role parents are taking in their child's success as supportive partners, rather than through top-down directives.

Layers of Justice in Writing: Grounding Philosophies and Influences

The personal philosophy that I bring to my community engagement work is that of justice over charity, solidarity over reinforced power dynamics. This is what grounds many of the above choices: framing our work with the expertise of longtime local players and residents, adapting to community needs as they arise, and providing youth leaders with structure to take an active role in their neighborhood's success. My background is in Catholic education, particularly the Lasallian tradition, an order that emphasizes educational equity with a social justice bent.

While these decisions are no doubt based in scholarship and theory, I've been driven to them most clearly through experience. In the first week of our teens' summer internship, one of my colleagues, a lifelong Camden resident, remarked at how much she wished she'd had a similar opportunity as a youth. I was privileged have such experiences: summer leadership camps and a spot in the teen section of the local newspaper. As a volunteer and then a nonprofit staff person, I learned that the most successful programs were consistently those driven in response to community needs, and which stayed committed for the long haul.

Much of my experience has been international. I read Paulo Freire and Ernesto Cardenal while leading volunteer groups in Nicaragua for an organization that makes no decisions without the direction of a locally elected governing board. I learned to push back against a banking model of education, and here, as elsewhere, saw the damage that can be done by well-intentioned visitors with no context for the dynamics of a place they seek to support. Earlier I participated in education-based volunteer trips to Kenya and Tanzania, for which I had no training as a teacher and learned much but contributed little. As an undergraduate, I was fortunate to be part of a program called 'Leadership and Global Understanding,' which framed international justice question first locally. We looked at each interconnected issue, including literacy, first in Philadelphia, then in the US as a whole, and finally in a global context. Two of our framing texts were Jeffrey Sachs' *The End of Poverty* and Hofstede's theory of cultural dimensions.

When I began to formally teach writing while earning my MFA at Rutgers—Camden, I embraced community-engaged pedagogy directly because of these influences. I chose to study in Camden because it was where I wanted to live and work long term. I'd seen that real change could not occur without permanent commitment, and it felt right to pursue this at home. I studied sociolinguistics and implemented understanding of the racism and classism inherent in writing education into my own teaching. As I emphasize with the K-12 students at Mighty Writers, in my composition classes I focused on the process of drafting and revision, along with building a sense of a writing community. I see self-expression as essential to justice.

When I taught composition (English 101 and 102) at Rutgers—Camden, it became clear that many students were more or less prepared for college writing directly because of the funding available to their previous schools. One of my driving motivators in my current role has then become working to supply Camden kids with the tools which they can use to succeed in higher academic settings.

It's also very clear that I cannot be the primary person to do this. Now in a managerial role, I've emphasized finding staff, guest speakers, and instructors who are people of color and, whenever possible, from Camden themselves. I can teach my students Black poets every day for a month, but this is much different than hearing original pieces performed by an artist who grew up three blocks away.

Through everything, it seems that the framing dynamic is power. Who gets to tell the stories, as Chimamanda Ngozi Adiche powerfully describes in her *Danger of A Single Story*: who listens, and who is heard? This is the politics inherent in all rhetoric. Who is the teacher and who is the student, who, even, is handing out the bags of diapers and who is receiving them? This ties into our current situation: who decides where the food bank sends school lunches, and why do we have an endless supply of books in the English language but almost none in Spanish?

These questions are not separate from writing education. In that same Russian doll of interconnected issues, the world, country, and now city have all been turned upside down. Gaps in educational access are set to skyrocket, and the basic needs of our students will likely continue to be unmet and exacerbated. As schools and political powers work to align resources where they deem most necessary, it is impossible to look at any one issue in a vacuum. Yet there is, indeed, a hierarchy of urgency. Our students cannot write if they are hungry, nor can parents and community leaders enter into equitable collaboration if they are facing down challenges that threaten their lives.

The New Normal: Future Plans and Visions

We know that change cannot happen without a sustained commitment, and we are now laying the groundwork for a more durable, locally based education program. There is no shortcut for trust. I hope that the relationships we are now building will continue, that parents who first found us because we were giving away baby formula will one day enroll their children in our Mighty Toddlers early literacy class. I hope the teens who are spending their summer going door to door handing out school supply packs will take pride in their impact, and that each kid who enters an online writing contest will take our words of affirmation to heart.

As of January 2021, it is still unclear what this year will look like for schools and educational nonprofits. The Nick Virgilio Haiku Association, which founded this Writers House and continues to maintain the legacy of their namesake poet, has also pivoted to maintain their mission and build community relationships. From livestreaming a poetry reading at Nick Virgilio's nearby gravesite to running online adult workshops, they too are finding new ways to engage their audience in this current moment. In reflecting the demographics of Camden city, they have also launched a social media series featuring Black haiku poets and are engaging Camden writers in a group of virtual poetry walks.

For Mighty Writers Camden, we've committed to continuing in-person food and diaper distribution through 2021 along with a full series of online workshops, contests, and individual mentorships. Because of pandemic-related shifts in programming, we're reaching dozens of new families in the community, mostly with young children. It's our hope that when in-person programming does eventually resume, these community members who live within walking distance will be our primary audience, returning to the core mission of meeting kids where they are. In the months ahead, we also have plans for additional formal collaboration with longtime neighborhood institutions, including the Heart of Camden and Sacred Heart School. In all of our work, we'll continue to focus on strengthening our students with the resources directly around them. We are especially looking forward to more focused partnerships with the Writers House at Rutgers-Camden, including joint author events to provide our students and their families access to university spaces and programming. This is one of the primary strengths of having two Writers Houses in one city: the ability to share resources, expertise, and connections to bring together all members of the Camden writing community.

Conclusion

The two Camden Writers Houses share similar challenges: an ongoing negotiation between mission and practice, infrastructural questions of transportation in a city whose residents face ongoing mobility challenges, and the project of helping participants feel comfortable in spaces that are still adapting in response to their needs. Neither space can ignore the grassroots literary/literacy activity happening in Camden, which has been a city full of open mics and informal writers' gatherings, such as the long-running Brigid's House writers' collective run by Cassie MacDonald, before either Writers House was a reality.

Spaces like ours were dreamed of as physical meeting places, spaces to enable the kismet of a connection between readers, writers, and the material that inspires them. Before COVID-19, we navigated the above challenges with the goal of engineering those chance encounters and watching the results bloom in the form of new works created, new cohorts, mentorships, and friendships established, and new resources made available across a wide spectrum of participants and community partners.

In the new era the virus has engendered, we're backwards-engineering those encounters once again, imagining how it might be possible to invite participants to co-create the social, sharing spirit of our programs from a distance. In fact, participant co-creation seems even more vital as programs are removed from our centers' physical houses: the momentary absence of walls and doors makes the creation of a spiritual home for our writers essential. We feel that our strategy as programming directors must be to design programs that invite participants to build such a homelike structure with their voices, faces, and names while such construction is impossible with their bodies. We're in agreement that such an invitation must first acknowledge and reflect upon participants' primary needs, whether for food and clean water, housing, and reliable income and/or employment. Only when those needs are met can we ask them to reach beyond their own homes and make a meaningful connection to a text, to another writer, and to the world.

Works Cited

Adichie, Chimamanda Ngozi. "The Danger of A Single Story." TEDGlobal, October 7 2009, https://www.youtube.com/watch?v=D9Ihs241zeg. Accessed 15 July 2020.

Dalton, Roque, tr. Jack Hirshman. "Like You." *Poets.org*, Academy of American Poets, poets.org/poem/you-1. Accessed December 21, 2020.

Hofstede, Gert Jan. *Exploring Culture*. Intercultural Press, 2002.

Sachs, Jeffrey. *The End of Poverty: Economic Possibilities for Our Time*. Penguin Group, 2005.

Schneider, Pat. *Writing Alone and With Others*. Oxford UP, 2003.

Simon, Nina. "Chapter 4: Social Objects." *The Participatory Museum*. Museums 2.0, 2010, http://www.participatorymuseum.org/chapter4/. Accessed 1 July 2020.

Simon, Nina. "Opening Up the Museum." TEDx Santa Cruz, November 6 2012, https://www.youtube.com/watch?v=aIcwIH1vZ9w. Accessed 1 July 2020.

Author Bios

Catherine Buck is the program director of Mighty Writers Camden. She holds an MFA from Rutgers University - Camden in fiction writing. Previously, she taught composition and business writing at Rutgers - Camden, La Salle University, and Rowan College in Burlington County. She ran community service programs at Cathedral High School in El Paso, Texas, and coordinated immersion groups in Leon, Nicaragua. She has served as a board member of JustHope Nicaragua and as a contributing writer for New Ways Ministry.

Leah Falk directs the Writers House at Rutgers University—Camden. She earned her M.F.A. in creative writing from the University of Michigan, where she was a Zell Postgraduate Fellow. She is also the author of *To Look After and Use* (Finishing Line Press, 2019) and her writing has appeared in *The Kenyon Review, FIELD, Electric Literature,* and elsewhere. Her work has received support from the Yiddish Book Center, Vermont Studio Center, Asylum Arts, and elsewhere. She has been a board member of Emerging Arts Leaders: Philadelphia, a workshop leader for NY Writers Coalition, and a teaching artist for InsideOut Detroit.

Love and Poetic Anarchy: Establishing Mutual Care in Community Writing

Emily Marie Passos Duffy and Ellie Swensson

Abstract

This profile details the ethos and emergent growth of Writers Warehouse, a collective project founded in 2016 with a focus on creation, craft, collaboration, and community. Based in Colorado, Writers Warehouse now aims to position itself as a mutual care collective through curating inclusive, non-hierarchical spaces, developing open access resources, and establishing a microgrant program for local writers.

Keywords

mutual care, mutual aid, poetry, community writing, poetic anarchy

Introduction

The Writers Warehouse (WW) project began in July 2016 at the Boulder Creative Collective (BCC) as "Boulder Writers Warehouse," a culmination of three years of community conversations about establishing a local hub for writers. The warehouse was originally designed to meet three specific needs voiced by writers in the region—reading venues, workshop rooms and supplies, and studio space. After two years of this model, it became clear that there was something missing. Our workshops were well attended, our event calendar was consistently full, and our studio space fostered plenty of creation, yet we could not find a stable source of financial support that allowed us to keep the space open. Monthly memberships never broke $200/month, not nearly enough to cover our $850/month rent. We went through multiple grant hearings where we received high scores and complimentary notes, yet we did not receive any funding in these proceedings. It was evident that the models we were operating on and the systems we were advised to work within were not working for us. We had to adapt. And to adapt, we needed time; time which we quite literally could not afford. In 2018, we left our studio at BCC, and we took a year to listen harder, find out what went wrong, what went right, and, perhaps more importantly, what we had left unexplored and unimagined.

This pause was crucial to WW's development. By stepping out of funding hearings and larger projects for a year, we were able to witness our community and our work from a space of contemplation rather than reactivity. It became clear to us in this process that doing *the work* doesn't always look like "work" as it is defined in our American capitalistic frameworks. WW shifted our focus to see what our community was looking for, experiment with approaches to meet those needs, and also fundamentally question what—and who—was left out of conversations about the writing "community" in general. Our first logistical step was to stop limiting ourselves geographically to Boulder. We started brainstorming multiple infrastructure projects to further accessibility in the writing community. How could we be mobile and adaptable, offer open-access, egalitarian resources, and support place-based community writing projects and installations? By late 2019, we realized that our true goal was to establish a mutual care collective for writers, and we returned to our original physical studio as part of the BCC's inaugural sponsored artists-in-residence program[1] with this aim in mind.

This profile shares our experiences and the theory and poetry that inform our practice and our work to foster mutual aid in the writing community. Our aim is to illustrate how combining a revolution of intimacy with an adaptive strategy fosters powerful community collaborations. This paper is our perspective on how empathy, advocacy, ego moderation, and poetic anarchy are fundamental, revolutionary tools in supporting community connection in the literary world. Our hope is that these perspectives may be useful to those who are new to community writing projects and also may invite established practitioners to renegotiate their own relationships with academic and nonprofit institutions to imagine more liberatory possibilities and approaches.

In order to understand our goals, it is important to recognize WW's positionality within active systems of privilege and systems of oppression. Our geographic location inextricably links WW to Denver and Boulder's literary scene which is known for its connection to the Beats, a literary movement in the 1950s that celebrated ideals of social and literary experimentation while in practice perpetuating sexism, racism, and ego worship.[2] Unfortunately, this pattern of harmful contradictions between ideals and practice very much persists in the Front Range today.

The U.S. Census Bureau estimated Boulder's population in 2019 at 90.2% white and Denver County as a whole at 80.8% white. In such a demographic context, any "business as usual" approach to the arts inherently centers whiteness rather than engaging the necessary work of resource reallocation and anti-racism. In terms of literary representation, Colorado named Bobby LeFebre as the Poet Laureate in July 2019, and LeFebre is the first person of color to receive the title since its inception in 1919. For 100 years, the highest honor available to poets in the state was held exclusively by white writers. Without explicitly naming white privilege and willingly surrendering this privilege, Boulder and Denver's government funds, art commissions, and art nonprofits are incapable of nurturing meaningful representation and support for communities of color.

So where do we as co-directors of WW fall in this cultural context? We both have Masters of Fine Art degrees, allowing us access to local and national academic resources and networks that many are excluded from. As a white, femme, queer, cisgender woman, Ellie has a strong privilege of passing that allows her unquestioned access to many institutional spaces that are historically unwelcoming and/or inaccessible to marginalized and disenfranchised communities. As a white-passing Latinx cis-woman and a sex worker in a legal faction of the industry, Emily shares connections with grassroots organizing communities and is also employed within higher education. We both carry certain amounts of privilege[3] while simultaneously being a part of marginalized communities, and we believe our ability to pass through social sieves invites us to be strategic disruptors and voices of dissent. Adrienne maree brown writes "Where we are born into privilege, we are charged with dismantling any myth of supremacy. Where we were born into struggle, we are charged with claiming our dignity, joy, and liberation" (brown, "Report: Recommendations"). Our individual complexities within our own positionalities, and the attendant work we are tasked with, directly informs our approach to community writing.

Our theoretical foundation for WW's engagement with the writing community consists of poetry by women of color, black feminist theory, and case studies of mutual care. This particular combination is a demonstration of our belief that theory and praxis are intertwined. Two theorists that form the bedrock of our community literacy and intentions in this work are bell hooks and Gloria Anzaldúa. In particular, we turn to the liberatory thread between hooks's writing on feminism and Anzaldúa's ideas on dual consciousness/hybrid identity. Both thinkers move the reader away from divisive silos and identity politics towards a more holistic framework for liberation. Their works are situated in different cultural contexts and embodied experiences, but they are speaking to everyone. All advocate for solidarity and coalition-building—inviting those with different identities into the shared struggle. Hooks's style of scholarship is inherently disruptive, both in form and content. Anzaldúa uses poetry and theorizing to weave a fabric of text that is porous, nondual, and liberating. We draw from their work, not to reinforce a certain canonical understanding of these writers, but rather to articulate their presence in our own literacies and politics.

Gloria Anzaldúa writes, "At some point, on our way to a new consciousness, we will have to leave the opposite bank, the split between the two moral combatants somehow healed so that we are on both shores at once and, at once, see through serpent and eagle eyes" (78-79). Anzaldúa's positioning of this both/and approach as a path towards true liberation—and not a lock—is situated within the framework of *la mestiza* identity and brings with it the respective cultural consciousness that Anzaldúa carries. This perspective on liberation can also be applied within the context of community writing projects and relationship building because it encourages us to see through a nondual lens of complexity. We need to embrace complexity and contradiction and reject rigidity in order to move towards a liberatory praxis of community writing.

Feminist theory and practice, as articulated by hooks in *Feminism is for Everybody*, corresponds with our vision for community writing and inviting folks to self-identify as writers. Hooks advocates for a "mass-based" visionary feminist movement, one that is not ignorant to identity-based differences but situated within them and connected to a broader movement towards total liberation: "Radical visionary feminism encourages all of us to courageously examine our lives from the standpoint of gender, race, and class so that we can accurately understand our position within the imperialist white supremacist capitalist patriarchy" (116). This invitation to the table is a call to examine one's own complacency and role in, to recall brown, dismantling supremacy and/or reclaiming dignity and joy, and it is a critical part of that practice.

Hooks understands that there are different paths to literacy. She also argues for solidarity and coalition-building—inviting those with different identities into the shared struggle. She emphasizes the importance of cultivating a politics and literacy that is far-reaching and unbound by the institution of the university:

> Mass-based feminist education for critical consciousness is needed. Unfortunately class elitism has shaped the direction of feminist thought. Most feminist thinkers/theorists do their work in the elite setting of the university. For the most part we do not write children's books, teach in grade schools, or sustain a powerful lobby which has a constructive impact on what is taught in the public school. I began to write books for children precisely because I wanted to be a part of a feminist movement making feminist thought available to everyone. Books on tape help extend the message to individuals of all ages who do not read or write. (113)

Embracing complexity and valuing accessibility of resources outside of institutional bounds, whether that means financial resources or sharing information, resists gatekeeping and moves towards a culture of community care.

This is where our theoretical boots meet practical ground in our engagement with mutual care. The practice of mutual care is a foundation of resistance movements spanning multiple generations, continents, and cultural contexts. At its core, mutual care is co-created by communities to heal the experienced socio-economic damage of industrial complexes. Two successful and currently active examples of mutual care are The Icarus Project, which supports the mental health community, and Lysistrata, which supports marginalized sex workers. The Icarus Project focuses on collective healing and liberation through offering peer support spaces, rapid response webinars, training, publications, and workshops. Their model focuses on combating the medical industrial complex through resource sharing to increase access to services and education ("What We Do."). Lysistrata Mutual Care Collective and Fund supports marginalized sex workers, indiviuals who are criminalized by the justice system and stigmatized by the nonprofit industrial complex, by distributing emergency funds to workers in crisis to help meet immediate survival needs. Both Lysistrata and The Icarus Project operate outside of traditional, institutional bounds, and therefore can move in ways that are adaptable and responsive to community needs. The type of care they offer their communities is a kind of radical intimacy that values people, their agency, and their wellbeing above all else.

Revolution of Intimacy

The revolution of intimacy in our work is boundaried empathy and advocacy in practice; it is an ethos of mutual care and inclusivity. In *Pleasure Activism: The Politics Of Feeling Good*, adrienne maree brown posits a crucial alternative to the scarcity mentality used by various institutions to limit and destroy us. She writes, "Liberated relationships are one of the ways we actually create abundant justice, the understanding that there is enough attention, care, resource, and connection for all of us to access belonging, to be in our dignity, and to be safe in community" (407). Brown's ideas are intricately connected with mutual care as well as our view that erotic empowerment is a critical component of presence and embodiment in the work. As Audre Lorde states, "the erotic is not a question only of what we do. It is a question of how acutely and fully we can feel in the doing" (2). Lorde positions the erotic as "a measure between the beginnings of our sense of self, and the chaos of our strongest feelings" (2).[4] Both Lorde's articulation of the erotic and brown's emphasis on liberated relationships demonstrate how intimacy, creative expression, and embodied joy and sensation can serve as radical reclamations of autonomy.

This freedom and promise of "abundant justice" connects the personal with the political. Radical self care ripples outwards; it becomes radical community care. And, when a community is radically caring for itself, there is little room for the active violence of gentrification, poverty, etc. Outside the bounds of institutions and organizations, "Mutual aid is real work. Caring for others is real work. Distributing free resources & building resource networks is real work. Creating and sharing content for liberatory pedagogy is real work" (The Comrade Closet). At the time of writing this, COVID-19 has made its way to our community, and we are seeing the urgency of multiple and emergent mutual aid endeavors intending to support community members in meeting basic needs, maintaining connection to creative communities, and staving off the loneliness and feelings of isolation that CDC-recommended social distancing may produce. These emergent mutual aid strategies, on large and small scales, within artistic communities, are revolutions of intimacy.

Part of intimacy and work that emphasizes relationships is a recognition of writers as fully human, fallible, and situated within their cultural moment. Writers, then, must remain self-aware and name the positionality of their identities in order to prevent a false and oppressive sense of authority. In her poem, "Revolutionary Letter #11," Dianne Diprima pleads for such authenticity: "we got to/ come out from behind the image" (21). We often forget, as Ostriker reminds us, that "[t]he poet is not simply a phantom manipulator of words but a confused actual person" (320). It may seem obvious, but explicitly recognizing writers as flawed human beings is a radical act toward liberation.[5] When we do so, we highlight our moral obligation to interrogate the literary canon and hold it accountable for its harms. Similarly, we have an obligation to hold new and emerging writers to the same standards.[6] For example, as hosts of community events we do not have to hold space for a bigoted poet at an open mic for the sake of creative expression. Voices invested in perpetuating systemic violence against oppressed people are not valid in community space. If "compromise is a coffin nail," (26) as Audre Lorde aptly states, then radical accountability of self and of one's peers is a life-affirming act.

A necessary part of intimacy is self-care and survival, which requires knowing and naming what we are fundamentally against. This delineation is a charged topic in conversations on community building about the effectiveness of "cancel culture" and the distinctions between "calling in" and "calling out." We affectionately refer to this kind of boundary setting as strategically burning bridges. Creative communities so often operate from a place of scarcity that we tend to collaborate with organizations or individuals that aren't aligned with our goals—or even, on a more fundamental level, our survival—in favor of sponsorship, fiscal support, promotion, and overall clout. Saying no is a crucial part of a revolution of intimacy in that it allows for healthy and sustainable partnerships where creativity can truly thrive.

This work of dissent and accountability is not something that can be done in isolation. WW, therefore, views writing in all its embodiments as inherently communal. None of us lives in a vacuum. We are inextricably, unquestionably linked, and our efforts to use language intentionally connects us to both our present community and the many overlapping literary lineages of the past. As Kimberly Blaeser writes in "The Voices We Carry":

> [...] no voice arises from one person. I know I write out of a place, a center, that is greater than what I alone am or could be [...] What I speak and write comes to me dank and tangled among the years and lives I carry. I write not only out of a knowledge of the past, but within a chamber of voices from the past. (269)

Acknowledging a tangled, polyvocal lineage of poets, theory, and practice in this way is central to our mission as a project and collective.

As believers in the inherently communal nature of writing practice, we see collaboration and partnership as fundamental. The term *partnered projects*—instead of community partnerships—reflects our experience that singular projects unbound by expectations of longevity or profitability allow for clear, honest, and sustainable communication. These partnered projects also make it far easier to set boundaries that foster genuine reciprocity and accountability in collaboration. WW has engaged in partnered projects with Boulder Housing Partners, City of Boulder Office of Arts and Culture, Jaipur Literature Festival, Boulder Public Library, CU Art Museum, Boulder Creative Collective, Boulder Museum of Contemporary Art, Boulder Fringe Festival, Punch Drunk Press, Kleft Jaw Press, Writers for Migrant Justice, and multiple traditional and non-traditional venues for performances, workshops, and gatherings.

One example of a partnered project that exemplified the revolution of intimacy is Krewhouse, a reading series created with local press Kleft Jaw. The series focused on sharing writing in a non-hierarchical environment and offered a public reading space where "the table is always big enough and the doors stay open." Each show featured local writers as well as artists from around the country. We used "introduction anarchy" to disrupt the genre of the literary bio and introduction. One example of this introduction anarchy was asking every poet to submit a poetic line prior to the reading. During the reading, each reader would say the name of the next poet and draw one of the poetic lines at random to introduce the next reader. This practice created a more cohesive group atmosphere and affirmed that no matter how credentialed each reader was, every poet had a platform to share their work in this non-hierarchical space.

Another aspect of care present in this reading series was that the community as a whole housed readers from out of town and offered transportation to and from the reading and to house parties afterwards. Through this event we held the tenet that poets are people, and that "Justice is what love looks like in public, just like tenderness is what love feels like in private" (West). Krewhouse offered an experience of both the justice—the public event through the content of the readings and the diverse backgrounds of readers themselves—and the tenderness—through the personal connections, private conversations, family reunion-ness of it all—of love.

If the point of the writing is the people, the first step to viable resistance and change is palpable support in practical ways that values an individual's survival and well-being first and foremost. How are you going to find the strength to write that poem, to show up for the workshop, to patron the reading, to contact that publisher, or to initiate that collaboration, if you don't have the support of your community in ways that actually empower you? We acknowledge that as writers we are implicated in both the perpetuation and dismantling of oppressive systems. Language shapes our world, and language is the vehicle through which we express, communicate, build, and also challenge and deconstruct. As writers, we have to choose how we want to use our positionalities in our creative and community work. We have to ask ourselves day in and day out: Do we want to perpetuate the status quo or imagine a new future? Do we want to be stagnant or agile? And we need to recognize that the asking, the reflecting, and the actions we take are all equal parts of the work.

Adaptive Strategy

We define adaptive strategy as logistical agility which centers the immediate needs of the community over organizational recognition or ego. Our story is full of examples of this approach to community work, in our overall organizational structure as well as specific projects. In September of 2019, WW co-organized the Denver iteration of Writers for Migrant Justice, a national movement spearheaded by four writers of color that utilized readings as community fundraisers for Immigrant Families Together. This event took place against a backdrop of increased white supremacist activity in the Denver area, and we were vigilant about potential violence or harassment. After our second reader finished their set, we were asked to vacate the premises upon which we'd previously had permission to host the event (see Fig. 1). As organizers, we had to decide how to proceed with safety and accessibility in mind. We moved the remainder of the event to a different location and still managed to raise $200. This was a testament to how adaptive strategy can function in the moment, and it was a powerful reminder of the collective power of the creative community on both local and national scales (see Fig. 2).

Since our inception, WW has viewed events like poetry reading series and workshops as opportunities to decentralize ego and redistribute intellectual and cultural capital. We plan to take that a few steps further with a fundraising campaign titled "Talk About Our Sh*t 2020." This campaign will raise money for a writers' microgrant program geared toward funding individual writers' needs for anything from food and rent to workshop fees or publication supplies. Our criteria for distributing funds is inspired by *collective aporia*, an online artist collective and international festival. Their website states: "Please note that we will never accept any applicants whose content promotes harmful, hateful, oppressive, or prejudice rhetoric, especially towards marginalized and vulnerable communities" ("Volunteer"). This statement is an example of the aforementioned strategically burned bridges we aim to uphold in our emerging projects.

In addition to the microgrant program, we intend to offer WW as a publication imprint for self-publishing writers. Many literary awards stipulate that eligible works must be published by a press. Our idea is to offer our name and imprint, no strings attached, so that self-published writers can enter the gated conversation of book awards and better distribution opportunities. Again, following the example of *collective aporia*, our stipulations will be that in order to receive this creative commons copyright, we will read the work and ensure it isn't harmful and/or perpetuating messages that are racist, homophobic, sexist, classist, ableist, transphobic, etc. If submitted work does perpetuate such ideologies and cannot carry the WW imprint, the writer will be notified with a clear explanation of our concern and why we can't endorse their piece.

Another concrete way in which we wish to mitigate gatekeeping in the poetry community is to create a "Lit Event Listserv"—an accessible email and cell phone listserv for people who want to stay informed of literary community events and wish to divest from social media. Social media platforms can be democratizing, but they also contribute to commodification of identity, invasions of privacy, and censorship. This Listserv will be an open access resource available to everyone regardless of institutional or social affiliation. We believe this kind of communication can be a tool for empowerment and liberation by increasing access and opportunity.

Mutual Care and Call to Action

By offering mutual care through a microgrant program, a publication imprint, and an open source Listserv, Writers Warehouse aims to disrupt hierarchies and foment poetic anarchy through radical accountability, revolutions of intimacy, and adaptive strategy. We have offered some of our reflections, strategies, and language in the hope that others engaged in community literacy work may be inspired to consider how mutual care and liberatory strategies apply to their particular contexts and communities of practice. Our advice for folks wanting to start their own community writing projects is to look around and see what's already going on. Is there a program that's under-resourced? A reading series that doesn't get a lot of attention? Instead of being concerned with being first/best/etc., figure out how to be in a mutualistic relationship with what's already happening. How can you show up and support? In particular, how can you leverage existing privileges and institutional access to address inequities and continue building and strengthening relationships within your literary communities? How might you continually emphasize the importance of pause, rest, and taking stock of what your project is actually up to as opposed to being beholden to institutional timelines/grant cycles—and in turn, gradually create more freedom for yourself and your organization? How can you invite more people into the practice and craft of writing? There are no easy answers here, but the more frequently we are willing to ask complex questions and be continually accountable and receptive to the causes and community we care about, the more possibilities will open for deeper relationships, transformative projects, and community care.

Appendix

Bolder Writers Warehouse
@bolderwriterswarehouse

This past Tuesday we collaborated with @nataliexearnhart to host a reading as a part of the national #writersformigrantjustice fundraiser. Thank you to @short_sharp_shock @chrisdrosales @duffylala and @michaelagisela for performing and contributing your voice. Thank you to our audience who supported us through a mid-event venue change and who helped us raise over $200 to date. To be displaced by a landlord of an empty lot in the midst of an event about displacement and deportation was a powerful experience and we appreciate everyone there who helped us with the transition. 📷 photo by @emilyyatesmusic

Fig. 1 Image from Writers for Migrant Justice Denver Reading from: Writers Warehouse (@writers.warehouse).

Fig. 2 Screenshot of national Writers for Migrant Justice fundraising progress from:

Fig. 3 Poetry cookies made by community member, Jona Fine, for Jaipur Literature Festival, supported by funding from the city and Boulder Public Library. This is an example of using resources to connect existing dot sin the community and empower writers. WW saw JLF's need for an interactive activity, a local poet needing financial support who had a passion for baking, and using our connections to make something happen in which the poet received full funding for their materials and their time.

Works Cited

Anzaldúa, Gloria. *Borderlands/La Frontera: The New Mestiza*. Aunt Lute, 1987.
Blaeser, Kimberly. "The Voices We Carry." *After Confession: Poetry as Autobiography*, edited by David Graham and Kate Santog. Graywolf Press, 2001.
brown, adrienne maree. *Pleasure Activism: The Politics of Feeling Good*. Later printing ed., AK Press, 2019.
—. "Report: Recommendations For Us Right Now From a Future." *Sublevel Mag*, 26 Nov. 2019, https://sublevelmag.com/report-recommendations-for-us-right-now-from-a-future/. Accessed 28 May 2020.
Diprima, Dianne. "Revolutionary Letter #11." *Revolutionary Letters*, Last Gasp of San Francisco, 2007.
Hooks, bell. *Feminism is for Everybody: Passionate Politics*. Routledge, 2015.
Lorde, Audre. *Uses of the Erotic: The Erotic as Power*. Out & Out Books, 1978. .

"Lysistrata." *Lysistrata*, www.lysistratamccf.org/.
Ostriker, Alicia. "Beyond Confession: The Poetics of Postmodern Witness." *The American Poetry Review*, vol. 30, no. 2, 2001, pp. 35-39.
The Comrade Closet. (@thecomradecloset). "Some thoughts on 'Real Work.'" Instagram, 19 August 2019, https://www.instagram.com/thecomradecloset/?hl=en.
"Volunteer." COLLECTIVE.APORIA, collectiveaporia.weebly.com/volunteer.html
West, Cornel. "Justice is What Love Looks Like in Public." Sermon at Howard University. *YouTube,* uploaded by Supernegromagic, 17 Apr 2011, https://www.youtube.com/watch?v=nGqP7S_WO6o&feature=youtu.be&t=21s
"What We Do." The Icarus Project, 3 Aug. 2017, theicarusproject.net/what-we-do/.
Writers Warehouse (@writers.warehouse) "This past Tuesday." Instagram, 7 Sept 2019.
Writers Warehouse (@writers.warehouse) "The next time someone tells you." Instagram, 10 Sept 2019.

Notes

1. As the only resident writers at BCC, we work to bridge the gap between writers and visual artists by nurturing new ideas and collaborations that push the boundaries of artistic disciplines. We understand deeply that all arts communities share the struggle for space and resources. WW believes that more collaboration across mediums and disciplines on individual and organizational bases not only creates engaging art but also increases our ability for surviving/thriving.

2. There are multiple essays and stories about the inherent sexism of the Beats movement and also how their elevation of the white male ego often led to sexual assault (see the lack of women's voices and POC voices in Beat writings, Allen Ginsberg's association with NAMBLA, etc).

3. Neither of us depend on this work for our financial livelihood, and this financial distancing allows us to refuse projects if they are not in line with our values. It also empowers us to be very intentional in avoiding any kind of long-term funding that would require us to answer to anyone other than the community we serve.

4. This acute and full feeling in the doing is inherently anticapitalist. Capitalism asks bodies to operate automatically—performing labor.

5. Idolizing well known poets and theorists perpetuates a culture of exceptionalism and discourages community members who may want to identify as writers and participate in writing communities.

6. If our goal is liberation, regression by way of apathy is not an option. Apathy is not what opens the door to creativity . . . it isn't a LACK of action that empowers people to speak (unless they are the privileged folks). Creativity for all requires an intentional unlocking of the gate.

Author Bios

Ellie Swensson is a queer southerner currently writing poems in Denver, CO. She earned her MFA from Jack Kerouac School of Disembodied Poetics at Naropa University in 2015. She is the founder and co-director of Writers Warehouse, a mutual care collective for the writers' community. She has over 6 years of program experience including the reading series Bouldering Poets and Krewhouse, collaborations with the City of Boulder's Office and Art + Culture, Boulder Public Library, Denver's Small Press Fest, Jaipur Literature Festival, Boulder Creative Collective, and more. Swensson is a firm believer that poetics is what occurs where eros, divinity, activism, and careful craft intersect. Her poems are published in a handful of places you may know, but she prefers her words alive in the mouth and the body. Her debut collection of poems, salt of us, was published in 2019.

Emily Marie Passos Duffy is a Colorado-based poet, teacher, and performing artist. Her written work has been published in Boulder Weekly, Portland Review, Cigar City Poetry Journal, Spit Poet Zine, and Iron Horse Literary Review. She is a contributing member of The Daily Camera's Community Editorial Board and a 2020 **artist-in-residence at Boulder Creative Collective.** A 2020 finalist for the Noemi Press Book Award and a finalist of the 2020 Inverted Syntax Sublingua Prize for Poetry, she was also named a 2020 Disquiet International Luso-American Fellow. She earned her MFA in Creative Writing and Poetics from Naropa University in 2018. Her ongoing community collaborations include work with Writers Warehouse, Boulder Burlesque, and Tart Parlor.

fall 2020

Neighborhood Writing: Developing Drop-In Writing Consultations in Philadelphia Public Libraries

Dana M. Walker, Patrick Manning, and John Kehayias

Abstract

> In this project profile we discuss a drop-in writing project initiated by the University of Pennsylvania's Critical Writing Program in partnership with the Free Library of Philadelphia. We explain our drop-in writing project and rationale for a model embedded in the neighborhoods in which we live. Aware of our own constraints and opportunities living in a diverse urban area, we examine how an approach of practicing in place has allowed us to gain some success, but the nature of this flexible approach has also created a series of challenges.

Keywords

> community writing; library partnerships; rhetoric of respect; university-community outreach programs; adult literacy

Introduction

Founded in 2003, the Critical Writing Program (CWP) of the University of Pennsylvania has been involved in a number of on-going community writing projects in Philadelphia. Building on this commitment, CWP faculty implemented a community writing project to offer one-on-one drop-in writing sessions for Philadelphians. The project's aim has been to create a space for community members to work on their writing within their own neighborhoods. Motivated to work in our community, faculty at CWP partnered with branches of the Free Library of Philadelphia (FLP) as well as some of Philadelphia's regional public libraries.

In 2018, CWP director Valerie Ross conceived of a community writing project that could be based in the local public libraries and had the advantage of being replicable across different places and for different populations. One of CWP's faculty members, Dana Walker, took lead of the new initiative, coordinating a team of faculty members, connecting with local libraries, and establishing the first meeting with a branch librarian from the Free Library of Philadelphia. Since then, the project has grown in size and number of people involved. Presently, our faculty volunteers spend two to three hours a week in a FLP branch working with writers on the project, idea, or need that brought them to their neighborhood library. After one and a half years, ten faculty, about a quarter of our instructional staff, have been active in the project. We have started programs in five distinct library branches in the city and two surrounding suburbs and are currently staffing approximately twelve hours of neighborhood writing sessions each week.

In this project profile, we begin by explaining our drop-in writing project and rationale for a model embedded in the neighborhood. We then describe the ways in which the project has shifted and adapted, ultimately being built by the clients who have been using it. Throughout the development and implementation of the project, we have been sensitive to the constantly negotiated boundaries between the university and community, the publicly-funded spaces of the library that are both inclusionary and exclusionary, and our own changing and often challenged expectations of what writing problems and needs we would encounter. As such, we remain cognizant of the scholarship that notes the potential of well-meaning community-engaged work to go awry (Brizee and Wells). We do not presume to solve such tensions, but draw on writing studies literature and community literacy projects rooted in place (e.g. Doggart et al.; Rousculp) as a way to think about community writing projects that might best work at these interstices. Aware of our own constraints and opportunities living in a diverse urban area, we examine how a kind of in-between yet place-based approach has allowed us to achieve some success, but the nature of this adaptable, flexible model has also created a series of challenges.

Community Writing Library Project

Penn's Critical Writing Program has been involved in community writing projects since its founding. Our Community Writing Library Project emerged from that larger commitment, with our writing program director and instructional faculty looking at different ways to work in the community. Our approach was akin to the University of Wisconsin-Madison's Community Writing Assistance (CWA) program, especially in their early iterations where volunteers staffed a "writing help" table in the public library system (Doggart et al.). Not as large as CWA, nor with external funding, the Penn program has been more focused on creating small, distributed sites of writing assistance.

When we initiated the project, we knew two things. First, we would be operating as unpaid volunteers, and second, we would be aiming to create a drop-in model that could be replicated by others. From the outset, then, it was important that the design of the program was economical, sustainable, and replicable by our own faculty and perhaps other writing faculty across the region. Given these three goals, we determined that the Free Library of Philadelphia would be an optimal partner in this project.

We were determined to produce an economical model that did not require external funding or paid staff. We knew that the FLP system, in turn, has an architecture of literacy that was capable of providing in-place support for this budget-minded approach. In the Philadelphia region, the library system is a relatively well-known, recognized, and trusted public space. Many of the branches are sites for community programming as much as they are for collections. And, like many public libraries in the U.S., the FLP branches bring together communities of interest (Willingham). For example, while we are providing writing consultation at a branch, there may be other groups meeting for a crochet club, chair yoga, or cooking classes. Providing an additional project to the library branches' calendar helped us attract interested writers without the need to find a space or develop extensive project advertising.

Our project also has low overhead, allowing for a minimal upfront cost to set up the programs. To initiate a writing drop-in program, faculty have reached out to the librarians at their local branch. The librarians have been welcoming, seeing this as fulfilling a need in the community, providing an additional free service in a public library system that has scarce funding. We also decided to focus on operating a drop-in service rather than put our main effort into developing workshops or lectures to deliver to community members. In part, this was a response to the need to keep the project economical and sustainable. All of our volunteers are full-time writing instructors or administrators who have teaching responsibilities that would make prepping workshops or lectures difficult. We were also aware that imposing a curriculum on our neighbors could be problematic. We were negotiating an in-between space between ourselves as writing experts at a university and ourselves as neighbors and writers. We did not know nor could we anticipate the diverse writing needs in our various communities. Though our specific project is not in the writing center itself, we were guided by what Nichols and Williams call "writing center values," especially an ideal of collaborative agenda or goal-setting with our writing clients. We are not constrained to a semester or class timeline and "can start our work with writers where they are, not where a course imagines they will be" (Nichols and Williams 90).

Moreover, demographics and discussions with neighborhood leaders and local librarians demonstrated that there was a need for writing support. Philadelphia has one of the highest poverty rates in the country. Anecdotally, librarians told us in our initial planning meetings that job seekers often came to them for help. These realities emphasized the need for additional services in Philadelphia, with writing assistance being one that is often overlooked but underlies many needs, like navigating social services, applying for schools, or securing employment.

Being embedded in and adaptive to a neighborhood and the diverse writing needs in our communities also meant we had to think about how to meet those needs as they emerged, a reflection of the community information model of many libraries. Library scholars have long pointed out the role of public libraries as institutions for community engagement (Goulding). Researchers have found that libraries, especially post-Internet, are repositioning themselves as physical locations of community and assets for diverse interaction (Audunson; Scott). Our project was similarly situated in place; faculty determined, then, that it was important to work in the neighborhoods where they lived. Because the FLP is an expansive and well-used library system with over fifty local branches situated throughout the city of Philadelphia, it was well-positioned to help our writing project accomplish some of our goals.

This embedded approach, where faculty members initiated programs in communities they were already a part of, allowed for a certain distance between the university and the neighborhood. The University of Pennsylvania is in University City, a West Philadelphia neighborhood, but most of our drop-in locations are in South Philadelphia. While University City is a diverse area, the overall education level is much higher than Philadelphia as a whole: less than 50% of Philadelphians over the age of 25 have some education beyond high school, while 75% of University City residents do ("The State of University City"). The movement from university to neighborhood has been a focal point of recent research, where those like Doggart et al. emphasize the importance of "minding the gap" between these spaces. In our project, we tried to respond to this difference through this embedded model, volunteering where we live. In other words, we did not go to a community: We were in our community.

Another benefit of this embedded model is that it has helped us navigate some of the tensions between university and neighborhood. This is perhaps exemplified in the reactions of writers who make use of our writing sessions. Many who seek our services value the university imprint as evidence of the sessions'—and, indeed, the faculty volunteers'—legitimacy. This can lead to a complex discussion about expertise, where the writer will insist on their own deficit when encountering a "real" writer from the university. However, more often than not—and, indeed, much to our surprise—many people who utilize the drop-in writing session do so without realizing it is staffed by university writing instructors. Instead, for these writers, it is the library itself that provides legitimacy to the program. Many times, patrons of the library will assume we are library staff and ask non-writing related questions: how to get a library card, how to check out a book, and what programs are upcoming. Given the diversity of responses to our position vis-a-vis the institutional spaces we represent and inhabit, our writing project has tried to operate not as one or the other, but in the in-between, interstitial position of neighbor.

Writing in Place

Despite knowing the neighborhoods well, we could not anticipate the diverse writing projects in our communities. In this, we joined others who have had questions and concerns about what community literacy located in place could look like. Nearly half of our clients are looking for job-search writing skills, commonly resumes, application forms, or cover letters. Less anticipated by the critical writing faculty, but also common, are Philadelphians who have been working on creative writing projects including novels and short stories. We expected, but have had fewer clients, who come to the writing drop-in service for help on student papers. Finally, we have had a handful of clients who are coming just to write or to talk about writing—and sometimes, really, just to talk.

All these projects have given us insight into the rich writing lives that our neighbors are living. As we reflected on these different writing encounters, we have found Rousculp's framework of a "rhetoric of respect" useful in understanding our own work. Rousculp defines a rhetoric of respect as "draw[ing] attention to how we use language in relation with others: how we name and classify, how we collaborate, how we problem-solve" (25). Drawing on ecocomposition theory, Rousculp emphasizes the importance of place in developing and understanding her analytic framework.

For Rousculp, this place-based rhetoric of respect describes the responsive and flexible operations often required in community writing work.

Because we work at diverse locations across the city, our tactics need to be responsive to the needs of different library patrons and neighborhood expectations. Our model is constructed collaboratively, through a rhetoric of respect that allows each session to be developed by the writer and the needs, desires, and expectations that writer brings to the session. We enact this *in place* and are, therefore, attuned specifically to the way that neighborhood differences impact how each session is constructed. This has led to each location developing idiosyncratic differences, or personalities.

The authors all live and volunteer in South Philadelphia, yet at different branch locations. The Fumo Family Library is located on a main thoroughfare in the city, within blocks of a subway stop. Led by a branch librarian who has been a champion of our program, many of Fumo's patrons live in the surrounding neighborhood. The Charles Santore Library is located in a quieter, more residential area, home especially to young families and professionals. The Whitman Library is the newest addition to our writing project; it is located on a main avenue of South Philadelphia and easily accessible by public transit. Most of its patrons live in the neighborhood, and there is a small yet active contingent of young people who frequent the library.

Across all of our experiences, the branch librarians have become vocal advocates and partners of the program. In each branch, the librarians let patrons know about the project and encourage people to use the service. Our partnership with the branch librarians has been critical to any claim to success this project can make, and we have greatly appreciated their frank insights and conversations about what has been working and what needed to be amended to best collaborate with the library patrons.

The writing drop-in program at the Whitman Library is staffed by Patrick Manning. The Whitman Library has a large dedicated children's area on the west side of the building and a shared adult and teen section on the east side. The writing sessions at Whitman occur in the adult/teen section. In this section, there are rectangular tables nestled between the bookshelves with four chairs each, and there is one area with more comfortable seating. When multiple writers attend, Patrick typically moves from table to table to work with the different writers, so there isn't always one set location where sessions occur.

The Whitman Branch sees a diverse population of writers and sees writers working on resumes, essays, journalism, application materials, and even a self-help book. And while attendance can fluctuate, there have been two dedicated writers who have attended every session and formed a de facto writing group. One writer spends afternoons at the library after school and another comes to the library as part of her home-schooling curriculum. At a shared table, the two work on different creative writing projects. One writer has been working on an epic poem about the past and present of American racism; another writer has hundreds of pages of fan fiction set in a video game universe. Together, these two writers ask for writing prompts and share their writing with each other. Periodically, Patrick checks in on their work but gives them space to think and write without constantly reading over their shoulders. This organic writing group has been visible in the library, and it has served as an advertisement for the writing project, encouraging other writers to inquire about the writing sessions.

One of the writers who approached upon seeing this writing group was a high school student applying to an SAT-prep course. The writer needed to write a personal statement, a genre she hadn't written before. With Patrick, she went over the expectations of the genre, and she decided to begin with her personal experience in a refugee camp. She asked—unsure and concerned—if it was all right to discuss this aspect of her life in a personal statement. This question was asked with a deep complexity. Not only: is the refugee camp experience genre-appropriate; but also: will it hurt my chances at getting into the program? Will it be overly problematic? Overly pathetic? Here, it is possible to see Rousculp's rhetoric of respect enacted. In this circumstance, such a framework describes the importance of an open dialogue about what the writer was comfortable with sharing and to what purpose.

In a different part of South Philadelphia, the Fumo Branch has developed its own distinct personality as well. It serves a different population, located as it is along a main thoroughfare and at a convenient public transit stop. At Fumo, two faculty (including Dana Walker) have been working with a range of writers. The Fumo branch is small, with about eight tables in the teen/adult section that are available for people to sit and work. Because of the library's size, we always have a visible place there. Depending on the number of clients, the writing consultant will usually rotate between tables—starting a project with one writer, then moving to the next while the other works independently, then looping back to check in.

At this branch, we have seen writing projects that we were anticipating such as resumes and cover letters. Indeed, about half our clients are doing some kind of career-related writing. Most frequently, these encounters have been one-offs. Someone comes to get feedback on their resume, and we never see them again. For example, in one session Dana worked with a woman on her resume and cover letters. Going through a mid-career transition, the majority of the session was spent talking about audience and how to portray previous experiences in a way that could match the employer's needs. At the end of the session, the writer laughed and said that she hoped she would never have to come back again, adding that if she did it would mean she hadn't gotten a job.

Other clients have often arrived with projects that we couldn't have anticipated. We have residents who are working on short stories and novels, writing school papers, or struggling with how to cite sources. We have also worked with retirees who just want to improve their writing as a goal in itself. One client has started writing a journal in his spiral notebook and when he comes to the session he often asks for a prompt and writes for about thirty minutes. When asked what he wants to write, he says that he just wants "to practice and get better." As with our colleagues at other branches, we are working to define each session in collaboration with the writer and what would best help each reach their goals. Many of those who seek our services are, unlike students, working without the pressure of a deadline. They can come back at any time if they are finding the service useful.

Just a few blocks north, at the Santore Branch, located in a residential part of the city, the Community Writing Library Project has developed in some ways similarly to our other branches, and in other ways, unique to the particular location and clientele. This is a smaller branch, with one large central room with books and tables where people work and groups meet. This is where John Kehayias sits at a table with a sign informing people of the drop-in service. While this branch has also primarily seen one-off sessions for resume updates and cover letters, as well as the occasional creative writer, one client has been attending the two-hour weekly sessions to work on English literacy. This has involved providing writing prompts for both in-person sessions and for practice at home, as well as responding to a variety of materials the client brings in. In this and some other branches, we are continually trying to assess what role we should play for language learners. While some of our faculty have experience in teaching English as a second language, our shared expertise is in teaching writing—distinct areas of expertise. Typically, multilingual clients are not seeking instruction in English, but rather assistance with a writing project, such as a cover letter.

In all branches, we have encountered writing interactions that we had not predicted. As writers, and instructors of writing, we know—in fact we teach—the importance of writing. But even we did not truly examine the community-building role of writing. In our case, this has not necessarily been in a large-scale community action or engagement. Rather, it has been more in building "community of relationships" (Morse). For some of our clients, writing serves as a means of connection, a basis for conversation and discussion. Perhaps never having had a writing community before, our drop-in clients can use the service to engage in a meaningful discussion of their work.

In addition, we have noted how we as faculty have become *embedded* in our own neighborhood libraries, which has led us to become more deeply involved in our communities. This has occurred in accidental, random ways through the building of a community of relationships. For example, our faculty have seen writing partners at children's soccer games and at local bars and restaurants. These connections are brief, to be sure, but they do suggest how writing builds neighborhood intersections both outside of standard institutions *and* beyond the practice of writing itself.

Conclusion: Limitations and Future Directions

The strength of the project has been its ability to adapt and spread. Indeed, in many ways the project has been collaboratively designed by those who use it—the writers and our library partners. While this flexible architecture has enabled some success, we are hitting some of the limits of this approach.

For example, the decision to partner with the public library system has made this project feasible, both because of their infrastructure and because the librarians have been central to promoting the drop-in hours. Nonetheless, we are also aware that we are working with a small subsection of our neighbors as a result. Our hours are constrained by not only our own teaching and other responsibilities, but the hours of each branch. For some, the publicly-funded, neighborhood-based library system may not feel like a comfortable place to seek writing support. Many might feel more secure seeking help within their community churches and social clubs. Additionally, we tend to work in public areas of the libraries, which may not be the best fit for everyone.

Also, we haven't struck the right balance in terms of utilization. At times we are at, and even over, capacity in terms of writers. At other times, we sit alone or with one other person. Attendance can also vary widely across branches, where one branch is regularly over-capacity while another is frequently under-utilized. As a result, we have begun exploring possibilities to introduce more neighbors to the drop-in writing project. For example, we have discussed the possibility of introducing workshops which might increase foot traffic and word-of-mouth, but also increases our own costs to prepare materials and workshops. In addition, we are looking into doing a better job of marketing the project. We may reach out to students in Penn's Wharton Business School to help us develop marketing materials for our community writing project. We have also explored putting up posters and visiting local churches, bodegas, pizza shops, and other places that offer an opportunity to get the word out about our writing project.

Finally, because we focused on an embedded approach, our project has been limited to the neighborhoods where faculty live. Although the neighborhood library branches where we work do serve a diverse community, our project is not reaching many of the city's neighborhoods, particularly those in North Philadelphia. In addition, this embedded approach has limited the staffing options. Most writing drop-in sessions are staffed by only one CWP faculty member. This means that if a volunteer is ill or otherwise unable to attend, then the writing drop-in session is cancelled. Likewise, if a volunteer decides to no longer continue with the project, then the library is left without the writing drop-in project altogether.

Because of this, we continue to grapple with the question of expansion. Whereas we had hoped to navigate the university-community divide by committing to an embedded model—where we worked in the neighborhoods where we lived—we now see the limitations of this model insofar as we do not have faculty who live in every neighborhood in the city. We need to think of how to serve more libraries across the city and how to do that with limited resources. Pursuing external funding may be an option, but figuring out personnel continues to be a challenge. We hope to find ways to meaningfully expand to other neighborhoods while preserving the benefits of the embedded approach.

As we navigate these changes and adjustments, we are aware that in many ways we cannot apply ready-made solutions given the unique experiences of each community and neighborhood. Thus far, our flexible, place-based approach has allowed us the ability to accommodate each new writing project a writer brings to the session. We are encouraged by these outcomes and look forward to continuing to work, revise, and develop this project as a place for writers to write in their own neighborhood.

Acknowledgments

While there are too many to name in this space, the authors would like to acknowledge all of our wonderful and hardworking colleagues at the Critical Writing Program, especially those that have helped initiate and keep this project going. In particular, we would like to acknowledge Valerie Ross for the inception of this project and her continued guidance throughout. We would also like to thank the librarians at the Free Library for being welcoming and supporting our time sharing their space. Finally, none of this would be possible without the writers who find their way to a table at their local library to sit down and share what they are working on.

Works Cited

Audunson, Ragnar. "The Public Library as a Meeting-Place in a Multicultural and Digital Context: The Necessity of Low-Intensive Meeting-Places." *Journal of Documentation*, vol. 61, no. 3, 2005, pp. 429-441, doi:10.1108/00220410510598562.

Brizee, Allen and Jaclyn M. Wells. *Partners in Literacy: A Writing Center Model for Civic Engagement*. Rowman & Littlefield, 2016.

Doggart, Julia et al. "Minding the Gap: Realizing Our Ideal Community Writing Center." *Community Literacy Journal*, vol. 1, no. 2, 2007, pp. 71-80.

Goulding, Anne. "Engaging with Community Engagement: Public Libraries and Citizen Involvement." *New Library World*, vol. 110, no. 1/2, 2009, pp. 37-51, doi:https://doi.org/10.1108/03074800910928577.

Morse, Suzanne W. *Smart Communities*. Jossey-Bass, 2014.

Nichols, Amy McCleese and Bronwyn T. Williams. "Centering Partnerships: A Case for Writing Centers as Sites of Community Engagement." *Community Literacy Journal*, vol. 13, no. 2, 2019, pp. 88-106, doi:0.1353/clj.2019.0009.

Rousculp, Tiffany. *A Rhetoric of Respect: Recognizing Change at a Community Writing Center*. NCTE, 2014.

Scott, Rachel. "The Role of Public Libraries in Community Building." *Public Library Quarterly*, vol. 30, no. 3, 2011, pp. 191-227, doi:10.1080/01616846.2011.599283.

"The State of University City 2020 Philadelphia." University City District. 2020. https://www.universitycity.org/sites/default/files/documents/The%20State%20of%20University%20City%202020_0.pdf. Accessed 10 February 2020.

Willingham, Taylor L. "Libraries as Civic Agents." *Public Library Quarterly*, vol. 27, no. 2, 2008, pp. 97-110.

Author Bios

Dana Walker, who holds a PhD in Information Science, is a Lecturer in Critical Writing at the University of Pennsylvania. Her current research focuses on information literacy. At Penn she teaches undergraduate writing seminars in communications and psychology, with experience working with a range of students from different writing backgrounds and needs. She also enjoys exploring the varied cuisines of her South Philadelphia neighborhood.

Patrick Manning is a Lecturer in Critical Writing at the University of Pennsylvania. He earned his PhD at McMaster University in English and Cultural Studies. His current research examines the cultural geography of the US Rust Belt, and he is working on a collection of short stories that considers the relationship between place, class, and gender. He lives in South Philadelphia with his spouse and two sons.

John Kehayias received a BA in Physics and Mathematics from Columbia University and a PhD in Physics from the University of California, Santa Cruz. After working for five years as a postdoctoral researcher in theoretical physics in Japan and the US, he joined the faculty of the Critical Writing Program at the University of Pennsylvania in 2017.

Reflection on "the Field"

Tiffany Rousculp

Tomorrow morning, I'm planning to talk with an old friend I haven't seen for nearly two decades. It's become commonplace to reach out like this during the COVID-19 pandemic; perhaps it's a kind of inventorying of our lives while we move through the months of uncertainty, reckoning, fear, loss, and more uncertainty. Along with many others, I've been building digital connections with people I used to (and still) love.

I've found most of these friends (or they've found me) through internet searches or a hopeful message sent to an old email address. Not this one. This one I found in the articles that you've just read. You might think I'm waxing poetic, but I'm not.

I sat down to read through the manuscripts in this collection to prepare to write this reflection. I learned about new programs and smiled as I read the words of friends and colleagues: some nearby, some on the other side of the country. Then, I opened a manuscript and saw that "Dana M. Walker" was the lead author. Seriously? She and I were friends in a different life, and the last time I had seen her was in Washington, D. C. when she helped me through a very difficult experience. Dana wasn't in community writing: she was a history major, working for some government-y thing. She was thinking of going to graduate school. I vaguely knew she had done so and that she had gotten married. It had been a long time.

During the summer, I wanted to COVID-connect with her, but there are literally hundreds of Dana Walkers in the U.S. Looking at the manuscript, I wondered if it could actually be her. How many had "M" for their middle initial? I put her name and "UPenn" into the search box and clicked on the second link.

Her picture popped up. It was her.

My mind blew. I returned to the article and read quickly. Their program in the Philadelphia Free Library system reminded me of the Salt Lake Community College Community Writing Center's (SLCC CWC) work with the Salt Lake City public library system. Then, their manuscript quoted my book, *Rhetoric of Respect*. My mind blew more. Dana (Dana M. Walker!) was working and writing in the same field that I loved so much, quoting me, while I was reading her. I sent an overexcited, entirely unprofessional email to her UPenn address and waited.

A day later she wrote back, "TIFFER!!!" She explained her career changes in a sentence and wrote that when she saw her co-author reference my book, she meant to get in touch but "pandemic…protests…etc." took her attention elsewhere. Understandable. I can't seem to keep an intention in my head longer than the time it takes to walk from the couch to the kitchen. But there she was, in my inbox, and, tomorrow, we get to talk to each other.

When Mark Latta asked me to write this piece for this collection, I was honored . . . and hesitant. Mark specifically asked me to "reflect on the state of the field." This seemed to be a request more appropriately made to one of those I had aspired to emulate, such as Linda Flower, Eli Goldblatt, Ellen Cushman, or Steve Parks. Who was I to reflect on this field, especially when I've been absent from it for nearly five years? But, as you must know (or if you don't, you should know), Mark is one of the kindest and most generous spirits I have ever met, so I said yes, not having a clue as to what I would say.

The obvious observation to start out with is that the field of community writing (or community literacy or community-engaged writing…it has forever been a challenge to name this network of nodes that are tightly and loosely connected) is maturing into a respected status within academic environments. At the same time, it continues a dance of defiance and of acquiescence to institutional expectations and exclusions in order to survive materially, and also to make new work possible. What I notice most about the field is that it has always—and likely always will—sway within the poles of defining its boundaries and breaking them. What follows is what is left of memories of my experiences in community writing and is certainly not a full—or necessarily accurate—rendering.

As I have experienced it, the academic "field" of community writing and the people within it have long both sought and rejected such an identity. In 2008, Eli Goldblatt invited me to the first-ever "symposium on community literacy" in Philadelphia.[1] I was one of about 20 people, feeling out of place as the only person from a community college. I had met a few of the participants previously, but many seemed to know each other well: Paula Mathieu, David Jolliffe, David Coogan, Linda Flower, Tom Deans (and more I can't remember…it was a long time ago). As we explored the possibility of creating a community literacy and writing network, arguments flew about who and what belonged in it and who and what did not. It could not belong only to academic institutions, but how would such a network benefit community partners (as they were referred to)? Community literacy and writing certainly included service-learning work, but it was more than that. Deans defined it as writing "about, for, and with" community, but then there were programs, like the CWC that I directed, where the community was doing the writing. It was a thrilling mess of ideas and people and possibility, but we didn't come to any conclusions.

A few years later, during CCCCs in Atlanta, Goldblatt and Parks brought together a small group of people for a lunch at Mary Mac's Tea Room. Goldblatt said there was enough happening around the country to get a group together. I participated, but mostly took notes, while Jackie Jones Royster, Juan Guerra, Kevin Reuss, Carlos Salinas, and Michelle Hall Kells talked about the possibilities of developing a national consortium. Dubbed the "National Consortium of Writing Across Communities" (NCWAC) and based on the work of Kells and Guerra (and specifically, the initiatives that Kells was leading at the University of New Mexico), this group would start with a small number of sponsor member institutions, no more than 20, with representation from all parts of the U.S. The conversations that we had in Philadelphia about who and what belonged continued: why sponsor institutions? What modalities and literacies should be included? Written, oral, visual, woven, earth? Perhaps the focus should be "semiotics across communities"? Royster argued that we needed to break down the binaries and hierarchies of research/practice/service/community, but if research wasn't a vibrant part of the NCWAC, it wouldn't survive. Still, this was a next step in a beginning. Brian Hendrickson, then a graduate student at UNM, would coordinate the development of a wiki-space for any and all interested programs, academic or otherwise. In a year, our progress would be examined at the first "National Consortium of Writing Across Communities Summit" in Santa Fe, coinciding with the WPA conference held there that year.

The year before the meeting in Mary Mac's, I had stepped down from the director position of the SLCC CWC. So that it could grow separately from me, I stepped fully away from the center, choosing not to serve on the advisory board. I was looking forward to building different community partnerships with the community college and supporting community writing colleagues within our metropolitan area and nationally. I chaired the formation of the Utah Community Literacy and Writing Coalition, which was invited to be a sponsoring member of the NCWAC, but, an insecure director forced a change of course, and I found myself divorced from the local community writing scene.

At the NCWAC Summit the next summer, some people from the Philadelphia group were in attendance, and so were Writing Across the Curriculum practitioners and teacher-scholar-activist proponents. Michelle Cox and Linda Adler-Kassner, among about 25 others, joined the cacophony about just what it was that we were trying to do. During the summit, the boundaries of community literacy and writing showed more potential—and also became even murkier. Adding to the modalities question, we now discussed what "community" was and how anyone or any group could possibly be outside it. Then, if that was the case, what was the point of belonging or not belonging to a network, consortium, or any other grouping? While Writing Across Communities had been an effective multi-functional initiative at UNM, it was too diffuse to succeed on a multi-institutional level. At the end of the summit, everyone needed a break from trying to define it.

For the next couple of years, I tried to stay involved with the national community literacy and writing conversation. I wrote *Rhetoric of Respect* based on what I'd learned from the SLCC CWC, consulted with new programs in other states, and attempted to remain a part of the developing field while not able to participate in it locally.

Then came Veronica House and the Conference on Community Writing (CCW) in 2015. The first conference, at the University of Colorado Boulder, was thrilling! Though I still felt a bit of an outsider, participating in the conference was delightful, sharing time with old friends like Beth Godbee, Tobi Jacobi, Eliana Schonberg, and Thomas Ferrell (the latter two, like me, worked at the crossroads of writing centers and community writing), and meeting new ones like Erec Smith, Lauren Rosenberg, and Paul Feigenbaum. These new friends led to other connections, including Mark Latta and Glenn Hutchinson (also writing center/community writing people), and a cyclical joy of knowing people who were passionate about the same kind of work that I was.

At the end of the first CCW, a meeting was held to consider steps towards forming a national organization. There were familiar faces (some who had always been there like Goldblatt and Parks) and new ones: some I'd heard of, some I'd read, all seemingly ready to take this collection of connections to a new level. And, with that came the same debates and arguments about what belonged in community writing and what didn't. Whose voices, what institutions, what scholarship, which practitioners? If everything belonged, then was there a field at all? And, if there wasn't a distinct field, how would the work benefit the academics who were participating in it? But, if the priority was on how it benefitted academics, wasn't that counter to the standards of reciprocity and partnership? Similar to the Santa Fe summit, emotions occasionally got heated, trying to forge the amorphous into a shape that had meaning for multiple distinct stakeholders. Again, we left unsure.

And, then it was over for me. During the next couple of years, I tried to hang on to the fringes of the developing Coalition of Community Writing, but it just wasn't possible. I had taken on a new position, founding a WAC program at the community college. I spun it off into a version of community writing, renaming it Writing Across the College, and providing similar programming to the members of the college that the CWC provided to the Salt Lake community (e.g. writing support, workshops, partnerships). Though I had tried to connect my work to the community writing field, presenting at the CCW and at CCCCs, this single boundary was clear: community writing did not take place within the boundaries of an academic institution. While the type of work and the modalities could vary—research, service-learning, partnerships, visual, oral, digital, textual, woven—the locale for community writing was not on campus. Right when it was becoming a field, I discovered I no longer belonged in it.

However, I continued to watch from loosely defined roles on editorial or advisory boards, as community writing became organized, institutionalized, and disciplinary. It found its shape, under the determined guidance of House, Mathieu, Feigenbaum, Cushman, Jacobi, Jenn Fishman, Seth Myers, Cristina Kirklighter, Shannon Carter, Deborah Mutnick, Laurie Grobman, Melody Bowdon, Smith, Elaine Richardson, Beverly Moss, Iris Ruiz, Godbee, Steven Alvarez, and, as always, Goldblatt and Parks. Many others (whom, sadly, I don't know because I've not been there; I apologize for what I know are many omissions) have been there too, pushing this project along, into what it is now. The Coalition of Community Writing's conferences and resources, working together with the (now) long-standing journals, *Reflections* and the one you are reading now, *Community Literacy Journal*, attest to the successful evolution of disparate (and desperate for connection) beginnings into a powerful and institutionalized group of scholar-activists and community partners.

The dozens of scholars, scholar-activists, teacher-scholar-activists, and community partners that currently serve on the CCW team, Board of Directors, and Advisory Board, the *Reflections* Editorial Team and Board, and the *Community Literacy Journal* Editorial Team and Board reflect the history and the future of this field. Again, familiar faces intermix with new (to me) faces in tightly and loosely connected nodes, and now with a depth that ensures a long and healthy future. The questions of who and what belong in this field—and the resistance towards codification—will likely always be a part of "community writing," but that tension, to me, is this field's beating heart. I hope it never stops.

I did get to talk to Dana M. Walker over Labor Day weekend. As expected, after the initial cries of "It's you!" and "I can't believe this!," Dana and I were who and what we used to be with each other. The only difference was that we now had the chance to talk about what we newly shared: community writing.

As I read through the other manuscripts that were sent to me, I felt kinship and admiration alongside nostalgia and loss. I learned about developments in the local Salt Lake community writing scene that I couldn't know before. I met new, passionate poets and community builders. I finally had the chance to drink in details about the detention/writing center campaigns that I learned about several years ago. And, frankly, I felt vindicated by the critique of the neo-colonial crusading of 826 Valencia. (I shed real tears while reading it.)

Even though I no longer actively participate in this beautiful field, being given the chance to do so for this moment brought me the same joy of spending some time with a dear old friend. I am grateful for the opportunity and look forward to witnessing what else is to come.

Note

1. After having learned from Eli through his writing and work with Steve Parks within the Institute of Literacy, Literature, and Culture, I finally met him in 2007 when we invited him to conduct a program review of the SLCC Community Writing Center.

Author Bio

Tiffany Rousculp was the founding director of the Salt Lake Community College Community Writing Center. After leaving the CWC a decade ago, Rousculp founded SLCC Writing Across the College, a WAC program built through community writing & literacy praxis. She is the author of the award-winning *Rhetoric of Respect: Recognizing Change in a Community Writing Center.*

Book Reviews

From the Book and New Media Review Editor's Desk

Jessica Shumake, Editor
University of Notre Dame

The reviews featured in this issue fill me with joy and pride to share because they all engage in timely conversations at the intersection of literacy, progressive coalition, pedagogy, community writing, and rhetoric and composition studies. The opportunity to learn from all four reviewers has expanded my understanding of what meaningful change and action—especially in the face of ongoing institutional, political, pedagogical, and fiscal challenges and limitations—look like *in situ* and I am grateful for each writer's time, energy, and investment. It has been a pleasure to work with Sarah Moon, Jessica Nalani Lee, Jenna Morris Harte, and Natalie Kopp on their thoughtful contributions, which advance our collective understanding of scholarship in the field of community writing.

All four of these reviews were written in the midst of the ongoing global pandemic, as racial violence, health care and educational disparities, political discord, deliberate mistruth, and ever starker socioeconomic inequities challenge us to develop more asset-based, human-centered, and ethical relationships in our communities, neighborhoods, institutions, workplaces, health care sites, correctional facilities, classrooms, and families. It is my hope that this issue's reviews serve as a call to new writers to interpret and assess work, activism, and art-based inquiry in the field of community literacy, broadly speaking, to ask questions that invite us to create a more inclusive future where more voices and perspectives can invent new conversations and spaces for belonging.

Writing Democracy: The Political Turn in and Beyond the Trump Era

Shannon Carter, Deborah Mutnick, Stephen Parks, and Jessica Pauszek, Eds.
Routledge, 2019, pp. 320

Reviewed by Sarah Moon
Massachusetts Maritime Academy

While *Writing Democracy: The Political Turn in and Beyond the Trump Era* has been assembled in direct response to Trump's America, it obviously predates the more severe democratic crisis that has flared since the spread of COVID-19 and the wave of protests in the wake of George Floyd's death. But the way our nation has responded to both of these events only heightens the urgency of the "political turn" in rhetoric and composition for which the authors call. The editors define "political turn" as they use it as "informed by Marx's theory of historical materialism and his critique of capitalism as inherently exploitative and unequal" and raise the question of whether "previous academic 'turns,' despite their acuity in some respects, have often obscured rather than clarified the historical tasks of achieving true democracy" (2–3). They write that their overarching goal is "to contribute to efforts to reclaim (or redefine) democracy as an egalitarian, inclusive, political economic system that supports human and all planetary life and well-being," while recognizing the seeming impossibility of this reclamation in the face of "climate change, unprecedented economic inequality, deeply rooted racist, sexist, and homophobic ideologies, and resurgent fascist movements and world leaders like Donald Trump and Jay Bolsonaro" (3). A list like this is enough to deflate anyone seeking to make change through their work, but the editors of this collection inspire us to try. These authors ask us to be accountable for the fact that the political commitment we exhibit as academics often "ends at the classroom door" and to commit to change that (7). Paul Feigenbaum's chapter, in this collection, focuses on inspiring progressive students to engage in activism, but one could say that *Writing Democracy* as a whole works to inspire progressive writing instructors—who are not yet doing so—to take the political turn in their classrooms. The collection, in sum, is asking teachers of writing who are already politically aligned with these authors to be brave in acting on their beliefs in their own pedagogy.

Important to those working in community literacy, the authors offer that "community engagement work—despite the best of intentions—too often underscores the problem of supporting social justice movements absent a critique of systemic inequality, escalating state repression and surveillance, and a rapacious market indifferent to human suffering" (13). The authors are clear in stressing the importance of rooting our political action in the theoretical "model of critique offered by an inclusive, consciously feminist, anti-racist Marxism" (13). Whether or not one identifies one's scholarship or teaching with a Marxist philosophy, their argument for doing so is compelling and there is much to be gained from the variety of material approaches to politically motivated teaching described in the chapters here. *Writing Democracy* is broken up into three sections: "Mapping the Political Turn," "Variations on the Political Turn," and "Taking the Political Turn."

Part I, "Mapping the Political Turn," offers primarily historical and theoretical reflections that reflect on our discipline's history of being political and helps support the Writing Democracy project's mission of troubling "democracy." The first chapter in Part I, "Composition's Left and the Struggle for Revolutionary Consciousness" by John Trimbur, serves as a powerful foundational text by debunking rhetoric and composition's supposed "progressive" legacy. In it, Trimbur disabuses compositionists of the perception of a progressive disciplinary legacy and stresses, instead, a legacy of being used by and complying with the neoliberal university while sometimes being influenced by leftist interventions (35). Trimbur notes, specifically, the controversy around University of Illinois Urbana-Champaign cancelling Steven Salaita's appointment to associate professor because of lobbying by alumni and donors who did not approve of Salaita's public criticism of Israel. NCTE, CCCC, and WPA did not choose to join other major professional associations to protest what was perceived as a political move by the university. Trimbur argues that NCTE/CCCC's lack of support for Salaita felt like a betrayal of what *had* seemed to many as a longstanding commitment to progressive ideals. This is one striking example that supports Trimbur's argument "that composition is and probably always has been not so much on a special mission" but, instead, has served as "a normal bureaucratic unit in higher education, with assets that can be leveraged for institutional aims" (35). Trimbur argues that we should understand composition to be a moderate and compliant discipline that has sometimes been influenced by "radical interventions from the left" (35).

Trimbur's next section looks at some of the results of these interventions, such as Students' Right to Their Own Language (SRTOL) in 1974 and the National Language Policy (NLP) Statement of 1988. Trimbur calls the CCCC SRTOL resolution "a historical though partial victory" and, in practice, not more than a "qualified tactical gain in the language wars" (42). He explains that the NLP statement was in part a reaction to California being the first state in the nation to make English their official language. Trimbur writes that while the NLP took an "'internationalist perspective,'" it was "cosmopolitan rather than revolutionary in outlook" (43).

Trimbur finds greater hope in the work of Neville Alexander in South Africa who worked to "*re-represent* [languages] translingually as democratic channels of reciprocal exchange in the formation of a new body politic" (44). Trimbur's piece works to set a tone of honesty about the gap between who we have been as a discipline and who many of us would like to be. He knocks us down a bit so that we might be more open to the necessity of the chapters in this book.

In chapter three, "'Organize as If It Were Possible to Create a Movement That Will Change the World' An Interview with Angela Davis conducted by LaToya Lydia Snyder and Ben Kuebrich," we receive wise guidance and inspiration from longtime political activist and Marxist feminist Angela Davis regarding how to think about activism. The authors write that Davis "calls on us as writing teachers to help create a radical collective political imagination" (51). Davis provides useful insights about the role of social media in activism, saying, "I would caution us not to assume that these new social media can actually do the work . . . of organizing. I think that's the mistake to basically subordinate ourselves to the means of communication and assume that that is about organizing a radical, progressive community of struggle" (53). Davis asserts that "A movement consists of far more than the capacity to be organized" (53–54). This something "more" is a kind of political and emotional connectedness that she doubts social media allows us to cultivate (54).

In response to organizing failures, Davis discusses how it is important to "preserve moments of promise" (54). For example, Davis notes that Occupy Wall Street "created the conditions for us to speak publicly and critically about capitalism in a way that perhaps had not been possible since the 1930s" (54). Davis seems to want to reach everyday people who are struggling to keep working for change in the face of difficulty and hopelessness. She also stresses that rather than privilege any one movement, "I would say that what is most important is the recognition of the interconnectedness of all those movements" (56). An important message was spurred by an audience member of the public interview who inquired how we can create the next Bayard Rustin. Davis replied that while it is important to know the names of great leaders of the past, holding onto those names can send a false message that "the only way you can make a difference is to be an extraordinary individual. And for people who don't see themselves as extraordinary individuals, it's kind of a message that you don't really matter" (58). Instead, Davis asserts, we need to ask, "how can we create situations so that people recognize that everybody matters, everybody can help bring about change" (58). Davis's final message speaks directly to composition instructors: "What is needed, I think, is a greater reliance on creativity, a greater reliance on the imagination and, of course, writing teachers have to really emphasize the power of the imagination" (59). Davis's inspiring exhortation to emphasize the power of the imagination is taken up later in the collection by Steven Alvarez.

In "Marxist Ethics for Uncertain Times," Nancy Welch offers a thoughtful exploration of the ethics behind the impulse to act in solidarity with social justice and union struggles such as the 2018 West Virginia Teachers' Strike. To describe her own guide for choosing to take place in activist efforts, Welch uses the term "'gut sense' solidarity" (61). Welch writes that she turns to Marxist ethics to better understand this form of motivation. Through questions such as: "*In what world shall we live?And How do we get there?* with *according to whom?* and *in whose interests?*, the Marxist ethical compass provides at any given moment a place to stand, a place from which to gain one's bearing" (61). Reflecting on the value of Marx in helping guide our political action, Welch writes that the "bedrock to historical materialism is that lived experience sets consciousness' conditions and horizons," but we need rhetoric or "the articulation of a set of counter ideas enabling the exploited and oppressed to move from existing as 'a class of itself' to acting as 'a class for itself'" (64). However, Welch notes that "neoliberal reign has fortified itself against" oppressed people's articulation of their condition "through precarious employment, anti-union legislation, and deportation threats as well as though the solidarity-shredding discourses of white supremacy, misogyny, nativism and bellicose nationalism" (65). Central to Welch's argument is the significance of *standpoint* that Marxist ethics gives us. She explains that you cannot have a universal ethical standpoint within a capitalist system that denies most humans the ability to live in ways that are most attuned to our human nature. Instead, to assess decisions morally, you have to situate yourself either with the privileged or working class. Secondly, she asserts that sectionalism is "a breach of Marx's moral vision" (Welch 71). For an example of this, Welch offers the example of "major labor unions ally[ing] their workers' interests with the capitalist class in pipeline and other extraction projects" (71). Welch notes that "these alliances and agreements reinforce rather than point the way toward overcoming a destructive order" (71). Finally, Welch asserts the importance of "reciprocal fidelity" in working class movements, quoting Lenin that "'working-class consciousness . . . cannot be genuine political consciousness unless the workers are trained to respond to *all* cases of tyranny, oppression, violence and abuse, no matter *what* class is affected" (72).

Welch shares Dana Cloud and Kathleen Feyh's term "affective fidelity" that doesn't treat emotion as "rationality's Other" and defines it as "that gut sense of certainty in an appeal's social justice promise" (73). Welch argues, importantly, that "through a grasp of affective fidelity . . . we can distinguish between one emotional appeal and another without misidentifying the presence of pathos itself as the danger" (73). This is such an important distinction as many of us allow an aversion to emotion to shut us off to the possibility of empathy and, by doing so, we lose the potential of feeling the gut sense solidarity that Welch identifies as so central to determining one's engagement in political action.

In "A Pedagogy for the Political Turn," Deborah Mutnick works to forge a Marxist pedagogy to support the historic task of addressing climate change. Mutnick writes "interrelated environmental, economic, and social problems make clear the need to connect the environmental crisis to unfinished struggles for racial, gender, and wealth equality, in essence demanding a socialist alternative to capitalism" (83). Mutnick argues that education must play a major role in the global effort to end our destructive reliance on fossil fuels and exploitative relationship to nature (84). Countering those who have argued against class focus as erasing issues rooted in racism, Mutnick writes: "rather than a type of identity commensurable with race and gender, class represents the fundamental division between those who control the relations and forces of production and those whose labor is exploited by it in the form of surplus value" (86). Mutnick writes that identity politics is "an understandable but problematic response to the failure of capitalist nations to live up to the promises of democracy" and argues that because of it, activists and teachers have ended up embroiled in debates that only end up splintering groups that could have instead been united (86). Mutnick then spends time laying out a similar view of the university that Trimbur gave us in chapter two. Mutnick writes that "this managed university works to shape the consciousness of faculty and students alike who, fearful of losing or never attaining job security, submit to anti-union, pro-business regimes" (89). She argues that the present state of society requires a "three-pronged strategy of defending the university, resisting its further corporatization, and rethinking critical pedagogy on multiple fronts beyond its walls" (Mutnick 90). Mutnick concludes by reminding us of her belief that the "failure of world governments to reduce emissions" is the clearest reason for Marxist pedagogy (99). Though as an educator, Mutnick writes that she was always cautious about letting political beliefs come through in her teaching, "this changing zeitgeist and exigency of climate change have convinced me that the time to fight for a socialist world is very possibly now or never" (101–102).

Part II, "Variations on the Political Turn" offers a number of personal takes on doing the work of the political turn as a scholar or teacher. The section begins with Stephen Parks' interview with Dana Cloud, "I'd Like to Overthrow Capitalism, But Meanwhile I Would Like the Nazis to be Completely Demoralized." In it, Cloud calls out universities, especially Syracuse, for their conflict of interest and for courting students who can pay exorbitant costs. In response to Parks' question, "What would a political turn look like if you thought of it as on-campus work?", Cloud shares her friend Brian McCann's point that "campus is real life. There are people who are oppressed here," so one can "get involved in policy making and organizing on campus that would help their labor conditions" (114–115). Cloud notes that the reason this doesn't happen more is because the academic culture is so invested in civility, the majority of faculty want to avoid antagonism with administration (115). Parks takes this up to ask: "What do you see as the purpose and effect of claims about the need for civility to politics on campus and off campus" (115). Cloud takes the opportunity to share her experience being targeted by "Nazis and white supremacists after calling for reinforcements on Twitter during a protest," which she calls one example in a "trend of harassing critical and activist scholars" (115). But she notes that the AAUP and National Communication Association "have developed toolkits and model responses" (115). Cloud then notes that though her chancellor had come out in her support, that hasn't "stopped calls for 'civility' in political debates on and off campus" (115). Cloud asserts that "the demand for civility is a form of social control and a threat to academic freedom" (115). To Parks' question, "What do you think academics who think of themselves as in the political turn should do?", Cloud responds that academics should focus on "generating ideas, testing them through action, and assessing them with your allies . . . You have to be doing that all the time, assessing yourself, and being humble about it" (120–121). In conclusion, Cloud advocates for joining "a principled socialist organization" and understanding that the common denominator in so many instances of injustice is class (121).

In Seth Kahn's "Audience Addressed? Audience Invoked? Audience Organized!", the author shares his experience striking as part of the Association of Pennsylvania

State College and University Faculty in October 2016, emphasizing how striking teachers must know how to speak to students to gain their support. Kahn notes that, "the specific context of our strike offers some illuminating lessons about understanding specific audiences as people, rather than abstractions" (123). Kahn recounts how at an open forum for students, the first few students who spoke up "told them they were being greedy" and that they "obviously 'don't care about students'" (125). Kahn says he stood up and asked whether they thought the ones who really cared about them were more likely administrators or teachers who see them in class every other day (125). Kahn writes that once the striking teachers understood students as a real audience rather than an abstraction, their ability to establish a bond of trust with them improved and notes that student support was a huge factor in their ultimate success. He writes, "I hope the examples here show concretely various kinds of communication acts, posed not as *persuasive*, but as *humane* and *trust-building*, helped APSCUF build solidarity with constituencies that have the power to help or hurt their efforts" (Kahn 129). Kahn's points align with Feigenbaum's point later in this section that as rhetoricians, we should understand the need to focus most on the audiences who are open to being persuaded and, in Kahn's case, who have power to affect the outcome of a particular struggle.

In "Taking a Lead from Student Movements in a 'Political Turn,'" Vani Kannan looks at student organizing and what faculty can learn by supporting these efforts, beginning with her own student organizing experience at Syracuse. The "campus sexual assault advocacy center," she writes, had recently closed and "students were deeply upset" (Kannan 131). She reports that fifty student groups came together to form a coalition "called THE General Body," holding "an 18-day sit-in at the university's administration building," aiming to address a wide range of grievances (Kannan 131). She was on the media team working with other students on communications to amplify the protest. Kannan pays special attention to militarization on campus, noting that "as local police forces become more heavily militarized, so do campus police" (134). At University of Maryland, she shares, students protested the university's acquisition of "'16 shotguns, two M14 rifles, and 50 M16 rifles,' along with an armored vehicle and two high-mobility, multi-purpose wheeled vehicles," all claimed by the university to help protect students in the case of a mass shooting (134). As examples of effectives student organizing, Vannan reports that students at SUNY Binghamton held a successful sit-in against the school's multi-million-dollar expenditure "on so-called community 'safety' initiatives" (134). She also briefly adds that student organizers worked to oppose Amazon headquarters in Queens, New York, which did not end up being built. Kannan is moved by students' solidarity with striking teachers and urges that "[a]s faculty, we should show this level of solidarity in student-led struggles too" (135).

In chapter nine, "Nudging Ourselves Toward a Political Turn," Paul Feigenbaum gives us one of the most actionable directives in the collection: to nudge our progressive students toward acting on their political beliefs. Feigenbaum explains that he's interested in reaching those students who have learned a kind of "political quietism" that comes with neoliberal values (138). He elaborates on this with the point that "it is possible to recognize, and even denounce, neoliberalism's individualist ethos of personal responsibility and still live according to this ethos" (138). To help illustrate the potential of students to move from quietism to political activism, Feigenbaum shares his own story of being mobilized in graduate school. He writes how he noticed at the time how few of his professors were actually politically active outside their scholarship. Feigenbaum notes that the "chronic insecurity" of neoliberal society pushes everybody, including students, into a kind of tunnel vision focused almost exclusively on whatever hurdle is next (139). As a result, social change is considered by many to be "the niche endeavors of small, fairly exclusionary groups" (Feigenbaum 139). Feigenbaum explains how "activists" thus become "an Other from which the majority of people disassociate themselves, even many who are otherwise sympathetic to a particular cause or ideology" (139). Feigenbaum was inspired by the 2008 book by Cass Sunstein and Richard Thaler *Nudge: Improving Decisions about Health, Wealth, and Happiness*. While Thaler and Sunstein call the kind of choice engineering for which they advocate "libertarian paternalism," Feigenbaum sees potential in "severing the concept of nudging from libertarian paternalism and reorienting it toward progressive ends" (142). He explains how his own graduate school professors nudged him toward political action. Notably, he reports how his union work—while in graduate school—demanded he become more comfortable speaking in groups: "I struggled to develop this skill, but had I begun this process earlier in my educational career, I might have struggled less in future roles I took on with various community organizations" (Feigenbaum 143). Though Feigenbaum doesn't state it explicitly, his observation suggests that one way we can help nudge our students toward activist engagement is by giving them opportunities to become more comfortable vocally sharing their ideas in the classroom. Additionally, Feigenbaum writes that writing teachers can help students "reassess their affective relationship to behaviors they would have avoided in the past" (146). He makes an important side note that echoes Angela Davis's response to the Bayard Rustin question that, in addition to perceiving activists as the "Other," another inhibitor to political activism can be the "progressive perfect standard" in which activist leaders are elevated to a status of perfection that students cannot imagine reaching (Feigenbaum 146). Feigenbaum helps us see that we can nudge students toward political action by helping them recognize commonality with activists, rather than transforming activists into positive or negative icons who are difficult to relate to as human beings.

In "Sustainable Audiences/Renewable Products: Penn State's Student Farm, Business Writing, and Community Outreach," Geoffrey Clegg describes teaming his business writing courses up with Penn State's Student Farm as an opportunity to "expose [students] to work that was not bent on pure capitalistic or neoliberal technological profit" (151). He begins by establishing many of the same critiques as Deborah Mutnick of the neoliberal university, and asserts that "hope lies in creating leadership that resists neoliberal imperatives within higher education" (Clegg 150). He acknowledges that this goes against the attitude of many students. Like Feigenbaum, Clegg also understands that they have been taught to think this way: "they are following the case studies, advice and models presented to them within business curriculum or looking at what mainstream Western media hypes as the newest ideals of profit-oriented decision making" (151). In the partnership between his technical and a business writing course and the Student Farm at Penn State, Clegg asked students to work together with an Agriculture Dept. faculty member to create written documents serving the farm's needs. Clegg writes that their work fit within "the critical service-learning environment advocated for by Veronica House (2014)," which asks instructors to "'[shift] the focus to intellectual rigor, problem solving, critical thinking and higher order reasoning'" and argues that a "business writing classroom offers an ideal space for critical service-learning because of the wealth of genres it employs" (Clegg 153). Clegg concludes his chapter by writing eloquently that "[t]he political turn within writing and rhetoric asks both instructors and students to resist neoliberal policies of capitalist assent by reconceiving the classroom as a site of passive learning into an active space for collaboration and direct action" (160). While he acknowledges that business writing might seem like an unlikely space for this; however, "asking business students to think local, act in tandem with local needs, and think beyond profit offers a form of resistance to what we see within the cronyism of the Trump administration" (160).

In "The Political Turn and the Two-Year College: Equity-Centered Partnerships and the Opportunities of Democratic Reform," Darin L. Jensen, one of the founders of the Teacher-Scholar-Activist blog, brings attention to two-year colleges and the tension in them between democratic and capitalist missions. He notes that graduate programs do not prepare students to teach at two-year institutions (an issue that the Modern Language Association has recognized and just begun to address through their Summer Institute for Teaching Reading and Writing). Jensen argues that our failures to prepare professionals specifically for the community college setting are "political and ethical issues. They speak to our failure as a profession and as a discipline" (163). Jensen provides some historical context for the present state of things, including quoting the Truman Commission Report that discusses scholars and teachers who are invested in "'revivify[ing] the ideals of democracy'" (164). He comments that its "language, sadly, seems almost quaint in the second decade of the 21st Century when our language surrounding education is usually reduced to mere job preparation" (Jensen 164). Jensen writes, though, that there is a teacher-scholar-activist turn among composition instructors at two-year-colleges and invites their four-year colleagues "to join us and learn from us" (165). Jensen writes that one answer to better connecting the teaching across two-year and four-year institutions is "equity-centered partnerships" which he defines as "reciprocal local agreements and programs wherein two-year college English departments and four-year colleges and universities, especially graduate programs, collaborate in creating meaningful, sustainable reforms that aid in the political turn and teacher-scholar-activist movement" (166). Among other examples of equity-centered partnerships, Jensen notes a collaboration between Salt Lake City Community College (SLCC) and University of Utah which has helped create a writing studies associates degree at SLCC and two upper-level bridge classes for students transferring to the University of Utah (169). In the conclusion of his chapter, Jensen writes that two-year college writing instructors have some great allies in four-year institutions, but "for the political turn to be a serious movement, it must reckon with how it engages two-year colleges in this labor" (172).

The authors in Part III each write about a specific political turn they or others have taken, some outside and some within the university. The section begins with the powerful "How Does It Feel to Be a Problem at the 9/11 Museum?" in which Tamara Issak provides a stakes-framed rhetorical analysis of the 9/11 Memorial and Museum that opened in May of 2014. Issak shares that she was a Muslim high school student in New Jersey on 9/11 and remembers a classmate saying in class, "'We need to kill all Muslims. Wipe them out'" (177). She then skips forward to standing in line at the 9/11 Memorial and Museum, wearing a hijab, recognizing the "problem" she poses in her mere presence. Issak reminds us how Trump spouted hateful and false comments about Muslims in his election campaign and that there are real, terrible consequences to this rhetoric: "data shows that there is more of a correlation between anti-Muslim rhetoric and anti-Muslim attacks than there is between terrorist attacks and anti-Muslim incidents" (178). Issak states that "Given the rise of anti-Muslim and anti-Arab racism, it is crucial for composition and rhetoric scholars to examine Islamophobic rhetoric" (179). These life and death consequences of persistent anti-Muslim prejudice frame her argument that the 9/11 Memorial and Museum helps foment Islamophobia (Issak 179). Issak points out that the museum sets up a clear dichotomy between "an American 'us'" and "an un-American/Muslim 'them'" (181). Supporting her point, she shares that lesson plans on the museum's website, which suggest books by Afghani authors *The Kite Runner* and *A Thousand Splendid Suns*, pose questions that reinforce "the idea of Muslims as foreign, particularly with [their] focus on the status of women" (Issak 181). On the surface, the lesson plans purport to be about "'understanding others'" but ultimately work to reassert "the hierarchy of American cultures above other cultures" (Issak 181). Sharing that other scholars have taken issue with the approach of the museum, Issak writes that eleven members of the interfaith panel reviewing the film *The Rise of Al Qaeda*, shown in the historical exhibition section of the museum, wrote a letter outlining their concerns that the video "'may well leave viewers with the impression that all Muslims bear some collective guilt or responsibility for the actions of al-Qaeda" and could help spur anti-Muslim "'bigotry or even violence'" (182). Ultimately, Issak powerfully calls on rhetoric and composition scholars to take a critical approach to any 9/11 materials they incorporate in their classroom and to work to consciously oppose Muslim stereotypes both within and outside the university.

In "Dismantling the Wall: Analyzing the Rhetorics of Shock and Writing Political Transformation," Steven Alvarez connects the terror of shock politics with a call that echoes Angela Davis's earlier in the collection for writing teachers to tap into student imagination. Emphasizing walls as metaphors, Alvarez seeks to encourage writing teachers to help students imagine how they can help dismantle conceptual walls. Alvarez writes that Trump's wall "became a way to disparage the perceptions of Latinx and Latin American immigrant communities and question citizenship status, while using racism as a tactic for pushing through privatizing austerity measures" (192). He wants composition instructors to consider the kinds of projects they can assign that allow students to "imagine a social field that is inclusive of racial, ethnic, religious, and gender divides" (Alvarez 193) Taking inspiration from Naomi Klein's *The Shock Doctrine*, Alvarez argues that "the rhetorical analysis of neoliberal 'shock' politics is the first step for students to understand the utopian possibilities for political transformation and dissent, possibilities that reveal how the politics of division and separation have alienated collective action" (193). For student reading to introduce the work of breaking down internal walls, Alvarez suggests *Read Donald Duck: Imperialist Ideology in the Disney Comic* about Donald Duck cartoons that circulated in Latin America "that did propagandist work" (199). Students can, through analysis of this text, "understand how 'shock' can become a tool of the state to further a neoliberal agenda by a populace disoriented from disastrous events" (199). Alvarez proposes that writing classrooms be spaces where "students can potentially speak back to shock politics through speculative writing" (201). Students' fictional counterstories have the potential to counteract the hyper individualism of neoliberal America and, as Alvarez quotes Aja Y. Martínez, the power to "'help to strengthen traditions of social, political and cultural survival and resistance'" (202). An appendix to Alvarez's piece provides an assignment description for composing speculative fiction which instructors can adapt to their own classrooms.

In "Pass the Baton: Lessons from Historic Examples of the Political Turn, 1967–68," Shannon Carter explores the Silent Protest of Tommie Smith and John Carlos raising their fists on the medal platform at the 1968 Olympics with an emphasis on the networks that allow for the circulation of protest messages and images that inspire others. She writes that "the image of the silent protest is still helping "move the needle toward justice . . . *today*, as that iconic image circulates, gaining momentum in the aftermath of Trump's election" (221). Carter explains how the Silent Protest was an outgrowth of a proposed Olympic boycott that gained traction after officials stripped Mohammed Ali of his heavyweight title. Tommie Smith was asked by a Japanese reporter at the 1967 World Games in Tokyo about the potential of an Olympic boycott. Carter writes that Smith reports that being asked this question triggered his political engagement. Carter shares that Carlos notes reading a later interview with Smith in *Track and Field News* as activating his own engagement. Media coverage of the Olympic Project for Human Rights (OPHR) at a Western Black Youth Conference meeting over Thanksgiving 1967 further encouraged black political resistance to being used as pawns in the Olympics. Carter quotes Founder Henry Edwards speaking at the Conference: "'It is time for the black people to stand up as men and women and refuse to be utilized as performing animals for a little extra dog food'" (216). Carter reports how, for a number of reasons, including the death of Martin Luther King Jr., OPHR no longer existed by the time Smith and Carlos raced, but the Silent Protest would not likely have taken place without it. Carter uses the metaphor of passing the baton to stand for the nodes in circulating networks of ideas and images that serve as flashpoints to inspire new activists. She asks us to pay particular attention to the role the circulation of texts plays in mobilizing political action. Carter's piece stands out in the collection in its offer of an area rich with potential for further scholarship.

In "The Visa Border Labyrinths: 310 Colombian and U.S. Artists and Scholars Write Their Way Through," Tamera Marko helps readers consider with greater importance the process of composing a visa application. Marko's perspective on the significance of the visa-writing process is informed by her eleven years teaching "a transnational First-Year Writing class in which students in the United States and students in Colombia write U.S. visa applications together" (235). The project is called PBM "Proyecto Boston Medellín" (235). Marko explains that in this program Emerson students of writing and art students from Universidad Nacional de Colombia in Medellín collaborate across two semesters "to do the research and writing necessary for the Colombian students to come to the United States and exhibit their art" (236). Marko writes, "I believe that navigating visa labyrinths should be listed on a curriculum vitae and discussed in cover letters and job interviews" (258). She makes a compelling argument for writing teachers and students to understand the depth and complexity of the visa writing process that many of our colleagues must undergo to study and teach with us.

In their conclusion, Shannon Carter, Deborah Mutnick, Stephen Parks, and Jessica Pauszek return to the primary exigency for *Writing Democracy*: that Trump's election "emboldened" racism and race-related violence across the nation (262). The editors articulate that it is "imperative that we forge solidarity based on anti-racist, feminist, pro-labor, internationalist principles" if we hope to build a movement to oppose the current power structure that "persists even in the face of catastrophe in placing profit above human need" (Carter et al. 262). The collection editors concur on building from a foundation of Marxist ethics, which they stress alongside of the importance of intersectionality: "[t]he political turn we advocate will not work without a deep understanding of how racism and sexism and other specific forms of oppression are both interlocking and interwoven into the history and logic of capitalism" (Carter et al. 269). As pedagogues of the political turn, they view rhetoric and composition's work as two-pronged: first, encouraging a critical consciousness of neoliberal capitalism and second, spurring action to join activist struggles. A third bridging-prong that emerges in the interview with Angela Davis and Steven Alvarez's piece is inspiring students' imaginative faculties to compose visions of alternative futures. The editors end by reminding us of "Davis's invocation 'to act as if it were possible' and Welch's description of a '"Marxist moral compass"' toward envisioning a society designed to "meet human need rather than reap private profits" (Carter et al. 271). The editors leave readers then with a hanging question that serves as its own generative entry point for pedagogues whose sense of purpose aligns with the authors in this collection: What *are* human needs? If the answer is not taken as manifest, this question could spur a powerful prelude to the kind of critical investigation which many of these authors encourage us to lead in our classrooms. In answering this question with our guidance and through consideration of additional resources, students can generate and perhaps debated their own lists of human needs, informed by each individual's distinct perspective and illustrating the places where perspectives overlap. We can then begin critique from a classroom-generated and openly discussed point of view in which everyone feels represented. In 2020, the U.S. is in dire need of the critical consciousness and activist intervention for which the authors in this collection call. The urgency for teaching toward a reclamation of democracy has not in our lifetimes been greater. The chapters in this collection provide reality checks, an ethical foundation, inspiration, and practical routes to action that can help us each be brave in taking our own political turn.

Transforming Ethos: Place and the Material in Rhetoric and Writing

Rosanne Carlo
Utah State University Press, 2020, pp. 208

Reviewed by Jessica Nalani Lee
Portland Community College

Recent social justice awakenings such as the "Me, too" movement and Black Lives Matter indicate a rising social consciousness that understands that perpetuating privilege is itself a form of complicity. In *Transforming Ethos: Place and the Material in Rhetoric and Writing*, Rosanne Carlo fortifies movement against complicity as she decries current undertakings in rhetoric and composition that would discount expressivist writing as integral to the desired outcomes for writing in higher education. In particular, Carlo implores rhetoric and composition scholars to consider the ways in which the field's preoccupation with outcomes and professionalization ignore the material realties of class and race consciousness. Through a careful synthesis of theory, personal explication, and pedagogical example, Carlo offers insight into how a transformative ethos—rooted in place and the material—is central to writing that produces identification across difference.

Transforming Ethos' introduction, "Rhetoric and Writing for Ethos Development, Not Transfer" establishes the relevance of 'transformative ethos' in light of three current discursive sites in field of rhetoric and composition: 1) the WPA Outcomes Statement (Council of Writing Program Administrators 2019); 2) *Naming What We Know: Threshold Concepts in Writing Studies* (Adler-Kassner and Wardle 2015) and its attendant theory of threshold concepts; and 3) *Writing Across Contexts: Transfer, Composition, and Sites of Writing* (Yancey, Robertson, and Taczak 2015) and its attendant curricular application of teaching for transfer. Through critical analysis, Carlo elucidates how all three promote an agenda that privileges skills and modes of professionalization that are demonstrable, quantifiably speaking, as transferrable to other writing done in the university. Carlo explains that she finds transfer pedagogies problematic in their single-minded focus on creating "expert" voices. Focusing on making students experts in their disciplines, Carlo warns, privileges a rhetoric that "becomes entrenched in the institutions where we teach, which many in the field have reminded us reflects a privileging of standard English, whiteness, middle classness, maleness" (20). Carlo concludes that consequently, "when we agree that the work of composition is teaching the disciplinary knowledge of writing for students to transfer to other disciplines, we may be opening a Pandora's Box that spews out white supremacist, violent rhetorics I think many people in the field do want to stand against" (20). The central argument of *Transforming Ethos* is an alternative to continuing to "kowtow to the needs of business rather than to the needs of community" (Carlo 16). Carlo aims to demonstrate that the "connections among ethos, materiality, and place are powerful instruments for writing and its teaching," to insist "on the relational and multimodal aspects of writing" and make "prominent its inherent ethical considerations and possibilities" (19).

Chapter one, "Finding a Transformative Definition of Ethos," shifts away from the introduction's spotlight on "extreme pragmatists that focus on datasets and outcomes" to elucidate the theoretical foundation upon which Carlo builds her definition. Carlo constructs a definition of ethos by drawing from the concept of Burkean identification, "contemporary and ancient discourse on ethos in relation to time (Kairos), space (gathering place), and Martin Heidegger's concept of dwelling, relying on his theories on the call of language" (27). Carlo expresses her desire to have her book "expand the term *ethos* beyond the Aristotelian definition—beyond a constructed appeal through words—and out into a theory of transforming identities" (33). Carlo explains that, given that Aristotle's *ethos* is based in textual appeal (constructed) and Plato and Isocrates' *ethos* is based in the character of the speaker (revealed), she suggests *ethos* be viewed as "three pronged: (1) character as lived experience, (2) character as expressed in text, and (3) character as expressed in the material (place and objects)" (36–37). It is this third facet of *ethos*, the material of place and objects, that Carlo explains is the focus of her book, with chapter two focusing on the ethos appeals as developed through interactions with objects, chapter three on places, and chapter four applying transformative theory of ethos to the first-year college writing classroom.

Chapter two, "Finding and Collecting: Stories on Material Objects and the Ethos Appeal" is a beautiful interweaving of personal narrative with textual analysis to enfold materialist writings such as Benjamin's "Unpacking My Library" (1969), Barthes's *Camera Lucida* (1980), and Corder's *Lost in West Texas* (1988) into a transformative theory of ethos. This chapter serves as a model of sorts for the type of writing Carlo is admonishing rhetoricians and compositionists to not overlook for the sake of neatly fitting into administrative-mandated outcomes. Chapter two carefully considers "writing that houses contradictions," (56) with the consideration itself acknowledging the limitations of Carlo's own knowledge. Through Carlo's synthesis of the materialist scholarship of philosophers (Barthes 1980; Benjamin 2002; Bennet 2001, 2010; Derrida 1996), rhetorical scholars (Corder; Kinneavy 1979; Shipka 2011, 2015), and literary theorists (hooks 1994, 2009; Sontag 1973; Stewart 1993), she contemplates how such works illuminate the material as both subject and object, interacted upon and themselves interacting (62). Recognizing the agency of material objects, in turn, allows us to "understand that inhabiting the world is a process" others undertake through their relationships to objects (Carlo 63). To discern this process, Carlo adopts the "provisional stance" (47) she recommends in chapter one, inviting rhetoricians and compositionists to discuss the material by considering how they already apply and have yet to apply the terms "thing-power, affect, character, narrative, time, and becoming" (67). After providing a brief commentary for each of these material key terms in relation to her larger discussion on ethos and identification from chapter one, Carlo notes the importance of this endeavor as "things ground us in the world, and though they cannot speak, they contribute to our inventive capacities as we speak of them and for them" (70). Next, Carlo proceeds to use the key terms she has defined to study the materialist musings of Corder, Benjamin, Barthes, and hooks in succession, in order to better understand how humans relate to things and, in turn, how this understanding can foster more meaningful connections between people. More specifically, this commonality brings people together because, "when we understand that inhabiting the world is a process others undertake through their objects, we begin to see others' values" and their character emerges (Carlo 93). In this way Carlo expands our rhetorical understanding of ethos as it is revealed through objects.

Chapter three, "Movement: The Possibilities of Place and Ethos Appeal," continues to explore how character is developed and communion with others is undertaken through engagements with the material, with a shift of focus from objects to places. What I find most compelling about Carlo's discussion of ethos in relationship to place is her illumination of "a continual attunement to place" through movement as rhetorical practice (28). Once again, Carlo pushes us to move beyond traditional, limiting conceptions, declaring that "getting into place is rhetorical, and not just in the sense of understanding the context of a rhetorical situation as a backdrop for speech acts" (97). Rather, Carlo states that she follows Thomas Rickert's (2013) lead in *Ambient Rhetoric*, where he argues that "rhetoric cannot and should not be contained, particularly to an agent's actions and even further to a system of linguistic or symbolic meaning that can only be perceived by human agents" (97). The process of getting into place, or dwelling, Carlo clarifies, is reciprocal, with human and place both having agency: "we are continually creating place and yet place's originary impulse of dwelling means place shapes us" (99). Carlo consults scholarship from Jim W. Corder and José Esteban Muñoz, elegantly interspersing her own narrative reflection in this chapter as well, this time including interactions with her dissertation advisor and mentor, Theresa Enos, to demonstrate the ways in which "we're compelled to write to not forget, to not forget places and loved ones and cultures" (104). Carlo confesses: "I keep thinking if I get Corder down, if I heed Theresa's imperative to write the book, he won't be lost, and neither will she," and it is admissions like these that add power to Carlo's injunctions, demonstrating that she is not only talking the talk of espousing expressivist writing, but walking the walk.

Central to her discussion of place is Carlo's use of the Greek term *chôra* in lieu of rhetoric and composition's more commonly used *topoi*. Carlo expounds on her preference for using *chôra* over *topoi*, stating that *chôra* is beyond the concept place in that it is a "generative place for the creation of places," taking on "the qualities of the places and things it holds, and thus it is a hard term to be 'reached' or 'touched,' as Jacques Derrida (1995) notes" (111). The elusive nature imbued in *chôra* is what Carlo is drawn to, as she "desire[s] to shift the thinking of place" as *topoi* "to place as *chôra* in order to see place as a thing that withdraws from speakers and wanderers" (111). Carlo goes on to outline *chôra* as spatial, (non)discursive, and embodied and then posits a way into *chôra* by probing memory's etherealness (122). She uses the imagery of a fold to complicate our comprehension of our relationship to place, inviting us to envision our bodies folded into places: "subjective memory cannot exist without the sensuous perceptions of the body," as well as our memories (Carlo 125). Like chapter two's description of objects this conception of place has agency, though this agency appears to make place more elusive, necessitating movement—whether in mind or in body—or what Carlo terms "wandering" (130). For Carlo, wandering is a "practice for how to recover and understand ethos beyond its written manifestations" (132). Ultimately, Carlo promises, "learning these methods of tracing the self and others through place—practicing a hermeneutics through movement that interrogates the *chôra*, or that withdraws—can lead to a discourse that is rich in possibility and holds an inventive stance toward the self, others, and the future" (134). Furthermore, Carlo adds, this inventive stance toward the self, others, and the future offers "reasons for writing outside the concept of transfer" (135).

Having demonstrated reasons for writing outside the concept of transfer, through an explication of a transformative ethos as expressed in the material of place and objects, Carlo concludes the book with a fourth chapter: "For an Affective, Embodied, Place-Based Writing Curriculum: Student Reflections on Gentrifying Neighborhoods in New York City." Carlo makes sure to clarify that this closing chapter is *not* a definitive guide for practicing a pedagogy with ethos and identification at its center, but rather is meant to "begin a dialogue for a different goal for composition—one for which we put aside issues of transfer [. . .] and take up subjects that remind us of rhetoric's ethical potentialities for being with and working to understand others" (136). Carlo summarizes the place-based curriculum she developed and taught at the College of Staten Island CUNY, which includes an overview of the theory, readings, and assignment activities for the following: a photo essay, a critical-response essay, and an argumentative essay. She also includes an analysis of student papers for both the photo essay and the argumentative essay. When describing her assignment of "place photo essays," Carlo discusses the ways in which expressive writing may well serve students in the "real world" more than academic writing ever could; how "remedial" students are served by valuing their ways of knowing and expertise (place-based pedagogy), rather than being rigidly made to conform to academic standards; and "writing to be understood" as alternative to—or further, more complex extension of—argumentative writing. Carlo's "critical analysis essay" assignment is a great model for how students can be introduced to a controversy in a scaffolded way. Herein Carlo's curriculum offers students a variety of views on a topic (rather than requiring students to find those views themselves), as well as examples of questions that help students think critically about the various viewpoints provided. For her argumentative essay assignment, which she calls "the weigh-in essay," Carlo describes the transitioning students from analyzing a controversy to taking a stance in a public argument. She states that a goal for the weigh-in essay is "for students to view issues through a perspective that allows them to see and critique racial and class inequality" (Carlo 162–163).

Carlo's book, as a whole, drives home a timely message: by myopically focusing on how students can thrive inside the academy, we devalue the ways the literacy of their everyday lives can sustain them in the day-to-day, perpetuating a system that privileges academic ways of knowing and being over other equally valid ways. Critics of the book may take issue with Carlo's staunch insistence on the negative implications of threshold concepts and teaching for transfer, arguing that such approaches allow students to gain access to a system that, for better or worse, is necessary to abide within in order to succeed. Yet attempts to improve students' economic mobility at the expense of erasing their material reality can be self-defeating. Community literacy scholars will do well to read this book and discover insights that can help them implement a transformational curriculum that celebrates, rather than attempts to assimilate the community members with whom we engage.

Conceptions of Literacy: Graduate Instructors and the Teaching of First-Year Composition

Meaghan Brewer
Utah State University Press, 2020, pp. 170

Reviewed by Jenna Morris Harte
Georgia State University

Most teachers can likely recall a host of "rookie mistakes" they made as they began their careers. Indeed, while one's level of preparedness for teaching varies depending on the context, Meaghan Brewer in *Conceptions of Literacy: Graduate Instructors and the Teaching of First-Year Composition* acknowledges the particular challenges graduate students face when teaching composition for the first time. As Brewer points out, graduate instructors often do not have a foundational understanding of composition theory, and in many cases, have never before taken a first-year composition course. Despite these challenges, Brewer points out that graduate instructors teach nearly a quarter of all composition classes, making her work in *Conceptions* particularly relevant to the state of the field (3). Too, well known within the discipline of rhetoric and composition, and another challenge for graduate instructors, is that there are many approaches to teaching first-year writing. Navigating the dynamics of a classroom for the first time, and also coming to terms with the multiplicity inherent to composition studies, can be daunting.

To help graduate instructors reconcile their past experiences in education, their personal ideas about teaching, and the myriad approaches to composition pedagogy, Brewer suggests providing graduate instructors with a background in literacy studies. Brewer makes the case that approaches to teaching composition stem from the individual teacher's preconceived conceptions of literacy. In doing so, Brewer provides a nuanced, theoretical framework for helping new and seasoned teachers alike to reconcile what might initially seem like variations or inconsistencies in the discipline. While researchers have certainly articulated that identity and prior experience shape pedagogy, Brewer's attention to literacy studies, and the dimensions of literacy, offers an original and innovative interpretation for how a metacognitive awareness of literacy practices can empower a graduate student instructor to begin to conceptualize his or her own framework for teaching writing. Brewer hopes that her book will be useful to graduate instructors and writing program administrators, and I have full confidence in Brewer's ability to reach her intended audience. Beyond the audience Brewer addresses directly, though, I personally have been teaching composition for five years and still found that her work challenged my own conceptions of literacy in relation to teaching. Brewer's book is critical to composition pedagogy and literacy studies, as it makes visible the ways that personal beliefs regarding literacy—along with one's past experiences—impact the choices we make as teachers of writing.

Brewer defines conceptions of literacy by leaning on scholarship from Peter Goggin and focuses on three positions: literacy for personal growth, cultural literacy, and social/critical literacy. To illustrate these conceptions, Brewer presents case studies of six individual English graduate students who were teaching composition as instructors of record for the first time. Brewer acknowledges the limitations of the scope of her inquiry, pointing out that the small group of graduate instructors does not represent diverse perspectives in terms of race and gender, but rather that they reflect the demographics of the practicum course she observed at her "Public University." Interestingly, Brewer analyzed students with creative writing, literature, and rhetoric and composition foci to make visible the way that allegiance to a particular discipline influences one's perception of what it means to be "literate." Through conducting interviews, observing their teaching, and analyzing their literacy narratives, Brewer concludes that the prior experiences the graduate students had—experiences connected to their disciplines of choice and also personal life events—influenced how the graduate instructors took on the task of teaching composition. Indeed, even more than the theory learned from the teaching practicum course, prior conceptions of literacy dictated what graduate instructors privileged when teaching composition. With this knowledge, Brewer emphasizes the importance of recognizing the connections between an instructor's existing conceptions of literacy and composition pedagogy practices.

In examining the pedagogical perspectives of the graduate instructors, Brewer carefully strikes a balance of valuing the work done by new instructors, and also critiquing it, to model how a WPA or composition practicum professor might provide support. First, in a chapter titled "Yoga Ashrams and Mother-Teachers," Brewer explains that "literacy for personal growth" relates to expressivist pedagogy in that it foregrounds the personally transformative nature of writing in a quasi-mystical way. A teacher drawn to valuing this conception of literacy might avoid being formulaic or espouse that writing "cannot be taught" (39). Candidly, Brewer explains that she does not align herself pedagogically with the students she analyzes here; she instead mentions that the perception might be "problematic . . . particularly if [the instructors] implicitly believe composition courses can't foster 'real' writing (which isn't learned or learnable but inspired)" (35). Yet, in drawing connections between expressivist pedagogies and literacy for personal growth, Brewer helps to justify the viewpoints of the graduate instructors that she analyzes, even while simultaneously critiquing their methodologies; Brewer notes that these particular students are focused on the pursuit of doctorates in Rhetoric and Composition, and she posits that this disciplinary focus influences the conception of literacy made visible through pedagogical choices to enforce what she terms as "dated" perceptions of the power of writing (57). Brewer analyzes the graduate instructors in action, and in a couple of instances, argues that a few teaching moments could have been reconstructed not to replace their expressivist proclivities, but to realign them with more critical, teachable notions of writing, such as genre awareness or the importance of workshopping (56). In the end, Brewer explains both the values and limitations of the conceptions of literacy for personal growth, and also provides advice for how to help further develop these ideologies to bolster instructors' efficacy as teachers of writing.

In addition to valuing and critiquing the graduate instructors' methodologies, Brewer is interested in the origins of the conceptions of literacy espoused, and also investigates how willing instructors are to challenge their own long-held beliefs about literacy. In "Texts, Hierarchy, and Ritual," Brewer moves on to showcase how perceptions of literacy as "cultural," as more rooted to textual analysis and, in some cases, the stereotypes of "ivory tower" academia can develop based on past experiences and personally held philosophical beliefs that privilege the superiority of literature. In particular, Brewer analyzes a graduate instructor who self-identifies as a conservative Presbyterian. This student happened to be studying literature for his PhD; as such, his religious reverence of biblical text had, according to Brewer, manifested in an ideology that seemed equate literacy with "salvation" (78). Brewer warns of the exclusionary nature of this kind of literacy, making suggestions that a focus on the perception of literacy as not just an ability to analyze literature could provide a broader appreciation of the many ways to be literate. Though Brewer followed these graduate students for only one semester, she tracks growth in their perceptions of literacy, but the growth did not necessarily develop based on their encounters with composition theory—she mentions that one student in particular "both changed and stayed the same" (60). Later in the book, Brewer mentions that the instructors had a "tendency to not mention the practicum" as being influential, which "suggests the power of their literacy conceptions" (138). Here, Brewer points out that the focus on providing the graduate instructors with theory in a composition practicum had less influence on their development of teaching practices than what the students already believed about literacy. In making the strength of conceptions of literacy visible, Brewer does not discount the work performed by practicum professors, but instead emphasizes the command of personally held beliefs about literacy.

In her final case study, "Graduate Students at the Threshold," Brewer discusses two creative writing graduate students and makes the case that their focus on creative writing allowed them to be more open to what Brewer calls "social/critical" conceptions of literacy. Quoting Goggin, Brewer explains that this line of thinking focuses on literacy as being "ideologically situated in social contexts" (99). For Brewer, this is the ideal perception of literacy to hold as a composition instructor; moreover, she makes the case that the creative writing students were more willing to adopt this ideological viewpoint than their peers in literature or rhetoric and composition. Brewer found that the creative writing graduate students were more willing to see identity as "fluid," and to think about how "literature can forward arguments" and be considered contextually (107). Brewer argues that composition engages with "practical and political concerns," and, therefore, thinking about the social constructions that determine literacy is key for composition instruction (107). Worth noting is that by situating the creative writing students as, perhaps, best suited to teach composition, Brewer advances an inclusive perspective regarding the teaching of composition. Brewer also emphasizes the ideological nature of literacy and underscores that literacy is situated socially, which she sees as a key perspective to embrace to teach writing well.

Though she values the work performed by graduate students, due to her focus on the ways in which literacy studies improves graduate student teaching, Brewer ignores labor concerns in First-Year Composition, particularly considering the instability of graduate student labor in general, and the misuse of adjunct labor in the field more broadly. Furthermore, Brewer neglects to develop an additional line of inquiry that might more carefully observe Harvey Graff's *The Literacy Myth* and Michael Harker's *The Lure of Literacy*. While Brewer mentions each of these works, she pivots each time, choosing a more optimistic perspective of literacy, especially in light of Harker's insinuation that debates surrounding compulsory composition are ever-present in higher education because we expect "too much" of both literacy and those who teach it (24). Further, Harker's outright criticism of systemic inequalities in higher education implicitly calls for a reimagining of what educators and administrators should expect to have students achieve in writing and rhetoric courses. While Brewer acknowledges Harker's position in the closing lines of her manuscript, a more in-depth consideration of literacy myths could be explored in her next book project.

Brewer begins and ends *Conceptions of Literacy* by discussing transfer theory and threshold concepts to make visible the challenges of being a new composition instructor. Generally, both transfer theory and threshold concepts are ways of thinking about the work undergraduate students perform as they encounter college writing for the first time. Yet Brewer does not align "novice" teachers with freshmen writers to demean their expertise. Instead, Brewer points out what is at stake if graduate students are not supported: the inherent difficulty of encountering threshold concepts involved with the teaching of reading, writing, and argumentation might cause graduate instructors to "abandon these views [of literacy] and the teaching that stems from them" (117). Worth noting is that Brewer's book, besides its omission of the labor crises and its optimism regarding the power of literacy, does empower graduate instructors, WPAs, and those who teach writing and rhetoric practicum courses to consider the factors—including literacy—that contribute to our long-held beliefs about what matters most in composition courses. In doing so, Brewer's book refreshingly explores writing pedagogy—and the voices of those teaching it—in meaningful and personal ways that will engage readers from start to finish.

Works Cited

Graff, Harvey. *The Literacy Myth: Cultural Integration and Social Structure in the Nineteenth Century*. Taylor & Francis, 1991.

Harker, Michael. *The Lure of Literacy: A Critical Reception of the Compulsory Composition Debate*. SUNY Press, 2015.

Beyond Progress in the Prison Classroom: Options and Opportunities

Anna Plemons
CCCC/NCTE Studies in Writing
and Rhetoric, 2019, pp. 185

Reviewed by Natalie Kopp
The Ohio State University

"After three hours I will go out the way I came in, but while I am here, we will write from deep wells, some recently discovered under the concrete strewn with broken glass and bits of bone" (Plemons 7). The concrete upon which Anna Plemons and her students write is that of California's New Folsom Prison, and the aforementioned sentence—from one of her nonfiction essays—is a near-perfect encapsulation of what brought her to write *Beyond Progress in the Prison Classroom*. As a long-time community writing instructor in the Arts in Corrections program at New Folsom, Plemons has spent years thinking not only about the "deep wells" discovered by her incarcerated students but also about how these students must play an active role in shaping their writing curriculum—how it should not be defined solely by people who can come and go at will "the same way they came in" (7). Plemons' classroom space is one in which, for different incarcerated writers, the act of "writing in community will fall somewhere between fully transformative and merely entertaining" (7). And yet, Plemons and her students exist in a world in which personal "transformation," as defined by non-incarcerated people, is often the required outcome for all incarcerated writing and for the continued existence and funding of prison arts programming. It is Plemons' personal experience with and reflection on these issues that inform this book.

In *Beyond Progress*, Plemons makes the case for a classroom pedagogy that moves beyond colonially-driven narratives of transformation. She argues that, when we as teachers and compositionists stop prioritizing student narratives based on individual transformation—narratives that position incarcerated students as personally responsible for their incarceration and in need of self-driven transformation through writing and education—we can begin to recognize larger webs of relationality that inform the lives of our students and the social factors that lead to incarceration.

While Plemons' study focuses on the teaching and writing done in the Arts in Corrections (AIC) program, her aim is to view the program as a microcosm for rhetoric and composition classrooms at large and the change that must be made in them to move beyond colonial ways of thinking. The theoretical framework of Plemons' book is one based in Indigenous scholarship rooted in relationality and respect. Plemons' writing combines theory and storytelling, and the book's four chapters are separated and introduced by four "Writers and Teachers" sections, composed of topical creative prose and poetry by AIC participants and Plemons.

Plemons begins in the first chapter, "Getting Inside: Measuring Something Other Than Progress", with a review of scholarship explaining the problem with the transformation narratives and emancipatory projects that remain prevalent in prison and college composition classrooms. She does not merely disavow these narratives through theory but brings to light some of the real-world reasons they persist, highlighting, for one, that many prison writing programs must adhere to the desires of funding organizations that commodify incarcerated students by requiring proof of transformative outcomes such as reduced recidivism. Instead of coercing incarcerated writers to produce the non-nuanced narratives others often expect, Plemons, in the book's second chapter, builds "The Case for Relationality as Decolonial Practice." Some scholar-teachers fail to recognize or envision their incarcerated students outside of prison, in turn failing to understand the many ways in which students seek to reconnect to their place in the outside world. Plemons calls for the work of "re-membering"—as opposed to dismembering, or separating parts from a whole—in the classroom. A strength in these first two chapters is the way in which Plemons allows her experiences as a community teacher-scholar to strengthen and add nuance to her theoretical framework. Plemons acknowledges, for one, that students themselves sometimes perpetuate transformation narratives and may desire to envision their stories in this way. She writes about the "need to show respect for incarcerated writers even when and perhaps especially when they do not share my own philosophical orientation" and demonstrates a respect for student writing that is not outshined by adherence to any one theoretical perspective (Plemons 28). At the same time, she describes the "yes/and" complications revealed by some of her students when writing proves "transformational *and* yet not quite so" and stresses the harsh reality that, while writing may prove personally rewarding for incarcerated student writers, it cannot lead to freedom from incarceration (Plemons 52). In these chapters, Plemons speaks openly about her own positionality in her work and the personal history of her involvement with AIC, and she embraces the personal and its influence on our scholarship.

In the third chapter, "Toward Relational Methodologies: Learning from the Work of Indigenous Scholars", Plemons outlines the Indigenous scholarship that influences her theory of the prison as a relational space and cites Indigenous scholars directly without, in the words of Zoe Todd, "filtering ideas through white intermediaries" (87). She proposes a relational methodology, based on the work of Margaret Kovach, for other prison scholar-teachers to consider adopting. This five-point methodological model calls for decolonial intention and ethic, research preparation, community accountability, reciprocity/community benefit, and knowledge gathering/meaning-making (Plemons 102).

The fourth chapter, "Opportunities and Options: Relationality at New Folsom", takes this five-point methodology and uses it to evaluate some of the specific programs at AIC, namely the family arts (FA) program, which includes initiatives such as a writing exchange between incarcerated students and family members and guitar lessons with concerts held during visiting hours. Instead of relying on a deficit model to justify its existence, the FA program aims to "position incarcerated people as cultural assets in their respective communities and actively support them in that role" (Plemons 122). Until this chapter, the book relied primarily on theory and storytelling to make its pedagogical suggestions and included few specifics from the AIC classroom. This chapter gives readers who work or are interested in doing work as prison teacher-scholars concrete pedagogical examples and a way to measure their impact quantitatively that does not commodify incarcerated students.

Beyond Progress concludes with an afterword in which series editor Steve Parks facilitates a conversation between author and Indigenous scholar Kristin L. Arola in order to discuss the ethical issues that arise when non-Indigenous scholars work to implement Indigenous and decolonial theories. The conversation provides additional insight into Plemons' positionality as a white scholar relying on Indigenous scholarship and digs into complex questions about citing the stories and scholarship of those with different traditions, backgrounds, and histories than those of the writer. While these questions cannot be answered fully in a short afterward, the section does provide a uniquely personal view of Plemons' writing and research process alongside the perspectives of Parks and Arola.

Beyond Progress excels in many ways. Plemons presents a useful model for those looking to add creative and narrative elements to academic writing. Within the text, Plemons' roles as a scholar, teacher, and creative writer inform each other, and the book represents a wonderful example of what can be accomplished by embracing interrelated writerly identities in academic scholarship. Additionally, the student writings included in the "Writers and Teachers" sections work not only as examples of student writing that elucidate and complement the book's themes, but also serve in their own right as pieces worthy of anthologizing and analyzing.

The strength of Plemons' inclusion of personal elements in her scholarship goes beyond just the "Teachers and Writers" sections. Her frank discussions of her IRB process and the conflicts that arose as she brought her community work at Folsom into the institutional context of academic research will be particularly useful for other community practitioners. Methodology sometimes remains hidden in academic texts, but Plemons gives voice to struggles faced by community researchers trying to conduct their work within the constraints of timed studies, grappling with the ethical precariousness of surveillance, or transitioning from collaborative community partnerships to more restrictive researcher-subject relationships. Plemons speaks openly about these struggles while also recognizing the undeniable importance of the IRB process, and many scholars navigating these aspects of community work will benefit from her insights.

The nuance of Plemons' arguments and the honesty of her prose make her book a valuable contribution to the recent influx of texts detailing prison writing programs.

Beyond Progress in the Prison Classroom is an important and pressing book for all prison teacher-scholars as well as anyone in the fields of rhetoric, composition, or creative writing doing community-based writing and research. The book will also be of interest to scholars and students of autobiography studies, narrative, or literacy studies. Plemons' storytelling skills, clear prose, and succinct explanations of her theoretical framework also make this a useful and accessible book for graduate students new to these areas of inquiry.

One place *Beyond Progress* falls slightly short of its ambitious aims is in making the case for the prison classroom as a microcosm for the rhetoric and composition classroom at large. While a decolonial framework is urgently and undeniably necessary in the university setting, and Plemons effectively reminds us of this, her book speaks most directly to the issues most relevant to sites of incarceration and community collaboration; in fact, her book addresses these important issues so well that it would be unreasonable to ask or expect it to do more. Plemons leaves it in the hands of future rhetoric and compositionist teacher-scholars to apply her pedagogical methods to their classrooms and write about it, which I hope they will. Ultimately, Plemons book is a gift that we should make use of in our own teaching and research.

PARLOR PRESS
EQUIPMENT FOR LIVING

New Releases

James A. Berlin and Social-Epistemic Rhetorics by Victor J. Vitanza

The Art of Public Writing by Zachary Michael Jack

The Naylor Report on Undergraduate Research in Writing Studies edited by Dominic DelliCarpini, Jenn Fishman, and Jane Greer

Internationalizing the Writing Center: A Guide for Developing a Multilingual Writing Center by Noreen Lape

Writing Spaces: Readings on Writing Volume 3 edited by Dana Driscoll, Mary Stewart, and Matthew Vetter

Forthcoming

Collaborative Writing Playbook: An Instructor's Guide to Designing Writing Projects for Student Teams by Joe Moses and Jason Tham

The Best of the Journals in Rhetoric and Composition 2020

Check Out Our New Website!

Discounts, open access titles, instant ebook downloads, and more.

And new series:

Comics and Graphic Narratives. Series Editors: Sergio Figueiredo, Jason Helms, and Anastasia Salter

Inkshed: Writing Studies in Canada. Series Editors: Heather Graves and Roger Graves

www.parlorpress.com

CLJ **Discount:** Use CLJ20 at checkout to receive a 20% discount on all titles not on sale through March 15, 2021.

www.ingramcontent.com/pod-product-compliance
Lightning Source LLC
Chambersburg PA
CBHW031319160426
43196CB00007B/589